AF653730

Concept Publishing Co.
Rs. 400/-

# CEREAL SUBSTITUTES IN A DEVELOPING ECONOMY

# CEREAL SUBSTITUTES IN A DEVELOPING ECONOMY

A Study of Tapioca

(Kerala State)

K N NINAN

CONCEPT PUBLISHING COMPANY, NEW DELHI

The Indian Council of Social Science Research gave the financial support towards the publication of this work. However, the responsibility for the contents of the book—facts, opinions, conclusions, etc.—is entirely that of the author and not of the ICSSR.

First Published 1986

© KN Ninan 1986
Karachepone Ninan Ninan (*b*. 1950- )

*Published by*

Naurang Rai
Concept Publishing Company
H-13, Bali Nagar
NEW DELHI-110015 (India)

*Printed in India by*

Bharat Enterprises
*at* Chetna Printers, Shastri Marg-3
Maujpur, Shahdara, Delhi-110053

Dedicated
to the
memory of my father
BEHANAN KARACHEPONE NINAN
Who sacrificed his todays
to secure my tomorrows;
Who shared my joy getting Ph D
but couldn't wait to see this book!

# FOREWORD

This is the first comprehensive study I have seen of a starchy root-crop that is acceptable, and in terms of calorie forms a useful supplement to the intake of cereals which form the main source of calorie intake in India. In my study on Food, Nutrition and Poverty in India, I had drawn attention to the fact that to reach targets of consumption in line with nutritional needs, we have to diversify our agricultural output and go in more for animal husbandry products, fruits and vegetables, and starch root crops like tapioca, potato and sweet potato which are heavy yielders in terms of per acre output and also substantial source of calorie. In order that this problem may be examined, it is necessary to have indepth studies of heavy yielding and calorie rich root crops; and tapioca is one example. In fact, the nutritional status of the poorer sections of the population in Kerala would have been very much below par but for the cultivation of tapioca and its wide use by the poor and marginal farmers to whom even rice crop is a cash crop.

I am glad that Dr Ninan has chosen for his subject such a comprehensive study of tapioca. The study brings out clearly the fact that this crop needs much more research attention and policy oriented action if tapioca is to continue to play an important role in meeting the food requirements of the growing population of Kerala and its component of the poorer sections. Tapioca seems to have served the purpose of an ideal subsistence crop in Kerala and it deserves more attention from our agricultural planners and scientists. Dr Ninan's work is a significant contribution to the understanding of the economy of a non-cereal subsistence crop and deserves the notice of all persons interested in improving the calorie intake in India, which is now recognised as India's major nutritional deficiency.

Dr Ninan's book also contains many other interesting details and analytical insights about subsistence economy in agriculture and what is sometimes called peasant farming. Altogether it is a comprehensive and painstaking work with a number of original insights and I would commend it to the attention of both nutritionists and agricultural planners in the country.

Institute for Social and
Economic Change,
BANGALORE
15th September, 1985

V K R V RAO
National Professor

# PREFACE

THIS is a revised version of a dissertation submitted to the Mysore University for the award of Ph D degree. The study is on Tapioca—a root crop which is cultivated in almost ninety countries of the tropical belt, including India which is the sixth largest producer of the commodity in the world. Despite its significance in the diet of the poor and also its usefulness as animal feed and an input for industries tapioca continues to receive a low priority in the development plans of less developed countries. Unlike other field crops it is also not well-researched, particularly its economic aspects.

This study presents a systematic and comprehensive enquiry into the economics of tapioca cultivation in Kerala State, which accounts for 70 per cent of the tapioca output in India, based on both secondary and primary data. Though the study is focused on tapioca it offers a comparative perspective of the crop vis-a-vis rice also both at the macro and micro level. Against the background of the world and Indian tapioca economies it analyses its growth behaviour in Kerala in respect of yields, area, output and prices. Its consumption vis-a-vis rice, nature of instability in yields and prices and price integration are also analysed. All these are done with the help of secondary data. The study then makes an indepth analysis of its economics in relation to rice, based on micro-level data covering different strata of farms and regions, analysing productivity, input structure and cost of cultivation, income and labour absorption. Other aspects like marketed surplus and market dependence, prices received by farmers, extent of processing, consumption at source and its role in the diet are also examined. The study thus provides valuable and original insights into the economy of a low value non-cereal subsistence crop grown mostly under rainfed conditions. It also gives empirical and theoretical insights into the working of a peasant economy where small holdings dominate.

At the outset let me place on record my deep sense of gratitude to Professor V K R V Rao who not only offered me a fellowship to pursue my doctoral studies but also encouraged me to work on this subject. I must thank him further for writing a foreword to this book despite his several commitments.

I profusely thank Professor M V Nadkarni, my supervisor, who took very keen interest in my work by sparing considerable time to go through successive drafts of the manuscript and also offering several useful suggestions and comments.

Several other individuals helped me at various stages of my work. In particular I wish to thank the following persons who responded to my request for copies of their publication on the crop. They are R O Diaz and the Librarian, Centre Internacional de Agricultura Tropical, Cali, Colombia; Dr Truman P Phillips, School of Agriculture Economics, University of Guelph, Canada; Dr Barry L Nestel, Associate Director, International Development Research Centre, Ottawa, Canada; Late Dr D G Coursey and Dr R A Noon, Tropical Products Institute, London; and Professor Leslie A Wilson, University of West Indies, Trinidad.

I have benefited much from the discussions I had with several persons particularly Prof V M Rao, ISEC, Bangalore; Prof N Krishnaji, Centre for Social Studies, Calcutta; Prof P V Sukhatme, Maharashtra Association for Cultivation of Science, Pune; Prof P G K Pannikar, Centre for Development Studies, Trivandrum; Dr K N S Nair, Chief, Agriculture Division, State Planning Board, Kerala (now with FAO); Dr Mathew Kurien, Director, Indian Institute for Regional Development Studies, Kottayam; Dr Gordon Banta, Associate Director, IDRC, Canada; Drs V G Rao, P M Kulkarni, R S Deshpande and H Chandrasekhar (my colleagues in the Institute). I also acknowledge with thanks the help and encouragements received from Messrs. V Manilal, Ramesh Kumar, Oommen Mathew,

D Nagaraj, Sridevi, Dr C C Abraham and Grace Abraham, Ronald Pereira, my mother Annamma and my wife Jane.

A special word of thanks to the officials of the Directorate of Economics and Statistics, Government of Kerala, particularly Dr R S Kurup (then Director) and Mr Somasekharan Nair (Additional Director); the Director and staff of Central Tuber Crops Research Institute, Trivandrum; and also the Director and Library staff of ISEC, Bangalore; Kerala Legislative Assembly, Trivandrum and University of Agricultural Sciences, Bangalore.

I will be failing in my duty if I do not express my deep sense of gratitude to the farmers and village officials who cooperated with me in my work and provided all the required information.

Finally, I express my thanks to the Indian Council of Social Science Research, New Delhi, for approving this study for award of an ICSSR publication grant.

Institute for Social and Economic Change,
BANGALORE
15th October, 1985

K N NINAN

# CONTENTS

# LIST OF TABLES

## LIST OF FIGURES

# 1

# INTRODUCTION

## THE CROP AND THE ISSUES

IMPROVED technology, appropriate economic incentives and selective institutional reforms have brought about a significant rise in the food output, especially in cereals, in a number of less developed countries (LDCs) in Asia and Latin America in the recent past. Consequently the aura of pessimism regarding the food prospects of these regions has given way to optimism. But several other countries especially in Africa continue to face an alarming food situation. And even in those regions which exude optimism on the food front, doubts persist as to whether, given the prevalent high rates of population growth and high income elasticity of demand for food, the supply of food can keep pace with the demand for it. In fact projections made by some studies suggest that food deficits may either continue to persist or show up in several LDCs in the not too distant future.[1] How to augment food production and whether cereals alone can meet this shortfall are interesting questions confronting the policy-maker. Apart from accelerating food production, improving the nutritional levels of low income people and also raising their effective demand for food are recognised as some of the major problems of LDCs. The importance and potential of cereal substitutes arises in this context. The present study focusses attention on one such promising cereal substitute, namely tapioca.

Tapioca (manihot esculenta, Crantz; syn, manihot utilissima, Pohl) or cassava, manioc, yuca, mandioca as the crop is commonly known is a root crop cultivated extensively in about eighty-seven countries that span the tropical belt.[2] The significance of the crop lies in the fact that it is a cheap cereal substitute and hence within the reach of those with limited purchasing power. Of particular interest to development planners in LDCs, is the role that tapioca could play in mitigating poverty and under-nutrition as also in increasing incomes. If calorie gap rather than protein inadequacy were the more serious problem confronting LDCs as visualised by some studies,[3] tapioca can play a positive role in combating it, being calorie rich. Though, per unit of weight, cereal crops like rice give more calories than tapioca (100 gm. of rice yields 346 calories compared to 157 calories from tapioca),[4] tapioca gives more calories than rice per unit of expenditure. Apart from containing large amounts of carbohydrates, tapioca is relatively rich in calcium and vitamin C and also contains nutritionally significant amounts of thiamine, riboflavin and niacine.[5] The leaves of the tapioca plant contains significant amounts of protein and vitamin A, but its consumptionis noticed only in Africa.[6]

Whatever be the significance of tapioca in meeting the food needs of the poor it can be produced in significant quantities only if it is economical or remunerative to produce. It can give high yield per unit area compared to most cereal crops.[7] Hence, despite its low unit value, returns from tapioca can be high. The wide gap between actual and potential yields of tapioca indicates a scope for increasing the returns from this crop through stepping up its yields. In the case of cereal crops like rice, actual yields are comparatively nearer potential yields. However, rice being a seasonal crop, it permits multiple cropping which could yield more income per annum. Tapioca does not have this advantage. The whole question of economics of tapioca production is involved here, particularly in relation to cereal crops like rice, which has to take note of productivity, price, inputs and their cost and possibilities of multiple cropping. The present study is an investigation into this. Pending further discussion later, we may note a few aspects of the economic significance of the crop.

The crop has a number of other attributes that make it well suited to poorly endowed regions and farms. It can withstand prolonged dry spells save for some moisture at the time of planting, and hence is recommended in regions with uncertain weather conditions.[8] It can realise economic yields on soils found unsuitable for most other crops, perhaps because of its feeder roots which penetrate to depths of 40-60 cm. in the soil.[9] Tapioca cultivation seems to be less risky than most other crops.[10] Thus despite its low unit value tapioca may yield a stable income and these reasons make its cultivation an attractive proposition to risk-averse farmers.

Unlike many tropical crops which fall easy prey to pests and diseases, tapioca is less susceptible on account of its hydrocyanic acid (HCN) content.[11] As a consequence the farmer need incur less expenditure on current inputs like pesticides and insecticides. The crop has no critical period for sowing and harvesting and so can be grown all round the year.[12] This is advantageous to farmers who primarily depend on family labour who in the case of other crops like rice have to hire in labour to complete sowing and harvesting operations in time. This is advantageous on two counts. Firstly, it reduces the requirements of working capital (like wages for hired labour) and proves beneficial to farmers with limited financial resources. Secondly, during peak seasons when labour is an effective constraint, tapioca growers can postpone sowing or harvesting and divert their attention to the pressing needs of other crops. This is beneficial to the farmer since the entrepreneurial factor is a limiting one relative to other factors. Further since harvesting of tapioca can be intermittent, dictated by demand, it can be stored in the ground itself thus reducing storage costs if not opportunity cost in terms of land use. All this would suggest that the crop should be of particular significance to small farmers. Whether it could go to the extent of making small holdings viable needs to be investigated, apart from the question of how far it is a subsistence crop and it meets their food needs.

Tapioca is also used in animal feeding and as an input in agro-based industries. It can substitute for costly cereal-based animal feeds (as being done in the EEC) without adverse effects on growth or yield of the animals, thereby releasing much needed cereals for human use. The crop's commercial value is enhanced by the fact that apart from being used as a raw material in food-based industries it is also used in starch and sago manufacture which find wide application in various industries engaged in paper making, textiles, dyes and chemicals, laundry adhesives, etc. Some countries like Thailand and Brazil are earning considerable foreign exchange by exporting tapioca meal, pellets, etc., to the EEC and USA where a large and growing market exists for tapioca-based animal feed industry.[13] New tapioca products like power alcohol and single cell proteins have been found.[14] Tapioca leaves seem to have the potential for being used in ericulture.[15] The by-products of tapioca like leaves and stems have value in use though not in exchange. Market outlets for the crop are now so wide and diversified, that it is a cash crop in its own right and its potential as a cheap source of food for thepoor may well be bypassed in its progress!

But an inhibiting factor for the crop's industrial utilisation asalso its marketability is the fact that it is highly perishable.[16] Once harvested the tubers deteriorate and can only be stored for about 48-72 hours. This rapid deterioration of tapioca renders them completely unacceptable for human consumption, reduces their acceptability for animal feed and, lowers the quality of the starch obtained from them.[17] This factor coupled with its low unit value have resulted in the markets for tapioca being localised. One method by which farmers meet this situation (of rapid deterioration) is to postpone harvesting by allowing the crop to remain in the ground as noted earlier. Though this reduces storage costs, as mentioned earlier, it represents an inefficient use of a scarce input like land.[18] Moreover, its susceptibility to loss is said to increase if the crop remains in the ground after it has matured. The other method by which growers meet this situation is to convert a major portion of the harvested produce into chips, either sun-dried chips or par-boiled dried chips as well as other processed products which have a longer storage life.

The foregoing discussion shows that tapioca has immense potentialities for growth. While on the one hand it can meet the food needs of a growing population, on the other, its large scale production can provide a cheap substitute for cereal-based animal feeds and also an input for the creation of agro-based industries. The crop, however, is neglected in most food economies and more so in India, which is the sixth largest producer of tapioca in the world. As such, the economics of tapioca cultivation also has been a relatively neglected area of economic enquiry and more so in India.

In evolving an appropriate policy framework for the development of tapioca, adequate knowledge about the crop's current status is needed. But equally important is the need to clear misconceptions and prejudices about the crop. Its HCN content for instance is cited as a cause of pellagroidic diseases like goitre (though no significant correlation between the two has been reported) while its low protein content is held out as the cause of nutritional diseases like kwashiorkor etc., in tapioca-consuming regions.[19] It is dubbed as an inferior food and hence the income elasticity of demand for tapioca is negative.[20] Apart from these factors, there are also prejudices against the crop. One is that it is a soil depleting crop, particularly of potash in the soil, and hence fertility of land has to be frequently replenished.[21] Another is that cultivation of tapioca on hill slopes (in the absence of proper tree cover, bunding and terracing) encourages soil erosion since the top soil has to be disturbed for harvesting the tubers.

An economic enquiry about the crop would obviously have to enlighten us on the role that it plays among different strata of farms and regions. A proper perspective on the tapioca economy should throw light on various issues like the pattern and intensity with which resources are used for cultivating the crop as also indicate the stresses and strains under which it is nurtured, the structure of costs and production, the factors limiting production and productivity on farms, the viability of the crop judged in terms of its relative rate of return as also its employment potential judged in terms of the labour absorbed by the crop, the cash and market orientation of production, the market outlets for the crop and its by-products as also the nature of market facing producers and consumers, prices received and relative importance of different market channels, the role of tapioca in the diet of producers, etc. All these are issues which could fall within the purview of this study.

Furthermore in a study of this nature, the crop's economy has to be viewed as part of an integrated perspective of the farm economy as a whole. A study of the other socio-economic activities will help place in proper perspective the role and importance of tapioca in the household economy. The extent of crop diversification as also overall diversification of the household economy are other issues that merit attention. Thus the present study would not only throw more light on the dimensions of the tapioca economy but also widen our understanding of peasant economies and farmer behaviour.

## TAPIOCA IN WORLD AND INDIAN ECONOMIES

Tapioca which is believed to be a crop of South American origin[22] is presently cultivated in most countries of the tropical belt, the ecological region most suited to its cultivation.[23] The relative position of selected major tapioca-producing countries and regions is given in Table 1.1. The table reveals that though Africa accounts for a major chunk of world's acreage and production of tapioca, productivity of tapioca is quite low there when compared to that in South America and Asia. Among countries Brazil ranks first both in terms of area and production of tapioca followed by Zaire, Indonesia and Nigeria. Though in terms of acreage India ranks tenth, owing to high productivity of tapioca (the highest in the table)[24] it ranks as the sixth largest producer of tapioca in the world. The table reveals large cross-section variations in the productivity of tapioca, ranging from 3 tonnes/hectare in Uganda to 17 tonnes/hectare in India.

TABLE 1.1: **Area, Production and Productivity of Tapioca: Relative Position of Selected Countries and Regions (average for three years, 1979 to 1981)**

| Countries/ Regions | Area harvested (in '000 hectares) | Per cent to world total | Production (in '000 metric tonnes) | Per cent to world total | Productivity (in tonnes/ hectare) |
|---|---|---|---|---|---|
| Brazil | 2070 | 15.0 | 24474 | 20.1 | 12 |
| Zaire | 1824* | 13.2 | 12400* | 10.2 | 7 |
| Indonesia | 1420 | 10.3 | 13670 | 11.3 | 10 |
| Nigeria | 1183* | 8.6 | 10833* | 8.9 | 9 |
| Thailand | 1005* | 7.3 | 14538* | 12.0 | 14 |
| Tanzania | 940* | 6.8 | 4600* | 3.8 | 5 |
| Mozambique | 601* | 4.3 | 2783* | 2.3 | 5 |
| Vietnam | 461 | 3.3 | 3378 | 2.8 | 7 |
| Uganda | 410* | 3.0 | 1390* | 1.1 | 3 |
| India | 353 | 2.6 | 5904 | 4.9 | 17 |
| Africa | 7315 | 52.9 | 46445 | 38.3 | 6 |
| Asia | 3798 | 27.5 | 43970 | 36.2 | 12 |
| South America | 2552 | 18.4 | 29933 | 24.6 | 13 |
| North-Central America | 151 | 1.1 | 900 | 0.7 | 6 |
| Oceania | 20 | 0.1 | 224 | 0.2 | 11 |
| WORLD | 13836 | 100.0 | 121472 | 100.0 | 9 |

*Note*: *FAO estimates.

*Source*: FAO Production Year-book, Vol. 35, 1981, FAO, Rome, 1982, pp. 116-117.

The history of tapioca in India is linked with the arrival of the Portuguese who are believed to have introduced the crop into Malabar, India in the 17th century. But there are other versions.[25] According to one the crop was introduced into India by Danes from the East Indies. Another version has attributed it to Spanish influence into the Philippines from where its cultivation spread to the neighbouring countries and to Assam and Eastern Bengal in India. Sawyer credits the Portuguese as having introduced it in their early settlement at Goa, while Padmanabha Iyer believes it to have been in Malabar.[26] But it was in the princely state of Travancore (comprising present-day Southern Kerala) that the cultivation of the crop gained impetus due to the active encouragement by Vishakham Tirunal, Maharajah of Travancore (1880-1885). To this day the Travancore region continues to be the dominant tapioca growing belt of the country. Table 1.2 presents the statewise distribution of area and production of tapioca. As obvious from the table Kerala enjoys a pre-eminent position in the tapioca economy of India accounting for more than 76 per cent of area and 70 per cent of production of tapioca in the country. Next to rice, tapioca is the most important food crop grown in Kerala accounting for almost a tenth of the state's gross sown area. Tapioca is an important staple food of the people in this region particularly of the low income groups. It is said to have provided 27 per cent of total calorie intake during the sixties.[27] Kerala state may be termed as a chronic rice deficit region. Production of rice is inadequate to meet the demand. But for the large scale availability of tapioca, the problem of undernutrition would have been even more acute in Kerala, particularly among low income groups. Kerala thus seems to be well suited for a study of tapioca economy. A more detailed description of the agricultural economy of Kerala in general and her tapioca economy in particular are given in subsequent chapters.

## A BRIEF REVIEW OF LITERATURE[28]

Before we spell out our objectives a review of the literature on tapioca would be worth attempting. We may study them under the following groups:

1. General Studies on tapioca mostly based on secondary data with a regional or historical perspective.
2. Farm level studies with a micro-perspective based on primary data.

TABLE 1.2: **Area and Production of Tapioca in India—Statewise Distribution (average for three years, 1979-80 to 1981-82)**

| State/Union Territory | Area under tapioca (in '000 hectares) | Per cent to All India figures | Production of tapioca (in '000 tonnes) | Per cent to All India figures |
|---|---|---|---|---|
| Kerala | 255.1 | 76.7 | 3964.1 | 69.9 |
| Tamil Nadu | 53.9 | 16.1 | 1527.5 | 27.0 |
| Andhra Pradesh | 12.7 | 3.8 | 121.7 | 2.1 |
| Arunachal Pradesh | 3.4 | 1.0 | 8.5 | 0.1 |
| Meghalaya | 3.1 | 0.9 | 16.0 | 0.3 |
| Karnataka | 1.4 | 0.4 | 13.7 | 0.2 |
| Assam | 1.3 | 0.4 | 6.0 | 0.1 |
| Pondicherry | 0.6 | 0.2 | 11.1 | 0.2 |
| Rajasthan | 0.3 | 0.1 | 0.4 | 0.01 |
| Nagaland | 0.3 | 0.1 | 1.1 | 0.02 |
| Mizoram | 0.3 | 0.1 | 0.8 | 0.02 |
| Tripura | 0.2 | 0.1 | 1.1 | 0.02 |
| Andaman and Nicobar Islands | 0.2 | 0.1 | 1.6 | 0.03 |
| All-India | 332.8 | 100.0 | 5673.6 | 100.0 |

*Source of Basic Data*: Area and Production of Principal Crops in India, 1980-81, Directorate of Economics and Statistics, Ministry of Agriculture, Government of India, 1982, and also, Agricultural Situation in India, December 1982, Directorate of Economics and Statistics, Ministry of Agriculture, Government of India, p. 626.

**(1) General Studies**

Given the limited coverage of secondary data the focus of the general studies on tapioca have been essentially confined to examining the behaviour of tapioca over time and space. This is done through trend fitting exercises or tabular analysis and in rare cases with the help of supply response models. Most of the studies are, however, too general in nature giving a descriptive account of the salient features of tapioca cultivation in different regions and also identifying the factors that have contributed to the growth of the crop. The emphasis of all these studies has been on aspects relating to production; questions relating to marketing and consumption have hardly received any attention.

Of the studies which examine the behaviour of the crop, we may refer to two by Butler, et al. and Diaz, who gave a global perspective of the tapioca economy.[29] Butler, et. al, examined linear trends in area, production and productivity of tapioca for the period 1948-52 to 1967 for different countries and regions and noted that tapioca production had increased in Africa, Asia and Latin America. But acreage increases were largely responsible for the trend in production than productivity increases. Yield per hectare had not shown much increase in Africa and only small increases were reported in Aisa and Latin America. Individual countries like Togo, India and Venezuela had increased yields by significant amounts. Diaz's finding pertaining to the sixties revealed that tapioca production per capita had increased by about 7.5 kgs. per annum in S. America but decreased in the rest of the world.

The other general studies restrict their analysis to specific regions. Though most of them tend to be impressionistic accounts, we do get interesting insights as to the role played by different factors in different regions. Though a lot of research input has gone into analysing the role of prices on agricultural growth, tapioca has figured only in two studies, one by Behrman, the other by Phillips. Behrman, using non-linear estimates of the Nerlovian type dynamic supply response model, observed that in Thailand tapioca was responsive to price changes.[30] But the increase in expected incomes due to increase in expected yields was stated to be a more important inducement than price expectation. Phillips, regressing production on tapioca selling prices, noted that though the supply of tapioca in the Brazilian states was responsive to price changes a six unit rise in prices was required to induce a unit change in production.[31] Some official Indian reports on tapioca have suggested a cobweb-type relation between prices and production but no empirical support is given to back these observations.[32]

The role of other factors too has been highlighted. Tapioca's intrinsic qualities, the demonstration effect and the catalystic role of the colonialists are some of the factors that hastened its easy assimilation in the African economies.[33] Its relative rate of return compared to other competing crops were cited for the spurt in tapioca cultivation in Brazil and Thailand.[34] Its growth in Travancore-Cochin (now in Kerala) and Java (Indonesia) was food-induced while in Madras (parts of North Kerala and Tamil Nadu) it was industry-induced.[35] In West Malaysia growth of tapioca industries and the export market contributed to tapioca's growth.[36] All this illustrates the diverse factors that have influenced the growth of the crop in different regions.

Unlike the general run of studies reviewed above, the study by Phillips was noteworthy for more reasons than one.[37] Apart from a detailed analysis of the demand-supply conditions in the tapioca market he has made region-specific studies on Brazil, Thailand and Kerala (by Angus Hones), based on secondary data. Projections made by Phillips revealed that demand for tapioca would increase for direct human consumption, use as industrial starch and animal feed, with largest increases being recorded in the animal feed market. But his demand models had the crucial assumption of constant price relativities and the results must be read in this light. Supply functions suggested that at the aggregate level supply of tapioca would meet demand for it but the disaggregated country-wise picture revealed that while countries like Indonesia, Philippines, Nigeria, would have tapioca deficits, others like India, Brazil, Thailand and Togo would have tapioca surpluses.

Another interesting finding was that tapioca is not a universally inferior food as is often believed. In 57 per cent of the producing countries the income elasticity of demand for tapioca was positive. In India, however, the coefficient was negative (—0.3) implying that it was an inferior good here. In his tapioca demand functions for human use, though Phillip's has incorporated the population and income effects, on account is taken of the substitution effect as also the cross-elasticity of demand.

Apart from the studies listed above we have a few more which are mostly impessionistic accounts or of no direct relevance to us.[38] Hence they are not reviewed here.

**(2) Farm Level Studies**

Studies on tapioca based on farm level data are very few indeed. We may refer here to three studies, two of which pertain to Kerala (hereafter FMS and AERC study) and third one to Colombia (hereafter CIAT Study).[39] In addition to these studies, there are two small research papers based on sample surveys in Trivandrum (Kerala) and Thailand. These studies differ from another in respect of their sample design, time frame of study and coverage of issues. These factors may be noted while comparing the findings of these studies. The issues discussed in these studies relate to yields, cost and returns or input-output relationships and, in some cases, on marketing of the crop.

Both FMS and CIAT studies noted that tapioca yields per unit area were generally higher among bigger holdings as compared to smaller ones, though no clear relationship could be established. The use of new inputs like fertiliser was one reason for relatively higher yields among bigger holdings in Colombia. In contrast to the findings of the above two studies, the AERC study found an inverse relationship between tapioca yields per acre and size of holdings, though the trend was not smooth. But the study does not spell out any reason for this trend. Perhaps the higher intensity of labour input among small holdings may explain this trend. Furthermore, fertiliser users were able to secure 20 per cent higher yields than non-fertiliser users. Inadequacy of water, attacks from insects and diseases were important factors that contributed to low tapioca yields among Thai farms whereas roofed storage of tapioca stems (kept for next planting) had a positive effect on yields.[40]

Land and Labour were the most important resources used in tapioca cultivation in Kerala as well as Colombia. As per the FMS, land and labour accounted for about 40 and 30 per cent of total costs (including imputed value of owned inputs). It also observed that total inputs in rupees per hectare (including imputed value of owned inputs) appeared to have an inverse relationship with size of holdings; output per hectare appeared to vary directly with farm size. According to AERC study, labour and capital (manure and fertiliser) accounted for 68 and 33 per cent of total expenditure (excluding the rental value of owned land) respectively. Here also the total value of inputs per acre varied inversely with size of holdings. As per the CIAT study, labour costs accounted for about 60 per cent of total variable costs on farms where machinery was used for land preparation and 90-95 per cent when the land was prepared manually. Total variable costs were found to be higher on farms where land was prepared with machinery due to higher costs of mechanised land preparation and higher levels of input use. Labour use per hectare was found to increase with an increase in size of tapioca holdings in Colombia. Investments on fertilisers and insecticides increased with an increase in farm size in Colombia whereas the use of pesticides or insecticides were not reported by Kerala farmers, as per AERC Study.

The impact of new technology on yields and employment has received some attention in these studies. The AERC study observed that at an additional cost of Rs. 261 (i.e., 30 per cent) HYV of tapioca would give an additional yield of 4.7 tonnes/acre, i.e., 43 per cent higher yield compared to local varieties. It also observed that HYVs were less labour intensive than local varieties of tapioca i.e., 65 mandays/acre for HYV as against 76 mandays/acre for local varieties.[41] Andersen and Diaz,[42] using Colombian data, noted that mechanical land preparation andchemical weed control would reduce labour requirements per hectare by about 30 and 40 per cent respectively. In terms of labour demand the impact of yield increasing biological technology would be felt mostly in the harvesting and packing stages. The employment elasticity with respect to tapioca yield was 0.2. Their findings, thus indicated that though new technology may increase tapioca yields and net returns, it would result in a net reduction of labour use. The findings of a number of other studies have indicated that though mechanisation may reduce costs, it is also labour displacing and hence conflict with the social objective of employment generation.[43]

With respect to profitability the FMS noted that, on an average, during 1962-63 to 1964-65 tapioca cultivation resulted in a net loss of Rs. 82 per hectare (profits calculated with reference to total costs including imputed value of owned inputs). But big farmers were able to report profits. As per the AERC study tapioca was profitable in all strata of farms during 1975-76, with farmers operating holdings less than 2.5 acres making maximum profits as compared to big farmers, owing to lower receipts by big farmers. The average profits taking all farms together was Rs. 3751 per acre. The CIAT study also found it to be profitable to cultivate (US $1896/hectare in 1974) but no information is provided with respect to inter-farm differences.

The emphasis of the micro-level studies too have been on aspects relating to production; questions relating to marketing and consumption have received very little attention. But there are exceptions. The All-India Report cited earlier, on the basis of on the spot surveys, gave interesting insights into the marketing of tapioca. It observed that in Travancore-Cochin small holders retained a good portion of their tapioca for on-farm consumption while large farmers released a substantial portion of their produce for the market. On an average 30 per cent of produce was retained as against 37-49 per cent in Madras during 1944-45 to 1952-53. The nature of trade structure differed between the two states. In Travancore-Cochin tapioca was sold either directly by producers to consumers (25 per cent of raw tubers and 5 per cent of chips) or by village merchants who bought from producers (75 per cent of raw tubers and 95 per cent of chips). Other intermediaries like commission agents and wholesalers played little role in Travancore-Cochin but in Madras they dominated the trade which may be due to the industrial use of tapioca in Madras.

The report noted further that the grower's share in consumer rupee in Travancore-Cochin was 80 to 84 per cent in the case of chips; in Madras it varied from 59 per cent in Malabar to 78 per cent in Tanjore in the case of tubers. These differences were attributed to the distance of markets as well as number of agents engaged in the chain of distribution. Another study by Venugopalan et. al, pertaining to Trivandrum district noted that 82 per cent of raw tubers were marketed immediately after harvest though repurchases took place; 50 per cent of market arrivals in the district were brought by the cultivators (the rest by village merchants and dealers); the producer's share in the consumer rupee was 66 per cent.[44]

Marketing of tapioca in Colombia, as per the CIAT study, was localised with more than 50 per cent of sales at farm itself and the rest being brought to the market for sale. The study observed a considerable difference between prices paid to small farmers and those paid to large farmers. Farmers with a cassava area of less than 2 hectares received only 70 per cent of the prices paid to farmers with 10 hectares or more. The study suggested that economies of size in transportation and other marketing activities may partly explain the existence of these price differentials. On the basis of preliminary results it was suggested that with respect to economies of scale in tapioca production in Colombia, price differential might be more important than cost and yield differentials. Apart from these questions none of the studies reviewed above have thrown any light on market dependence and the role of tapioca in consumption.

The foregoing review indicates that as far as the general or macro-level studies are concerned they have confined their attention to only selected issues like examining the growth behaviour of the crop, which of course is due to the limited coverage of secondary data. The few available farm or micro-level studies fall short of what is warranted by the importance of the crop in terms of their coverage of holdings (particularly the Kerala Studies), regions and issues posed. None of these studies are unanimous as to whether it is the small or big farmers who are efficient in production of tapioca judged in terms of yields or returns secured. They also fail to provide an in-depth analysis of the factors limiting production and productivity on farms. On many issues like labour use pattern, marketable surplus, market dependence and consumption little or no light is shed. Furthermore attempts to relate empirical findings to issues of theoretical importance like the efficiency of small vs. large farms, the size-productivity debate, whether economies of scale operate in production, the viability of small holdings etc., are feeble or nil. These studies thus appear to be purely empirical in nature, devoid of any theoretical underpinnings. The limitations of these studies are further compounded by the fact that they tended to view the tapioca economy in isolation. Any meaningful study of the tapioca economy should be framed in the broader context of the farm economy. The proposed study seeks to overcome these limitations by covering more holdings and widening its scope to include a detailed analysis of the production, consumption and marketing of tapioca.

## OBJECTIVES AND APPROACH

In the light of the above discussion, the present study seeks to make a temporal and spatial analysis of the tapioca economy in Kerala and also offers a detailed farm level analysis of its economics taking into account the aspects referred above. The study provides a further dimension by giving a comparative perspective of the tapioca and rice economies in Kerala in the context of the linkages existing between the two. The specific objectives of the study are as follows:

1. To analyse the tapioca economy in Kerala over time and space, at state and district level in comparison to rice.
2. To examine the output and yield rates of tapioca in comparison with rice, along with the pattern and intensity of resource use and also to estimate gross income from tapioca by size groups of farmers.
3. To analyse the input and cost structure of tapioca vis-a-vis rice and also estimate the net income generated from tapioca cultivation in relation to other sources of income by size groups of farmers.
4. To examine marketing behaviour of farmers particularly marketed surplus and market dependence, consumption

at source, tapioca processing at farm level and also price received by size groups of farmers.

The study attempts a micro-level analysis of farm household data covering different strata of farms and regions in Kerala. Analysis of secondary data in connection with objective one above is more in the nature of a background to the detailed micro-level study. Farm households were selected on random sample basis from the enumerated list of tapioca cultivators with probability proportional to size of operated area. For purposes of analysis the farm households after selection have been startified into different size groups of holdings. Details of sample design are presented in Chapter III. The analysis in the present study will employ both intra-crop inter-farm and inter-farm inter-crop comparisons. More details about the methods, concepts, etc., used in the study are cited in the relevant chapters. We may, therefore, pass on to the analysis of our data.

## REFERENCES

1. Cf. *Food Needs of Developing Countries,* Research Report No. 3, IFPRI, December 1977; Peter Oram *et al.*: *Investment and Input Requirements for Accelerating Food Production in Low Income Countries by 1990,* Research Report No. 10, IFPRI, September 1979; John W Mellor: *The Changing World Food Situation,* Food Policy Statement, IFPRI, January 1985.
2. The plant is called cassava in English-speaking regions of North America, Europe and Africa; manioc in French-speaking areas; tapioca in English-speaking parts of South-east Asia; mandioca in Brazil; yuca in Spanish-speaking regions of South America. See Truman P Phillips: *Cassava Utilization and Potential Markets,* IDRC—020e, Ottawa, Canada, 1974, p. 1.
3. Cf: PV Sukhatme: Protein Strategy and Agriculture Development, *Indian Journal of Agricultural Economics,* January-March 1972, Vol. XXVII, No. 1; *Malnutrition and Poverty*, Lal Bahadur Shastri Memorial Lecture, IARI, New Delhi, 1977; C Gopalan, et al.: Effect of Calorie Supplementation on Growth of Undernourished Children, *American Journal of Clinical Nutrition,* 26 May, 1973, pp. 563-566; RA McCance and EM Widdonwson (ed), *Calorie Deficiencies and Protein Deficiencies,* J and A Churchill Ltd., London, 1968.

4. Cf: C Gopalan et al.: *Nutritive Value of Indian Foods*, National Institute of Nutrition, Indian Council of Medical Research, Hyderabad, 1977.
5. W O Jones: *Manioc in Africa*, Stanford University Press, 1959, p. 6.
6. "The eating of manioc leaves was considered as a mark of Poverty in an African Village, Evodoula, where Drs R Masseyeff and A Cambon (of ORSTOM) had conducted a dietary survey in 1954", See Jones, op. cit., p. 142.
7. In Kerala while local varieties of tapioca yield on the average about 10-16 tonnes per hectare, the hybrids like H-165, H-226, H-97 have recorded yields upto 40-50 tonnes per hectare. G Cours (vide Magoon) has reported average yield on European Plantations in Madagascar to be 40 tons per hectare. Cerighelli (vide Magoon) has also reported the case of exceptionally high yield of 150 tons/hectare in Brazil under special conditions.
8. D E Kay: Root Crops—Cassava in *TPI Crop and Product Digest*, No. 2, Tropical Products Institute, London, 1973, p. 25.
9. D E Kay, *Ibid.*, p. 25.
10. TJ Goering: *Tropical Root Crops and Rural Development*, World Bank Staff Working Paper No. 324, April 1979, p. 18.
11. Truman P Phillips, op. cit., p. 1.
12. Truman P Phillips, op. cit., p. 1.
13. R G Nair: *Utilisation of Tapioca* in Proceedings of Short Specialised Training Course on Tapioca Production Technology, October 14-18, 1974, Central Tuber Crops Research Institute (CTCRI), Trivandrum.
14. TJ Goering: op. cit., pp. 7; 52-57.
15. A Pilot Project for this was completed at the CTCRI, Trivandrum in 1982.
16. Jean S Ingram and J R O Humphries: Cassava Storage—A Review, *Tropical Science*, Vol. XIV, No. 2, pp. 132-133 (Reprint); and RH Booth: *Cassava Storage*, CIAT, Cali, Colombia, September 1975, Series EE-16.
17. D G Coursey and R H Booth: *Post-Harvest Losses in Perishable Tropical Produce*, in Proceedings of VI British Insecticides and Fung. Conference, London, 1971, p. 675.
18. Ingram and Humphries, op. cit., states: ". . . large areas are occupied by a crop which is already mature and are thus unavailable for further cropping". Ingram and Humphries estimate that globally about three quarters of a million hectares of land are occupied unnecessarily by the standing crop while Booth estimates it as 20 per cent of area under tapioca cultivation.
19. Cited in D E Kay, op. cit., p. 31.
20. Cited in Truman P Phillips, op. cit., p. 2.
21. Cited in Truman P Phillips, op. cit., p. 2.
22. Cf: Jones, op. cit., Barbara S Renvoize: The Area of Origin of

Manihot Esculenta as a Crop Plant—A Review of the Evidence, *Economic Botany*, 26(4): 352-360, 1973; C Earl Smith, Jr: The New World Centers of Origin of Cultivated Plants and the Archaelogical Evidence, *Economic Botany* 22(3): 253-366, 1968.

23. It grows best in warm humid climates and cannot withstand frosts. Under rainfed conditions it requires a minimum rainfall of 1200 mm to 1500 mm. But it can also be grown in areas with rainfall ranging from 500-2500 mm. It grows well in well-drained laterite, sandy loam or red loam soil with a PH between 4.5 to 6.5. It requires friable well-aerated soil for uniform tuber development. Saline soils and soils subject to water-logging are unsuitable as it affects the tubers. In very rich and clayish soils the plant is liable to produce more leaves and stems at the expense of tuberous roots. See, D E Kay: op. cit., p. 25 and *Package of Practices for Tapioca*, CTCRI, Trivandrum (Pamphlet).
24. The highest tapioca yields were, however, reported by some of the minor tapioca-producing countries like Cook Islands (32 tonnes/hectare), New Caledonia (28 tonnes/hectare), Barbados (25 tonnes/hectare), Cape Verde (24 tonnes/hectare) and Mauritius (18 tonnes/hectare). See FAO Production Year Book, Vol. 35, 1981, pp. 116-117.
25. See A K Yegna Narayan Aiyer: *Field Crops in India*, Bangalore Printing and Publishing Company Ltd., 1966, p. 264.
26. A M Sawyer: Tapioca Cultivation in Travancore, *Indian Forester*, Vol. XXI, 1895, pp. 290-296; A Padmanabha Iyer; The Cultivation of Tapioca in Travancore, *The Mysore Economic Journal*, October 1916, pp. 510-512.
27. *Poverty, Unemployment and Development Policy—A Study of Some Selected Issues with Reference to Kerala*, Centre for Development Studies, Trivandrum, United Nations, 1975 and Orient Longmans, 1977.
28. For a comprehensive review of literature on tapioca, see CH Hendershott, et al., *A Literature Review and Research Recommendations on Cassava*, AID Contract CSD/2497, University of Georgia, Athens, see in particular Chapter 1, *Cassava, the Plant*, *World Production and its Importance in World Food Supply*, by D G Rogers and S G Appan and Chapter IX, *Economics of Cassava Production and Marketing—Economic Considerations*, by S J Brannen. For a briefer review of literature on tapioca, see Barry L Nestel: *Current Trends in Cassava Research*, IDRC—036e, Monograph, IDRC, Ottawa, Canada, 1974.
29. E Joseph Butler, et al., *An Economic Analysis of the Production, Consumption and Marketing of Cassava (Tapioca)*, Department of Agricultural Economics, University of Georgia, College of Agriculture Experiment Stations, Research Bulletin 97, June 1971; R O Diaz: *World Cassava Production and Yield Trends, 1960-68*, Bulletin RB-1, CIAT, Columbia, October 1972.

30. JR Behrman: *Supply Response in Underdeveloped Agriculture: A Case Study of Four Major Annual Crops in Thailand*, 1937-1963, North-Holland Publishing Company, Amsterdam, 1968.
31. Truman Phillips, op. cit., Chapter 6.
32. Cf: *Report on the Marketing of Tapioca in India*, Directorate of Marketing and Inspection, Ministry of Food and Agriculture, Government of India, New Delhi, Marketing Series No. 88, October 1955 (All India Report); *Report of the Sub-Committee of the Tapioca Market Expansion Board*, TMEB, Board of Revenue (Civil Supplies), Department of Food, Government of Kerala, Trivandrum, 1972; *Report of the Tapioca Enquiry Committee*, Travancore-Cochin Government, 1952.
33. W O Jones: Op. cit., and also his Manioc: An Example of Innovation in African Economies, *Economic Development and Cultural Change*, Vol. V, No. 2, January 1957, pp. 97-117.
34. C H Hendershott, et al.: *A Feasibility Study on Manioc Production in North-east Brazil*, AID Contract No. AID/LA-681 (Brazil), University of Georgia, 1971; Truman Phillips, op. cit.
35. All-India Report, op. cit.; Walter P Falcon et al.: *The Cassava Economy of Java*, Stanford University Press, 1984.
36. Aw-Yong Kong Keong and Mooi Soong Wooi: *Cultivation and Production of Tapioca in Perak*, Jabatan Pertanian, Kementarian Pertanian Dan Perikanan, 1973.
37. Truman Phillips, Op. cit.
38. Cf: M Delcasso and P Silvestre: *Economic Problems Encountered in the Intensive Cultivation of Cassava by IRAT/TOGO*, Paper presented at Agricultural Research Seminar, in Roots and Tuber Crops, University of Ibadan, Nigeria, 22-26 February, 1971; *FAO: The EEC Tapioca Market—Possibiliteis and Limits*, FAO, Rome, 1971.
39. (i) *Studies in the Economics of Farm Management in Kerala* (*Alleppey and Quilon*) combined Report for the years 1962-63 to 1964-65, Directorate of Economics and Statistics, Ministry of Agriculture, New Delhi, 1973 (hereafter FMS).
    (ii) *Study on Tapioca Cultivation in Kerala*, Agricultural Economics Research Centre, Department of Economics, University of Madras, 1976 (hereafter AERC Study).
    (iii) RO Diaz, et al.: *Costs and Use of Inputs in Cassava Production in Colombia: A brief description*, Series EE-No. 5, September 1974, CIAT, Cali, Colombia (hereafter CIAT Study).
40. Truman Phillips: *A Profile of Thai Tapioca Production Practices*, Paper presented at the IV International Symposium on Tropical Root Crops, International Society of Tropical Root Crops and CIAT, Cali, Colombia, August 1-8, 1976.
41. The AERC results pertaining to HYVs must, however, be read with

caution as it is based on only 9 observations as against 66 in the case of local varieties.

42. Per Pinstrup Andersen and R O Diaz: ***Present and Potential Labour Use in Cassava Production in Colombia***, Paper presented at III International Symposium on Tropical Root Crops, Ibadan, Nigeria, December 2-9, 1973, CIAT, Colombia.
43. A Krochmal: Labour Input and Mechanisation of Cassava, ***World Crops***, London, September 1966; JM Beeny, ***Mechanisation for Tapioca***, University of Malaya, Kuala Lumpur, 1969; AB Catambay: Cost of Harvesting Cassava with a Plow, ***Philippine Agriculturist***, 21: 277-280, 1932; AB Catambay and CE Yango: Cost of Harvesting Cassava with Animal Drawn Plow, ***Philippine Agriculturist***, 23; 662-665, 1935.
44. S Venugopalan, et al.: A study of Marketing of Tapioca in Trivandrum district (Kerala), ***The Journal of Scientific Research***, Banaras Hindu University, Vol. XII (2), 1960-61, pp. 335-341.

# 2

# TAPIOCA ECONOMY IN KERALA
## A Macro View

BEFORE we go into the economics of production and marketing of tapioca at the farm level, it would be useful to study salient behavioural features of tapioca as reflected at the state level and also in terms of an inter-district picture.

Against the background of agricultural regions and crop pattern in Kerala, we may first of all try to know what kind of farmers contribute to growth in Kerala through a study of the Census of Agricultural Holdings for the State, particularly the data on crop pattern in different size-groups of holdings. It helps us to know about the agrarian structure of Kerala, which is the social base for agricultural production and growth rates therein.

The most important behavioural aspect of tapioca economy is the growth of the crop, in terms of area, productivity and production. This needs to be studied particularly in relation to paddy.

Growth determines supplies available to the consumer unless the crop or its manufactured products are exported. In particular, we give attention to changes over the years in comparative economics of tapioca from a consumer angle in this respect.

The price behaviour is of interest both to producers and consumers. Apart from a comparison with paddy/rice, the structure of tapioca prices at farm, retail and wholesale levels and the degree of integration between them would also be of interest. This can throw light on market integration and enable us to see whether increase in prices in wholesale markets reach the farmer? proportionately. In studying production and prices, instability therein is also of significance to farmers, to consumers and to the economy in general, and hence to us too.

A word as to why we shall keep paddy/rice in view, while studying tapioca. In the food economy of Kerala, the two are inter-linked both in consumption and production. They are substitutes in food, rice being considered superior. When rice prices increased in the sixties, a shift in consumption to tapioca appears to have taken place.[1] Strictly speaking, they are not good substitutes in production, since tapioca is a dry land crop while paddy is an immensely water-loving crop. Tapioca can be grown in relatively inferior areas, while paddy needs more fertile areas and needs much more greater care in cultivation. Inspite of this, there is competition between the two. Popularisation of paddy cultivation in uplands (grown in lower tracts of hills) constitutes a threat to tapioca cultivation. Also tapioca is sometimes grown in place of paddy particularly in mixed lands (dry-cum-wet). Both these practices are not uncommon in Kerala.

## NATURE OF SECONDARY DATA

Before analysing the data, we have to refer to some of its limitations. Unlike in most states of India where agricultural statistics are compiled on the basis of the returns filed by village-level staff, they are estimated from sample surveys in Kerala, Orissa and West Bengal. On the basis of land utilisation survey conducted twice a year, data pertaining to area under crops was collected. From 1975-76 onwards, the Timely Reporting Scheme (TRS) for collection of agricultural statistics was introduced whereby all the revenue villages in the state were to be completely enumerated on a phased programme spread over six years beginning with the year 1975-76. The TRS data are believed to be of higher precision on account of the bigger sample size.[2] Hence the area statistics of 1957-58 to 1974-75 are not strictly comparable with that of 1975-76 and thereafter. Crop cutting experiments were introduced in the former Travancore State in

1950 to estimate the yield of paddy crop. This was subsequently extended to Cochin and Malabar region upon the formation of Kerala State. In regard to tapioca, however, yield was estimated on the basis of conventional estimates and it was only from 1963-64 onwards that crop-cutting experiments were extended to estimate the yield of tapioca. The differences between the tapioca production figures of 1962-63 and 1963-64 are large and are obviously due to the change in the estimation procedure.[3] Hence the production figures of tapioca prior to 1963-64 are not comparable with the subsequent period. Taking all these factors into consideration our study analyses the data only for a recent period, beginning with the year 1963-64. The analysis is done separately for two periods, 1963-64 to 1974-75 and 1975-76 to 1981-82. This is because, apart from the data limitations cited earlier, our results suggested a structural break in the growth trends necessitating a categorisation in terms of these two sub-periods.

Two new districts, Malappuram and Idukki were formed in 1969 and 1972 respectively and since the data for these two districts are available only for a few years, a separate study on these two districts is not attempted.[4] The data used in the analysis is drawn from the publications of the Directorate of Economics and Statistics, Kerala. Area, production, productivity and price statistics are taken from various issues of the Season and Crop Reports supplemented with consolidated reports like Agricultural Statistics in Kerala (1975), Statistics for Planning (1972, 1977, 1980 and 1983). The sources of consumption and other data used in the analysis are cited in the text.

## AGRARIAN ECONOMY OF KERALA : A BRIEF DESCRIPTION

The diversity and heterogeneity in crops cultivated in Kerala in a way reflects the diversity in natural resource endowments apart from other factors. One thus finds in Kerala crops requiring diverse agro-climatic environments ranging from tropical crops like rice, tapioca, banana, cashew, rubber, spices, etc., to plantation crops like tea, coffee and cardamom that prefer cool temperate climate. As per 1961 census the State was divided into three natural zones viz., lowlands, midlands and highlands, on the basis of contour lines of altitude. These zones form parallel north-south lines running across the state.[5] Though the three natural zones are strictly speaking not homogeneous agro-climatic zones, one does find broad differences in soil type, cropping pattern and topography between the three zones.[6]

The highlands skirting the Western Ghats on the eastern boundary of the state accounts for about 48 per cent of the geographical area of the state. The region which is sparsely populated is physically featured as a land strewn with extensive, tall and steep hills interspersed with narrow valleys. It contains the forest resources of the state and is the abode of important plantation crops like tea, coffee, cardamom, rubber, etc. As one moves from the western ghats in the east to the sea coast on the west the hills become flatter with milder slopes and the dales become wider. This region, viz., midlands accounting for 42 per cent of the state's area is quite densely populated. A wide range of crops like rice, coconut, tapioca, banana, cashew, spices, etc., are grown here. The soil in the region is lateritic and its variants. Cashew processing provides employment to many in this region. The lowlands or coastal region which is densely populated is characterised by near level topography containing sandy to sandy loam soils. Rice is grown in the lowlying areas and coconut in garden lands. Apart from agriculture, allied agricultural activities like coir-making and fishing provide employment to many in this region.

The state has all the pre-requisites like favourable climate, soil, topography, etc., that are conducive to the growth of tapioca. Though tapioca is grown in the three natural zones, cultivation is mainly concentrated in the midlands. It grows well in well-drained laterite, sandy loam or red loam soil and the state abounds in these soils. Under rainfed conditions tapioca requires a minimum rainfall of 1200 mm to 1500 mm distributed evenly throughout the crop period. The state is blessed with abundant rainfall from both monsoons. Though planting of tapioca in Kerala is carried on throughout the year, the best time of planting is April-May and second best in the month of September with the onset of North-East Monsoon. Months of April-May are most favourable for planting tapioca as the crop can utilise both monsoons for growth as will as yield.[7] Excepting for the high ranges (falling in parts of Kottayam and Idukki districts) which lie at 1000 metres above MSL where cool temperate climates prevail, humid tropical climate prevails in the state. Tapioca is susceptible to frosty weather and therefore not grown in the high ranges. Mean temperature in the state varies between 75° F and 90° F and hence conducive to the growth of tapioca which is adversely affected when the temperature goes below 50° F. Severe droughts are rather unusual but heavy floods are of frequent occurrence and cause severe damage to crops.

Table 2.1 presents a comparative picture of selected economic indicators of the state in relation to the national economy. It is interesting to note that though the primary sector accounts for over 40 per cent of the NDP both for the state and country as a whole, the proportion of workers engaged in agriculture (cultivators and agricultural labourers by main activity) is lower in Kerala (41 per cent) compared to the country as a whole (68 per cent). Furthermore, the proportion of agricultural labourers to total workers is higher in Kerala than the same at national level; consequently the proportion of cultivators is lower in the state compared to the all-India figures. Allied agricultural activities absorb over 9 per cent of total workers in Kerala as against over 2 per cent at all-India level.

Another striking feature of the state's agricultural economy is the preponderance of small holdings when compared to the all-India picture. As per Agriculture Census 1976-77, 88 per cent of the operational holdings and 40 per cent of operated area in the state were in the size range below 0.5 hectares as against 55 and 11 per cent respectively for the country as a whole. For holdings above 10 hectares these proportions were 0.1 and 9 per cent respectively for the state and 3 and 26 per cent for the country. The average size of holdings in the state is 0.49 hectares, which is far below the national average of 2 hectares. It is noteworthy that the proportion of wholly owned holdings is higher in Kerala as compared to the national figure.

**TABLE 2.1: Selected Economic Indicators for Kerala State and India**

| Indicators | Reference year/period | Unit | Kerala | India |
|---|---|---|---|---|
| 1 | 2 | 3 | 4 | 5 |
| *Income* | | | | |
| Per Capita Income | Average for | | | |
| (a) At current prices | 1979-80 to | Rs. crores | 1366 | 1550 |
| (b) At 1970-71 prices | 1981-82 | do. | 622 | 691 |
| Share of primary sector in Net Domestic Product | | Percentage | 40.4 | 41.7 |
| *Occupational Structure* | Census 1981 | | | |
| Proportion of cultivators (main activity) to total work force | do. | do. | 13.2 | 42.1 |
| Proportion of Agricultural Labourers (main activity) to total work force | do. | do. | 28.2 | 26.3 |
| Proportion of workers in allied agricultural activities to total work force | do. | do. | 9.4 | 2.2 |
| *Operational Holding Particulars* | | | | |
| Proportion of operational holdings below 1 hectare to total holdings | Agricultural Census 1976-77 | Percentage | | |
| (a) Number | | | 87.7 | 55.2 |
| (b) Area | | | 40.0 | 10.7 |
| Proportion of operational holdings 10 acres and above | do. | do. | | |
| (a) Number | | | 0.1 | 2.9 |
| (b) Area | | | 8.9 | 26.2 |
| Average size of operational holdings | Agriculture Census 1976-77 | Hectares | 0.49 | 2.0 |

TABLE 2.1—(*Contd.*)

TABLE 2.1—(*Contd.*)

| 1 | 2 | 3 | 4 | 5 |
|---|---|---|---|---|
| Proportion of wholly owned holdings to total holdings | Agriculture Census 1976-77 | Percentage | | |
| (a) Number | | | 99.2 | 94.8 |
| (b) Area | | | 98.6 | 94.2 |
| Proportion of wholly rented holdings to total holdings | do. | do. | | |
| (a) Number | | | 0.5 | 1.2 |
| (b) Area | | | 0.5 | 0.9 |
| *Land Use* | | | | |
| (Proportion to total geographical area i.e., Reporting area) | Based on Average for 1979-80 to 1981-82 | | | |
| (a) Area under forests | | do. | 27.8 | 22.2 |
| (b) Not available for cultivation | | do. | 9.2 | 17.0 |
| (c) Cultivable area not sown | | do. | 5.1 | 13.7 |
| (d) Land under miscellaneous tree crops excluding net sown area | | do. | 1.7 | 3.5 |
| (e) Net area sown | | do. | 56.2 | 46.0 |
| (f) Multiple Cropping Index (i.e., Ratio of gross cropped area over net area sown) | | do. | 132 | 123 |
| Land-man ratio* | | Hectares | 0.8 | 2.0 |
| *Irrigation* | | | | |
| Proportion of Gross Irrigated Area to Gross Cropped Area | Based on Average for 1979-80 to 1981-82 | Percentage | 13.5 | 28.7 |
| Irrigation Intensity (i.e., ratio of gross irrigated area over net irrigated area) | | do. | 164 | 128 |
| *Cropping Pattern* | Based on Average for 1979-80 to 1981-82 | Percentage | | |

(*Table* 2.1—*Contd.*)

TABLE 2.1—(*Contd.*)

| 1 | 2 | 3 | 4 | 5 |
|---|---|---|---|---|
| (Proportion to total cropped area) | | | | |
| (a) Rice | | Percentage | 27.8 | 23.2 |
| (b) Total cereals | | do. | 27.9 | 60.2 |
| (c) All foodgrains | | do. | 29.0 | 73.7 |
| (d) Tapioca | | do. | 9.2 | 0.2 |
| (c) Coconut | | do. | 23.2 | 0.6 |
| (f) All food crops | | do. | 61.5 | 81.3 |
| (g) Plantation crops (i.e., Tea, Coffee, Rubber, Cardamom and Cocoa) | | do. | 14.5 | 0.6 |

*Note*: *Land-man ratio—it is the ratio of net cultivated area (i.e., net sown area plus current fallows) to workers engaged in agriculture (i.e., cultivators plus agricultural labourers by main activity).

*Source*: Computed from data in the publications of the Government of Kerala and India.

The third conspicuous feature is the extremely limited scope for extensive cultivation in the state. The proportion of cultivable area not sown to total geographical area was only about 5 per cent for the state as against about 14 per cent at the all-India level. About 56 per cent of the state's geographical area is sown as against 46 per cent in the all-India case. This indicates the limited scope for extending cultivation in the state. The problem is further compounded by the low land-man ratio in Kerala (0.8 hectares) as compared to the all-India figures (2 hectares). Scarcity of land is a severe constraint in increasing agricultural production in the state, particularly for rice. Future possibilities of increasing agricultural production depend more upon intensive cultivation through multiple cropping and inter-cropping. Northern districts of Kerala, however, offered some scope for extensive cultivation in the case of tapioca.

Though the proportion of gross irrigated area to gross sown area is lower in Kerala than in the country as a whole, it may be noted that the state falls within the high rainfall belt of the country.

Lastly, the cropping pattern of the state reveals some distinct features. The proportion of area devoted to foodgrains production is very low in the state as compared to the national picture. Foodgrains—virtually rice in Kerala—account for only a third of the state's gross cropped area, as against 74 per cent at the all-India level. The seemingly low per capita availability of food (rice) in Kerala is to some extent offset by the availability of tapioca, a cereal substitute which occupies almost a tenth of the gross cropped area. Coconut and plantation crops occupy a significant position in the state's agricultural economy.

Though, as noted earlier, tapioca accounts for only a tenth of the state's gross cropped area, its distribution among the districts is quite varied. Table 2.2 suggests that the four southern districts, Trivandrum, Quilon, Alleppey and Kottayam account for almost 65 per cent of total area and production of tapioca in the state. In other words, the districts comprising the Travancore region account for a sizeable proportion of area and production of tapioca in Kerala. Trivandrum, Quilon and Kottayam interestingly account for only 15 per cent of area and production of rice in the state. Almost 50 per cent of area and production of rice is accounted by the four northern districts, Palghat, Malappuram, Kozhikode and Cannanore with Palghat itself accounting for 22 per cent of rice area and 29 per cent of rice production in the state. Thus the main tapioca growing belt in the state is seen to fall within the districts comprising the Travancore region and the rice-growing belt in the districts comprising the Malabar region.

Of the various crops cultivated in the state rice, coconut and tapioca together account for about 60 per cent of the total cropped area. We may examine and find out the relative position of the three crops in different size classes of holdings using the Agriculture Census data for 1976-77. Table 2.3 reveals that more than 56 per cent of tapioca area is in holdings less than 1 hectare, 40 per cent in holdings between 1 and 5 hectares and the remaining 4 per cent in holdings more than 5 hectares. The same proportion in the case of rice is 29 per cent, 61 per cent and 10 per cent respectively. In the case of coconut these

TABLE 2.2: **Distribution of Area and Production of Tapioca and Rice in Kerala (based on average for 1979-80 to 1981-82)**

| Districts | Area under Tapioca % | Production of Tapioca % | Area under Rice % | Production of Rice % |
|---|---|---|---|---|
| Trivandrum | 21.6 | 21.6 | 4.0 | 3.5 |
| Quilon | 25.1 | 24.0 | 6.3 | 6.3 |
| Alleppey | 7.7 | 7.4 | 10.4 | 12.0 |
| Kottayam | 9.9 | 11.2 | 4.1 | 4.7 |
| Idukki | 3.9 | 5.3 | 1.1 | 1.2 |
| Ernakulam | 5.1 | 6.2 | 12.7 | 11.3 |
| Trichur | 2.8 | 2.4 | 14.0 | 11.7 |
| Palghat | 5.3 | 5.2 | 22.6 | 29.2 |
| Malappuram | 7.6 | 6.3 | 10.0 | 8.2 |
| Kozhikode | 2.6 | 2.0 | 5.7 | 4.1 |
| Cannanore | 8.4 | 8.4 | 9.1 | 7.8 |
| State | 100.0 (255) | 100.0 (3964) | 100.0 (802) | 100.0 (1304) |

*Note*: Figures in parentheses give absolute figures—Area in thousand hectares; Production in thousand tonnes.

proportions are 59, 36 and 5 per cents respectively. While tapioca and coconut cultivation is concentrated among marginal and small holdings, medium and large farmers account for a major portion of area under rice. Area under tapioca and coconut as a proportion of cropped area tends to decrease continuously with an increase in size of holdings. In the case of rice, there is no continuous tendency of either rise or fall, but the middle size classes with more than 1 hectare upto 10 hectares devote larger area under rice than either smaller or larger farmers. While farmers in the size group below 0.5 hectares devote 21 per cent and 27 per cent of their cropped area

TABLE 2.3: **Relative Position of Tapioca, Rice and Coconut in Crop Pattern of Different Size Classes of Holdings: Kerala Agriculture Census, 1976-77**

| Size classes of operational holdings in hectares | Gross Cropped Area % | Area under | | | Area under Crop as % of Gross Cropped Area in each size-class | | |
|---|---|---|---|---|---|---|---|
| | | Tapioca % | Rice % | Coconut % | Tapioca % | Rice % | Coconut % |
| Below 0.5 | 23.1 | 32.4 | 11.1 | 38.2 | 21.1 | 15.1 | 27.4 |
| 0.5— 1.0 | 18.8 | 24.2 | 18.2 | 21.2 | 19.4 | 30.5 | 18.6 |
| 1.0— 2.0 | 24.1 | 22.9 | 32.0 | 19.8 | 14.3 | 41.9 | 13.7 |
| 2.0— 3.0 | 12.4 | 9.6 | 15.7 | 9.0 | 11.6 | 39.6 | 12.0 |
| 3.0— 5.0 | 10.7 | 7.2 | 13.2 | 7.3 | 10.2 | 39.2 | 11.4 |
| 5.0—10.0 | 6.1 | 3.1 | 7.8 | 3.5 | 7.7 | 40.5 | 9.7 |
| 10.0 and above | 4.8 | 0.6 | 2.0 | 1.0 | 1.8 | 13.4 | 3.5 |
| All | 100<br>(1821) | 100<br>(274) | 100<br>(574) | 100<br>(302) | 15.1 | 31.5 | 16.6 |

*Note*: Land utilisation of holdings below 0.02 hectares and institutional holdings have not been recorded.
Figures in parentheses give area in thousand hectares.

*Source*: Directorate of Economics and Statistics, Government of Kerala, Trivandrum.

to tapioca and coconut cultivation respectively, the same proportion in the case of rice was only 15 per cent. On the other hand, farmers with 10 hectares and above devotedonly 2 per cent and 3.5 per cent of their cropped area to tapioca and coconut cultivation respectively; in the case of rice it was over 13 per cent. Thus, on the whole tapioca and coconut are seen to be relatively more important among small farms than on large farms, whereas rice was more important among medium and large farms. But what is interesting is that even big farmers do grow an inferior food crop like tapioca.

## GROWTH OF TAPIOCA AND RICE

Given the scale of food preferences in Kerala, support for programmes with emphasis on rice production have received priority over tapioca production both at the institutional and grass-root level. But technical constraints to augment production are more severe in the case of rice than tapioca. Land, for instance, is a severe constraint for extending rice cultivation but not to the same extent in the case of tapioca. Rice productivity too is fairly near its technical threshold but not so in the case of tapioca where vast potential exists to enhance tapioca productivity. The differences in the performance of the two crops in the different regions of Kerala, should as a rule, reflect on the differences in endowments as also the relative importance of tapioca and rice in the different regions. Of the available land in Kerala where there is still some scope for extending cultivation (i.e., cultivable area not sown), the northern districts accounted for 70 per cent of it, southern districts for 21 per cent and the remaining was shared by the other districts. Apart from increasing productivity per hectare in a given season there are other possibilities of increasing food production either through adjustments in cropping pattern or increasing the intensity of cropping which may be more relevant to a seasonal crop like rice. These factors seem to be the proper perspective within which any meaningful analysis of the growth behaviour of the two crops should be attempted.

**(i) State Level Performance**

Our analysis of the growth behaviour of tapioca and rice is done separately for the period 1963-64 to 1974-75 (Period I) and 1975-76 to 1981-82 (Period II) for reasons already stated. For measuring growth rates of tapioca and rice we have used linear trends with slope expressed as per cent at respective means. The detailed results pertaining to tapioca and rice are presented in Tables 2-A and 2-B at the end of this chapter. As is evident from both the tables, the growth in production of tapioca and rice has been significant during Period I. This was no doubt, due to a significant growth in area as well as productivity of the two crops. Though the growth rates in area, production and productivity of both tapioca and rice have been significant for the state as a whole, the rates of growth are higher in the case of tapioca. For the state as a whole, while tapioca production during this period recorded a growth of 7.32 per cent per annum, in the case of rice it was only 2.30 per cent per annum. Growth of area under tapioca was 3.63 per cent per annum, while for rice it was only 1.07 per cent per annum. Despite all encouragements (governmental and non-governmental) the productivity of rice registered a growth of mere 1.24 per cent per annum compared to 3.90 per cent in the case of tapioca.

The tremendous growth in tapioca production during period I as compared to rice would be more striking if we note the trends in production per capita which reveal that while tapioca production per capita has shown a positive growth of 5.13 per cent per annum (significant at 1 per cent level) rice production per capita has more or less remained static (in fact it showed a negative growth, —0.07 per cent per annum, but the trend was not significant). This suggests that supply of tapioca was more elastic than that of rice during this period. It is, therefore, quite apparent that tapioca has played a major role in increasing food availability in Kerala.

When we look at the trends for 1975-76 to 1981-82, we find a sudden downturn in the fortunes of both tapioca and rice. Production of tapioca registered a significant decline whereas that of rice was stagnant. In per capita terms both tapioca and rice production registered a significant decline (the trends were

—6.76 and —1.43 per centper annum respectively). A significant decline in area under both crops was the prime reason for the above trends. Yield of tapioca also declined slightly but the trend was not significant. However, the yield of tapioca in relation to rice yield recorded a significant decline in this period. Furthermore, the price of tapioca did not register any significant increase though the results must be read with caution on account of the limited observations available for analysis. Paddy price too did not register any significant increase. Apart from some of these factors increasing costs of paddy cultivation have made it unattractive leading to substitution of coconut, sugarcane and bananas in place of paddy. The factors that contributed to the decline in tapioca area may not be the same. Quite possibly the steep rise in tapioca production in the period upto 1975 may have led to a glut in the market, particularly in the absence of measures to absorb this increase in production. Furthermore, the remunerativeness of cocoa cultivation espoused by official and non-official agencies caught the imagination of cultivators; as a result cocoa cultivation may have replaced tapioca in some of the inter-cropped lands. Cashew and rubber are other crops which have been displacing tapioca.

As against this, during 1963-64 to 1974-75 there were a number of factors favourable to both crops. Apart from a significant growth in prices of both crops (see discussion later) yields of both crops recorded a significant increase, the increase being much higher in the case of tapioca. In fact trends fitted to the relative tapioca—rice yield indices were significant at 1 per cent level. High Yielding Varieties (HYV) of rice are finding wide acceptance but the introduction of HYVs of tapioca will help maintain, if not increase, the relative yield advantage for tapioca. Though trends fitted to the ratio of tapioca yield to rice yield indicate a significant decline in recent years (i.e., Period II), tapioca still continues to maintain its yield advantage over rice (refer Table 2-C).

**(ii) Districtwise Performance**

Of the districts, five—Kottayam, Cannanore, Ernakulam, Alleppey and Quilon, have yield rates of tapioca higher than the state average (high productivity districts) while Trivandrum, Trichur and the northern districts combine[8] (it includes Palghat, Malappuram and Kozhikode) have tapioca yield rates below the state average (hereafter low productivity districts). In the case of rice three districts, Palghat, Alleppey and Kottayam report yield rates higher than the state average with Quilon being a marginal case. Trivandrum, Ernakulam, Trichur, Cannanore and Kozhikode figured among the districts with relatively low yield rates of rice. Kottayam led the tally of districts with the highest yield rate of tapioca, almost 19 tonnes per hectare. At the other end of the spectrum we find the Northern districts combine with yield rate of tapioca around 13.6 tonnes per hectare. As far as rice was concerned Palghat was well ahead of the other districts with mean rice productivity being 1841 kgs/hectare. But neighbouring Kozhikode had the lowest yield rate of rice, being 1167 kgs/hectare.

The growth in productivity of tapioca during 1963-64 to 1974-75 has been tremendous in both high and low productivity level districts (see Table 2.4). Particularly, all districts with high productivity levels have registered a high and significant growth in productivity of tapioca. This means that the higher rates of growth here are not 'statistical', i.e., it is not merely due to a rise from a low base. Trivandrum, a low productivity district, stood solitary by recording a low and statistically not significant growth in tapioca productivity. The growth rates in productivity were noteworthy in Cannanore (9.47 per cent per annum) and Trichur (8.92 per cent per annum). Even in the other districts the growth in productivity was more than 4 per cent per annum. If we classify the districts with high rates of growth in productivity (i.e., all excluding Trivandrum) three of them registered a higher rate of growth in area as compared to the state average. They are Quilon, Trichur and the Northern districts combine. The remaining four registered lower growth rates in area, in fact three of them showing no growth in area (i.e., statistically not significant) and one showing a significant decline (see Table 2-A). It is heartening that in quite a few districts increase in tapioca production has been mainly through increase in productivity and not at the expense of area. This is a fact of significance in Kerala, where land is limited.

TABLE 2.4: **Classification of Districts according to Growth Performance of Tapioca during 1963-64 to 1974-75 and 1975-76 to 1981-82**

| Districts with | Rate of growth of productivity | |
|---|---|---|
| | High | Low or negative growth |
| | *1963-64 to 1974-75* | |
| High productivity levels | Kottayam, Cannanore, Ernakulam, Alleppey, Quilon | Nil |
| Low productivity levels | Trichur, Northern districts | Trivandrum |
| High growth in area | Quilon, Trichur, Northern districts | Trivandrum |
| Low or negative growth in area | Kottayam, Cannanore Ernakulam, Alleppey | Nil |
| | *1975-76 to 1981-82* | |
| High productivity levels | Nil | Kottayam, Cannanore, Ernakulam, Alleppey, Quilon |
| Low productivity levels | Nil | Trivandrum, Trichur, Northern districts |
| High growth in area | Nil | Nil |
| Low or negative growth in area | Nil | Kottayam, Cannanore, Ernakulam, Alleppey, Quilon, Trivandrum, Trichur, Northern districts |

*Note*: The state average has been used to demarcate low and high growth districts. If the state average is negative, only those districts with positive and significant trends are classified as high growth districts. Districts with other trends (i.e., positive but not significant and negative trends) are classified as low or negative growth districts. Northern districts include Palghat, Malappuram and Kottayam.

*Source*: Derived from Table 2-A presented at the end of this chapter.

Of the four districts which reported high growth rates in tapioca area two—Quilon and Trivandrum—fall within the Travancore region which, as noted earlier, contain the main tapioca-growing belt of the state. In absolute terms the increase in tapioca area between 1963-64 and 1974-75 was the highest in Quilon (44847 hectares) followed by the Northern districts combine (33304 hectares) and Trivandrum (28442 hectares). The potential for extensive cultivation was the maximum in the northern districts which accounted for about 70 per cent of total cultivable area not sown in the State. On the other hand the potential for extensive cultivation was relatively the least in Trivandrum and Quilon, both of which accounted for less than 3 and 4 per cent respectively of total cultivable area not sown in 1963-64. The increase in tapioca area here has been effected mainly through adjustments in cropping pattern. In fact a perusal of the land use data suggests that between 1963-64 and 1974-75, net area sown (under allcrops) increased by only 1818 and 11611 hectares in Trivandrum and Quilon districts respectively which is far less than the increase in tapioca area in these two districts. To some extent, part of the increase in tapioca area may have been effected through inter-cropping with other crops.

If we look at the trends for 1975-76 to 1981-82 we find a dramatic change in the growth scenario presented above. Both high as well as low productivity level districts registered either a low or declining trend in tapioca productivity. The declining trend in productivity was significant only in Cannanore, whereas in Kottayam, Alleppey, Quilon, and Trichur the negative trends were not significant. Ernakulam, Trivandrum and the Northern districts reported positive trends but they were not statistically significant. In other words, this indicates that unlike in the previous period, there has been no significant increase in the tapioca yields per hectare. In fact, they have declined though these trends were significant only in Cannanore. Even more disturbing to note is that all the districts reported a decline in tapioca area though the declining trends were not significant in Cannanore, Trivandrum and the Northern districts. The rates of decline were quite steep in Kottayam (−7.89 per cent per annum), Ernakulam (−4.26 per cent per annum), Alleppey (−5.91 per cent per annum), Quilon (−6.61

per cent per annum), and Trichur (−8.49 per cent per annum). Of these districts Kottayam, Ernakulam and Alleppey had reported declining trends in the previous period also, whereas other districts especially Quilon, Trivandrum, Trichur and Northern districts had earlier registered a positive and significant growth in tapioca area. In absolute terms the decline in tapioca area between 1975-76 and 1981-82 was the highest in Quilon (28090 hectares), Trivandrum (11720 hectares), Northern districts (11060 hectares) and Kottayam (10870 hectares). Thus unlike in the earlier period where area under tapioca had registered a positive and significant growth in both traditional and non-traditional areas, during 1975-76 to 1981-82 all the districts reported declines, though bulk of the decrease in tapioca area took place in the traditional tapioca-growing belt of the state, especially in Quilon, Trivandrum and Kottayam districts.

Table 2.5 gives a comparative picture of the changes in area under tapioca and rice during the two periods under review. It is quite obvious that the increase in area under tapioca during period I has not occurred at the expense of area under rice as borne by the fact that not a single district has reported any decline in area under rice cultivation. The converse may, however, seem to be true in Alleppey, Kottayam and Ernakulam where the decline in area under tapioca seem to be associated with the high growth in area under rice in these three districts. Both Alleppey and Kottayam are high rice productivity districts, as noted earlier. The declining trend in tapioca area was, however, significant only in Alleppey. It may be noted that a large portion of the lands in Alleppey may be classified as of the mixed category where with provision of infrastructure facilities, rice can be grown. In Cannanore also the growth in tapioca area was low and not significant. To the extent tapioca and rice are substitutable, any subsistence requirement of tapioca can be met with smaller area when productivity has increased. With tapioca registering a high rate of growth in productivity in these three districts, farmers may have preferred to curtail the area under an inferior and less remunerative food crop like tapioca and shift the area so saved to the cultivation of more lucrative crops. The case of ragi (eleusine coracana) in Karnataka State is

TABLE 2.5: **Classification of Districts according to Growth of Area under Tapioca and Rice during 1963-64 to 1974-75 and 1975-76 to 1981-82**

| Districts with | Declining area under tapioca | Low growth in area under tapioca | High growth in area under tapioca |
|---|---|---|---|
| | *1963-64 to 1974-75* | | |
| Declining area under rice | Nil | Nil | Nil |
| Low growth in area under rice | Nil | Cannanore | Trivandrum<br>Quilon<br>Trichur |
| High growth in area under rice | Alleppey<br>Kottayam<br>Ernakulam | Nil | Palghat<br>Kozhikode |
| | *1975-76 to 1981-82* | | |
| Declining area under rice | Alleppey<br>Kottayam<br>Quilon<br>Trivandrum<br>Cannanore<br>Kozhikode | Nil | Nil |
| Low growth in area under rice | Palghat<br>Ernakulam | Nil | Nil |
| High growth in area under rice | Nil | Nil | Nil |

*Source*: Derived from Table 2-A and 2-B presented at the end of this chapter.

an instance worth citing, where following adoption of HYVs of ragi, farmers have curtailed ragi area and shifted the area thus saved to cultivation of more lucrative crops like mulberry.

The rates of growth in area under rice during Period I are, however, relatively low in most of the districts compared to that of tapioca. This is understandable because land is a severe constraint to extending rice cultivation but not to the same extent in the case of tapioca. Except in Kottayam where the growth rate of rice area was 2.6 per cent per annum, the growth rates of rice area were less than 2 per cent per annum in other districts, with Trivandrum, Quilon, Trichur and Cannanore even reporting growth rates in rice area less than 0.5 per cent per annum. It seems even more likely that a large part of the increase in rice area during this period was achieved by raising additional crops from existing lands following augmented irrigation facilities. In fact, between 1963-64 and 1974-75 area sown more than once doubled from about 4.4 lakh hectares to 8.2 lakh hectares. Tapioca obviously could not have been the beneficiary of this increase in cropping intensity, being an annual crop.

During Period II i.e., 1975-76 to 1981-82, we find a change in this picture with all districts (excluding Palghat and Ernakulam) reporting a decline in area under both tapioca and rice. The declines were relatively high and significant for Kottayam, Trivandrum, Trichur, Cannanore and Kozhikode, whereas in the case of Alleppey and Quilon they were not statistically significant. Though Palghat and Ernakulam recorded a positive increase in rice area they were not statistically significant. The above results clearly suggest that unlike in the preceding period 1963-64 to 1974-75, during which there was a significant growth in area under tapioca and rice, during the latter period i.e., 1975-76 to 1981-82 both crops had entered a phase of deceleration.

Though both crops registered a decline in area, the factors that have contributed to this decline need not be the same for the two crops, as mentioned earlier. Further, whereas during the Period I area declines under a low value crop like tapioca (in some districts) were possibly in response to an increase in yields, the decline in tapioca area in Period II does not seem to be due to the same phenomenon. As mentioned already, the failure to diversify the market outlets for tapioca and its by-products has been a major factor as to why the crop was unable to sustain the growth momentum generated during the period 1963-64 to 1974-75. In other words, market constraint has prevented further stimulus to the crop's growth. Furthermore, there has been no significant increase in either yield or farm price of tapioca except in Kozhikode where prices rose significantly. The yield of tapioca, in fact, declined in a number of districts, though these trends were significant only in Cannanore. In the case of rice yields rose significantly in a number of districts (Alleppey, Quilon, Ernakulam and Kozhikode) whereas in other districts the increases were not significant (Palghat, Kottayam, Trichur). Only Trivandrum and Cannanore reported a decline in rice yields but they were not statistically significant. Price of paddy, however, did not register any significant growth in any district. In fact, quite a few districts reported a decline in paddy prices, though these trends were not statistically significant. In other words, paddy prices have more or less remained stagnant during this period. This factor coupled with the increasing cost of cultivation must have induced farmers to shift from rice to other remunerative crops like coconut, sugarcane, bananas etc.

We have already observed the impressive performance of tapioca relative to rice in the rates of growth of productivity during 1963-64 to 1974-75 and its unimpressive performance in this respect during the subsequent period i.e., 1975-76 to 1981-82. We may note here that during Period-I, districts which showed higher growth rates in rice productivity also registered higher growth rates in tapioca productivity (Quilon, Alleppey, Kottayam, Kozhikode and Ernakulam) and districts with low rates in one registered low rate of growth in the other too (Trivandrum). Other districts (Palghat, Trichur and Cannanore) recorded higher rate of growth in tapioca productivity but not in rice. Broadly growth rates in productivity of the two crops during Period-I have gone together (unlike in area) which suggests that productivity performance of tapioca has not been at the cost of rice or vice-versa.

But the same cannot be said about Period II, where we find that most of the districts which recorded a decline in tapioca productivity also registered a positive increase in rice productivity (though the trends in both cases were not statistically significant). It was only in Cannanore, Ernakulam and Palghat that the trends in tapioca/rice productivity (positive or negative) moved in the same direction. On the contrary in respect of area almost all districts recorded a decline in area under both crops. In other words, whereas in Period I productivity trends of both crops moved together (unlike area trends), in Period II, it is the area trends of the two crops which have moved together, unlike productivity trends. This suggests that in Period II, productivity performance of rice may have been at the cost of tapioca.

The better performance of tapioca during Period I could imply that more resources were being allocated to tapioca cultivation or that there was increasing use of modern inputs like HYV seeds and fertilisers than in rice. But given the policy underlying the priority for rice production in the state, yield augmenting factors are weighted in favour of rice rather than tapioca. In 1963-64 for instance almost 78 per cent of gross irrigated area in Kerala was accounted by rice alone, and in 1974-75 this proportion rose to 83 per cent but came down to 72 per cent in 1981-82. There are no separate figures for tapioca. But the Agriculture Census 1976-77 suggested that less than 3 per cent of tapioca area was irrigated, the remaining 97 per cent being rainfed. Irrigated tapioca, it may be noted, yields two to three times more than rainfed tapioca.[9] HYV seeds played a major role in augmenting rice production. By 1974-75 HYVs accounted for 19 per cent of total rice area and 22 per cent of rice production in the state. These proportions further rose to 32 and 40 per cent respectively in 1981-82. There is, however, no information as regards the extent of tapioca area under HYVs. Though HYVs of tapioca have been introduced by CTCRI, Trivandrum since 1963, there has not been much of an effort to spread it as done in the case of HYVs of rice. However, it is believed that the wide acceptance and popularisation of cultivation of M-4 an improved variety of tapioca was also responsible for enhancing tapioca productivity apart from HYVs of tapioca.

With regard to fertiliser use too, rice has been the main beneficiary. The NSS 26th round suggested that rice both irrigated and unirrigated accounted for the major chunk of fertilisers consumed in Kerala.[10] A sample study in 1967-68 revealed that 25.2 per cent of cultivators growing rice used fertilisers while only 5.5 per cent of cultivators growing tapioca used fertilisers.[11] The study revealed that 64.5 per cent of rice area was treated with fertilisers, while in the case of tapioca area it was only 15.1 per cent. The Agriculture Census 1970-71 and 1976-77 for Kerala also corroborated these evidences that rice was the main beneficiary of fertiliser use in Kerala.

Thus it is quite obvious that rice attracted more yield augmenting inputs compared to tapioca during both periods. In spite of this, as observed earlier, tapioca was able to register a faster rate of growth in yields during Period I possibly because the crop was more input responsive than rice. Constraints like pests, need for skills, etc. are more operative in rice. Besides, rice being an ancient crop, its actual yield is nearer potential yield, and response to inputs may be more limited.

A historical analysis of the factors behind the growth of tapioca in the different regions of Kerala provides interesting insights.[12] Though tapioca is believed to have been introduced into Malabar by the Portuguese during the 17th century the spurt in tapioca cultivation in Malabar seems to be only a recent phenomenon. This may partly be due to the influence of Travancore migrants to Malabar who imported with them their cultural affinity to tapioca. But growing use of tapioca as an industrial input may be the major factor. World War II resulted in the disruption of the imports of starch required for the Indian textile industry.[13] The country was thus forced to tap indigenous sources of starch like maize and wheat. But being staple foods their production could only be limited. It, therefore, became imperative to supplement this by indigenous production of starch from other sources like tapioca. In fact a large portion of the tapioca needs of the starch industry in Tamil Nadu until recently was being met from Malabar. If the growth of tapioca-based industries is any indication of the end-use of tapioca produced in Malabar we note that during the late sixties and early seventies Malappuram district in Malabar (part of northern districts combine) became the focal point of growth of at least 75 small scale tapioca-based industries.[14] Travancore provides a contrast to Malabar, with tapioca cultivation spreading fast partly due to the active encouragement of Maharaja Vishakham Tirunal (1880—85) and partly due to economic factors. Frequent occurrence of famines in Travancore, a region deficit in her foodgrain requirements hastened the spread of tapioca cultivation in Travancore. The Travancore region continues to be the predominant tapioca-growing belt in Kerala accounting for almost 65 per cent of the State's tapioca area, as noted earlier. Travancore provides a further contrast in that the once famous tapioca-based cottage starch industry at Balaramapuram near Trivandrum declined due to economic factors but more likely due to non-availability of tapioca suggesting that tapioca production is this region in mostly used for food purposes. Thus, while the growth of tapioca in Malabar can be described as industry-induced in the case of Travancore it was largely food-induced. The deceleration in the area and production of tapioca in recent years may suggest that tapioca production in the state had reached an optimum level by the mid-seventies and given the present level of demand for the commodity, it was not possible to sustain the growth momentum of the sixties and early seventies. The spurt in tapioca cultivation in the neighbouring Tamil Nadu state in recent years has curtailed the demand for Kerala tapioca by the starch and sago industries of that state. Further, an improvement in the availability of rice and other cereals from the public distribution system and open market, etc. has also depressed the demand for tapioca.

## CONSUMPTION OF TAPIOCA AND RICE

Given other factors, the growth of a crop depends upon the demand generated for the crop and its products. In the context of the importance of tapioca and rice in the food economy of Kerala, we may briefly examine its role in consumption in Kerala. Compared to production data, consumption data on tapioca are meagre. Excepting for the NSS data there does not appear to be any data on consumption from official sources. Some non-official sources like Centre for Development Studies, Trivandrum (CDS), Operation Research Group, Baroda (ORG) an Shubh Kumar of IFPRI, Washington (SKK) have given estimates of tapioca and rice consumption in the course of their studies.[15] The NSS data are based on consumer expenditure surveys, the ORG and SKK estimates on the basis of dietary surveys while the CDS estimates are based on Food Balance Sheets.[16] Though an advantage of the CDS data based on Food Balance Sheets is that consumption is related to production and its end uses, by its very nature it cannot shed any light on the consumption pattern across socio-economic groups. On the other hand, the NSS, ORG and SKK data give us some idea about the consumption pattern among different socio-economic groups. However, dietary and consumer expenditure surveys have their shortcomings particularly when the reference period for recording consumption details are not representative enough.[17]

We have presented these three sets of estimates for a comparative analysis (see Table 2.6). There is not much variation in the estimates of rice consumption between the three sets of estimates, being around 1000 calories per capita per day. But in regard to tapioca consumption the CDS estimates differ greatly from the other two. On the average during the sixties according to the CDS data, around 628 calories per capita per day were derived from tapioca consumption. The NSS and ORG estimates of tapioca consumption for rural Kerala were around 300 calories. An interesting feature of the NSS data is that consumption of rice has declined over the period under reference but that of tapioca has increased (though their estimates are still far below those of the CDS). Between rural and urban areas consumption of rice does not show much variation (though it is slightly higher in rural areas) but the difference is striking in the case of tapioca. The NSS 28th round revealed that in rural Kerala 366 calories per capita per day were derived from tapioca and only 190 in the case of urban Kerala. In the case of ORG estimates, it was 284 and 142 calories for rural and urban areas respectively. If the ORG and NSS estimates are accepted they would vary widely from the production data on tapioca based on its known end uses. This could mean that either production of tapioca is overestimated (though the yields of both rice and tapioca are based on crop-cutting surveys) or that a higher proportion of tapioca is being used for non-food purposes. But the CDS on the basis of empirical deductions suggested that around 70 to 80 per cent of tapioca production is available for human consumption.

TABLE 2.6: **Daily Per Capita Consumption of Tapioca and Rice in Calories for Kerala**

| Item | | | Rice | Tapioca |
|---|---|---|---|---|
| NSS Estimates (Based on consumer expenditure survey) | 17th Round, 1961-62 | Rural | 1134 | 270 |
| | | Urban | 1158 | 74 |
| | | State | 1136 | 182 |
| | 28th Round, 1973-74 | Rural | 845 | 366 |
| | | Urban | 834 | 190 |
| | | State | 840 | 278 |
| CDS Estimates (Based on Food Balance Sheets) | 1961-62 | State | 1059 | 575 |
| | 1970-71 | State | 1000 | 744 |
| | Average for 1961-62 to 1970-71 | State | 920 | 628 |
| ORG Estimates (Based on dietary survey) | 1971 | Rural | 959 | 284 |
| | | Urban | 835 | 142 |
| | | State | 938 | 260 |

*Note*: (1) With regard to NSS data, figures were given for cereal substitutes as a group. Since tapioca largely accounts for cereal substitute group in Kerala, these figures were assumed to represent those of tapioca consumption.

(2) The ORG data were given for Roots and Tuber group. But the report mentions that this group refers to tapioca mainly. Hence the figures were taken to represent tapioca consumption.

Table 2.7 presents the consumption pattern of tapioca and rice in terms of socio-economic groups as per ORG and SKK estimates. The ORG estimates clearly reveal that while tapioca consumption declines with an increase in income, consumption of rice increases with an increase in income. Shubh Kumar's sample study (1974) in the tapioca-dominant Trivandrum district also corroborates the ORG findings that the income elasticity of demand for tapioca is negative and for rice positive. But unlike ORG estimates, SKK estimates suggested that not only is per capita consumption of tapioca very high among the lowest income groups with per capita monthly income less than Rs. 50 but also tapioca outbids rice as the main source of calories in the diet of these income groups.

TABLE 2.7: **Consumption of Tapioca and Rice among Different Socio-Economic Groups in Calories Per Capita Per Day**

| Food commodity | Income Group | | | |
|---|---|---|---|---|
| | Rs. 100 | Rs. 101-200 | Rs. 201-500 | Above Rs. 500 |
| *ORG Estimates* | | | | |
| Rice | 810 | 1031 | 1068 | 1213 |
| Tapioca | 291 | 265 | 180 | 139 |

| Food Commodity | Monthly Per Capita Total Income (in Rs.) | | | | | |
|---|---|---|---|---|---|---|
| | Less than 15 | 15-24 | 25-34 | 35-49 | 50-74 | 75 or more |
| *SKK Estimates* | | | | | | |
| Rice calories (daily adult equivalent) | 396 | 616 | 750 | 777 | 839 | 970 |
| Tapioca calories (daily adult equivalent) | 1013 | 898 | 819 | 817 | 729 | 213 |

*Source*: 1. ORG Estimates, see Food Habits Survey, *op. cit.*
2. SKK Estimates, see Shubh K Kumar, *op. cit.*

Table 2.8 presents the NSS data on tapioca and rice consumption for two reference periods. However, no clear trends emerge except in the case of consumption of rice in rural and

TABLE 2.8: **Monthly Calorie Consumption Per Person of Tapioca and Rice: Kerala (in thousand calories)**

| Monthly per capita expenditure classes (in Rs.) | NSS 17th Round (September 1961 to July 1962) | | | | NSS 28th Round (October 1973 to June 1974) | | | |
|---|---|---|---|---|---|---|---|---|
| | Rural | | Urban | | Rural | | Urban | |
| | Rice | Tapioca | Rice | Tapioca | Rice | Tapioca | Rice | Tapioca |
| 0—13 | 21.0 | 8.0 | 18.9 | 2.0 | 6.8 | 7.9 | No Sample | |
| 13—15 | 45.5 | 3.8 | 31.6 | 1.0 | 6.1 | 13.1 | 12.5 | 0.3 |
| 15—18 | 32.1 | 11.9 | 31.8 | 0.6 | 11.8 | 7.3 | 5.8 | 19.6 |
| 18—21 | 41.3 | 5.9 | 37.4 | 6.1 | 11.0 | 11.9 | 10.2 | 5.1 |
| 21—24 | 33.0 | 11.1 | 36.8 | 2.4 | 15.0 | 10.1 | 14.6 | 4.8 |
| 24—28 | 43.6 | 6.2 | 45.7 | 1.1 | 17.2 | 8.1 | 14.1 | 8.8 |
| 28—34 | 42.5 | 7.9 | 42.1 | 2.5 | 17.5 | 11.8 | 19.4 | 4.8 |
| 34—43 | 60.9 | 14.2 | 39.0 | 1.1 | 20.9 | 10.2 | 19.3 | 6.4 |
| 43—55 | 43.9 | 3.3 | 49.7 | 1.1 | 25.1 | 12.2 | 27.0 | 6.3 |
| 55—75 | 38.7 | 0.2 | 46.3 | 5.1 | 29.2 | 11.3 | 25.3 | 7.4 |
| 75 & avobe | 45.0 | 5.2 | 36.0 | 2.1 | 40.7 | 11.3 | 33.1 | 4.1 |
| All Classes | 34.0 | 8.1 | 34.2 | 2.2 | 25.4 | 11.0 | 25.0 | 5.7 |

*Source*: (1) Computed from NSS 17th Round, September 1961 to July 1962, Integrated Household Survey (Sch.27), No. 184, Tables with Notes on Expenditure, Cabinet Secretariat, Government of India, 1974.

(2) NSS 28th Round, October 1973 to June 1974, No. 240, Tables on Consumer Expenditure, Department of Statistics, New Delhi, 1977.

urban areas (NSS 28th round) which shows that rice consumption increases with an increase in size of expenditure classes. In the case of tapioca there is no continuous tendency of either a rise or fall. Rice is seen to provide more calories than tapioca in most expenditure classes. Tapioca, however, outbids rice as the main source of calories in the two lowest expenditure classes in the NSS 28th round. It is also noted that while consumption of rice between rural and urban areas do not show much difference, it is quite striking in the case of tapioca. This seems to suggest that the impact of urban culture on tastes and preferences as also the demonstration effect are reflected in the food habits of the urbanites with relatively less tapioca being consumed. Also between the two NSS rounds per capita rice consumption seems to have declined in both rural and urban areas while that of tapioca seems to have increased slightly. If calorie intake has a direct relationship with per capita food production the above tendency, if correct, may seem to reflect the availability of the two foods in Kerala during the said period.

One of the reasons why tapioca figures prominently in the diet of the poor is that it is cheap compared to rice. Per rupee of expenditure calories derived from tapioca are higher than rice (See Table 2-C). A disquieting feature is that over the period 1963 to 1981, this advantage seems to be declining though the trend is not smooth. The class-specific nature of the demand for tapioca, confined as it is to low income groups, suggests that this factor may act as a constraint on the growth of the crop in the long run, unless markets for the crop and its products are diversified. The decline in the production of tapioca in the late seventies is a pointer in this direction.

## PRICE BEHAVIOUR

We may now examine the behaviour of prices of tapioca and paddy/rice and find out what role they have played in the growth of the two crops. The price trends for 1963-64 to 1974-75 suggest that price has not been an inhibiting factor to both crops. The farm prices of both crops registered a significant increase during this period both at the state and district levels. At the state level the farm price of tapioca increased at 8.48 per cent per annum while that of paddy increased at the rate of 10.19 per cent per annum. Though the prices of both crops increased, the rate of increase in price of tapioca was less than that of paddy at least at the state level. In fact trends fitted to the ratio of the respective tapioca-paddy price indices revealed that the relative price of tapioca had declined slightly at state level but this trend was not significant. At district levels too the relative price of tapioca did not show any significant growth (either positive or negative) in most districts. The disincentive, if any, to augment tapioca production on account of the slower or insignificant growth in tapioca prices compared to paddy prices was largely offset by the faster increase in tapioca yields compared to paddy yields during this period.

During Period II, i.e., 1975-76 to 1981-82, though the farm prices of both crops registered a positive growth, it was not statistically significant. At state level, the farm price of tapioca rose by 4.79 per cent per annum, whereas paddy prices increased only at the rate of 0.72 per cent per annum. Though tapioca prices apparently seem to have grown faster than paddy prices during this period, trends fitted to the ratio of the respective prices suggest that the increase in the relative price of tapioca was not statistically significant. Further, whatever advantage tapioca may have gained from the increase in its prices was offset by the fact that tapioca yields did not register any significant growth in any district. In fact, tapioca yields declined in many districts though these trends were not significant. In the case of paddy, yields rose significantly but this advantage was offset by its virtually stagnant prices during this period. At district levels too, though tapioca prices increased faster than paddy prices, the trends were not significant. It is quite obvious that unlike in Period I, in Period II the failure of the farm prices of both crops to rise significantly has been an important factor, apart from other factors, for the decline in area under both crops.

Being competing commodities in consumption an increase in the price of paddy/rice is bound to affect tapioca prices too. The demand for tapioca and rice, apart from other factors, depends not only on the production of the two crops but also on their relative prices. In order to find out the impact of changes in rice prices on tapioca prices, we have postulated a functional relationship between prices of tapioca and rice at farm and retail level. The wholesale price of rice has not been quoted from 1965 onwards and hence a similar analysis is not attempted at wholesale level. In our regression equations tapioca price is the dependent variable and paddy/rice price the independent variable. The derived 'b' estimates expressed in terms of the ratio of respective means of the two prices (i.e., $\hat{b} \times \frac{\overline{X}}{\overline{Y}}$) gives the elasticities. These elasticities indicate the extent of response in the price of tapioca to changes in the price of rice. The concept of elasticity assumes significance in economics in the context of commodities that have close substitutes as in the case of rice and tapioca. This is because when price of a commodity is elastic, people generally tend to substitute in favour of that substitute commodity which is relatively less priced.

Table 2.9 presents the results showing the impact of changes in farm and retail prices of paddy/rice on the corresponding prices for tapioca. The results suggest that in a majority of the districts the changes in tapioca prices both at farm and retail level in response to changes in paddy/rice prices were less than proportionate. In other words, when the price of paddy/rice rose by one per cent price of tapioca also rose but by less than one per cent. However, we may note that the elasticities for retail prices were either proportionate of more than proportionate for Alleppey and Kottayam respectively and near perfect in many other districts. This suggests that tapioca retail prices are highly sensitive to rice retail prices which indicates the importance of the two commodities in the food basket of Kerala. Nevertheless the fact that the elasticities are less than proportionate in most cases suggests that substitution between tapioca and rice is not perfect. This may be because tapioca is considered as an inferior commodity and hence competes with rice in consumption only among the low income people.

We may now examine how far tapioca markets are integrated by studying the price movements in the farm, retail and wholesale markets. In the published reports the price data for wholesale and retail prices were given in terms of calendar years while the farm prices were expressed in terms of agricultural year. Since month-wise price data are also available we have computed the farm prices in terms of calendar years to make the two sets of data comparable for the study. The farm and then retail price of tapioca have been regressed on the corresponding wholesale price of tapioca. The response in farm or retail prices of tapioca to changes in wholesale prices of tapioca are measured by deriving their elasticities in the same fashion as spelt out earlier. These elasticities measure the sensitivity of farm/retail prices of tapioca to changes in the wholesale prices of tapioca.

TABLE 2.9: **Classification of Districts in Kerala according to Price Response of Tapioca Farm/Retail Prices Corresponding to Changes in Paddy/Farm Retail Prices: 1963 to 1982**

| Range of price response | Regression result for Farm Price Equations* | Regression result for Retail Price Equations* |
|---|---|---|
| Less than 50 per cent | Nil | Nil |
| 50 to 75 per cent | Ernakulam** | Nil |
| 75 to 100 per cent | Trivandrum | Trivandrum |
| | Quilon | Quilon |
| | Alleppey** | Alleppey |
| | Kottayam | Ernakulam |
| | Trichur | Trichur |
| | Palghat** | Palghat |
| | Kozhikode | Kozhikode |
| | Cannanore** | Cannanore |
| More than 100 per cent | Nil | Kottayam |

*Note*: The farm price equations are based on data for the period 1963-64 to 1981-82. In the case of retail prices they refer to the period 1963 to 1982.

*The trends for all the districts were significant at 1 per cent level.

**Based on data for 1966-67 to 81-82.

*Source*: Derived from Table 2-D.

Table 2.10 classifies the districts on the basis of their price response in farm/retail prices to changes in wholesale prices of tapioca. By and large, in most districts the response in farm and retail prices to changes in wholesale prices has been less than proportionate. In other words, wholesale prices fluctuate more than farm and retail prices, except in Trivandrum and Kottayam where the farm prices responded better and Kottayam and Alleppey where the retail prices responded better. The response in farm prices to an increase in wholesale prices of tapioca in Cannanore and Ernakulam and for retail prices in Cannanore was relatively lower than in other districts. Among the districts Cannanore reported the lowest response in both farm and retail prices, 62 per cent, whereas in the case of other districts they exceeded 74 per cent. This is probably due to the fact that Cannanore has consistently reported the highest level of farm and retail price for tapioca, possibly on account of the better quality of

TABLE 2.10: **Classification of Districts in Kerala according to Price Response of Tapioca Farm/Retail Prices Corresponding to Changes in Wholesale Prices of Tapioca during 1963 to 1982**

| Range of price response | Regression results for Farm Price Equations* | Regression results for Retail Price Equations* |
|---|---|---|
| Less than 50 per cent | Nil | Nil |
| 50 to 75 per cent | Cannanore**<br>Ernakulam** | Cannanore** |
| 75 to 100 per cent | Quilon<br>Alleppey**<br>Trichur<br>Kozhikode** | Trivandrum<br>Quilon<br>Ernakulam<br>Kozhikode** |
| More than 100 per cent | Trivandrum<br>Kottayam | Alleppey<br>Kottayam |

*Note*: *The trends for all districts were significant at 1 per cent level.
**Based on data for 1966 to 1982.
Palghat district has been left out since wholesale prices of tapioca were quoted only for 4 years.

*Source*: Derived from Table 2-E.

tubers found in this district. On the contrary, in Kottayam the response in farm and retail prices to changes in tapioca wholesale prices were more than proportionate indicating that market integration was better here. Kottayam district is known for its progressive farmers who have a preference for commercial crops; and even in respect of the marketing oftapioca it enjoys a unique position in the state. The less than proportionate changes in farm and retail prices in response to an increase in tapioca wholesale prices in most districts suggests that there are market imperfections which inhibit farmers and retailers from benefiting fully from an increase in wholesale price of the commodity. It may be noted here that on account of the low value and perishable nature of tapioca there are disadvantages in marketing the commodity. This factor impedes the commercialisation and large scale industrial utilisation of tapioca particularly when large quantities of raw tapioca tubers have to be stored in processing centres.

## INSTABILITY IN YIELDS AND PRICES

A key element which influences producer decisions is the nature of risk and uncertainty associated with the cultivation of crops. Small farmers, by nature, are averse to cultivating crops which are subject to business-cycle type fluctuations. We may examine and see how far instability in yields per hectare and prices of the two crops has influenced their growth behaviour. To measure instability in yields and prices, coefficient of variation adjusting for trend wherever present (CV/CVT for short) have been calculated. The district-wise results presented in Table 2.11 suggest that instability in rice yields has been relatively lower compared to tapioca (with the exception of Kottayam). However, the state level picture for tapioca seems rather deceptive and does not adequately reflect the wide inter-district variations in the CVT values for tapioca yields. This could possibly indicate that inter-district instability is mutually offsetting to some extent more in the case of tapioca than in rice. Crop failure in one district in a year is offset by a good crop elsewhere.

**TABLE 2.11: Instability in Yields and Prices: Tapioca and Rice/Paddy during 1963-64 to 1981-82**

*(CV/CVT in percentages)*

| Districts | Instability in | | | |
|---|---|---|---|---|
| | Tapioca Yield | Rice Yield | Tapioca Price | Paddy Price |
| Trivandrum | 8.47 (11.14)* | 5.42* (5.92)* | 18.01 | 30.59 |
| Quilon | 17.31* (7.71) | 5.95 (6.39) | 18.22 | 26.75 |
| Alleppey | 22.97* (22.21) | 7.31 (8.85) | 19.77 | 26.70 |
| Kottayam | 12.70* (7.93) | 13.25 (15.69) | 19.65 | 29.80 |
| Ernakulam | 17.43 (22.04) | 5.03 (6.83) | 12.47 | 29.78 |
| Trichur | 22.22 (12.68) | 6.20* (7.31)* | 13.62 | 29.13 |
| Palghat | 15.68* (11.05) | 4.17 (4.28) | 15.16 | 26.95 |
| Kozhikode | 15.68* (11.05) | 8.71 (11.10) | 21.98 | 27.65 |
| Cannanore | 26.40 (22.06) | 5.29 (6.66)* | 14.49 | 24.67 |
| State | 10.56 (5.26) | 3.61 (4.61) | 14.34 | 26.72 |

*Note*: *CV in percentage; the rest are CVT in percentage.
Figures in parantheses present CV/CVT values in percentage for the period 1963-64 to 1974-75 (i.e., Period I).

A sharp and uneven increase in the yield rate of rice in Kottayam may explain the high instability in rice productivity in that district. The districtwise CVT values for tapioca yields are of a mixed character and prevents any attempts at a generalisation. However, the CV/CVT values for period I, i.e., for 1963-64 to 1974-75 givė some interesting clues at least as far as this period was concerned. Here Alleppey, Ernakulam and Cannanore which reported either a decline or a low and insignificant growth in tapioca area during this period were characterised by relatively high instability in tapioca productivity as indicated by the higher CVT values for the districts (being 22 per cent) compared to other districts. A possible inference stemming from this is that in the case of low value and inferior food crops high instability in yields may act as a disincentive to enhancing production of that crop.

The CVT values computed for the prices of the two crops suggest that price instability is quite high in the case of paddy compared to that of tapioca both at the state and district levels. This may be because paddy is more commercialised than tapioca and role of market is greater in paddy. The CVT values across districts more or less show a similar pattern except in Kozhikode where the price of tapioca appears to show relatively high instability almost nearing the CVT values noticed for paddy prices. The relative stability of tapioca prices compared to paddy prices seems to provide a clue to one of the reasons favouring tapioca cultivation. Obviously, the relatively higher stability of its prices seems to offset its relatively higher yield instability, and hence farmers are attracted to the crop because of relatively stable prices.

To sum up: our analysis suggests that there were two phases in the growth of tapioca and rice in Kerala. The first phase covering the 12 year period from 1963-64 to 1974-75 witnessed a significant increase in area, production and productivity of both crops, the rates being higher in the case of tapioca. What was remarkable about the growth of tapioca in this period was that growth was not confined to traditional tapioca-growing areas but extended to newer areas, particularly the northern region of the state. Secondly, the increase in tapioca area did not occur at the costs of rice area; on the contrary in some regions like Alleppey rice may have displaced tapioca in mixed lands. Thirdly, the growth did not occur just through area increases, but also through a significant rise in yields per hectare, a fact of significance to a state like Kerala, where land is limited. Though rice area and yields per hectare also grew at a significant rate, they were not as impressive as that of tapioca, owing to scarcity of lands suitable to cultivate rice and limited scope for enhancing rice yields under present technology. A significant rise in prices and yields of both crops were among the important factors that contributed to the growth of the two crops in this period.

The second phase covering a shorter period, viz., 1975-76 to 1981-82 witnessed a dramatic change with tapioca recording a decline in production while rice production was stagnant. This was primarily due to a significant decline in area under both crops. The factors that have contributed to the decline in area under tapioca and rice are not the same. As far as tapioca is concerned the class-specific nature of demand for the commodity, consumed as it is by low income people, may have inhibited the crop from sustaining the growth momentum observed during the period upto 1975. If this is true, it suggests that market is a severe constraint on the growth of tapioca in the long run, unless the market for the crop and its by-products are diversified. It is this fact which may explain why the crop has not been able to maintain the growth momentum of the late sixties and early seventies, as evinced by the decline in area and production of tapioca in the late seventies. Moreover, fascination for cocoa cultivation, particularly among big farmers, may have displaced tapioca in inter-cropped lands. Cashew and rubber cultivation also seem to have grown at the cost of tapioca. Other contributory factors were an insignificant growth in prices and a slight decline in yields. As for rice, a decline in paddy/rice prices, increasing costs of cultivation etc., have induced paddy cultivators to shift to more remunerative crops like coconut, sugarcane, etc.

Two singular features of Kerala's tapioca economy are that while tapioca is cultivated by all strata of farms, it figures more prominently in marginal and small holdings. Which factors have made the crop's cultivation attractive needs to probed into in detail when we analyse our farm data. On the basis of secondary data it appears that the high yields of the crop, relatively low instability in tapioca prices are some of the factors favouring tapioca cultivation. Secondly, it is mostly consumed by poor people because it is cheap relative to rice. A rupee of expenditure yielded more calories from tapioca than rice, though this advantage seems to be declining. Though tapioca and rice are competitive in consumption, substitution between the two crops is not perfect on account of its inferior nature. This explains why even though tapioca prices were sensitive to changes in paddy/rice prices, the changes in tapioca prices were less than proportionate. Prices of tapioca at farm, retail and wholesale markets have moved in unison though fluctuations in wholesale prices were more than in the case of farm and retial prices. An increase in wholesale price of tapioca did not reach farm and retail markets proportionately in most cases, perhaps due to market imperfections.

TABLE 2-A: Growth Performance of Tapioca in Kerala—1963-64 to 1974-75 and 1975-76 to 1981-82

| Districts | Mean tapioca productivity in tonnes per hectare** | | Growth Rates of Tapioca @ | | | |
|---|---|---|---|---|---|---|
| | | | In production | In area | In productivity | In yield relative to rice yield |
| Kottayam | 18.75 | (a) | 2.67[2] | —0.56 ns | 4.19[1] | 0.89 ns |
| | | (b) | —9.69[2] | —7.89[2] | —1.61 ns | —4.21 ns |
| Cannanore | 15.82 | (a) | 10.97[1] | 1.48 ns | 9.47[1] | 8.87[1] |
| | | (b) | —2.77 ns | —0.12 ns | —2.61[3] | —2.23[3] |
| Ernakulam | 15.75 | (a) | 3.17 ns | —1.53 ns | 5.01[2] | 3.75[2] |
| | | (b) | —3.11 ns | —4.26[2] | 1.48 ns | 0.25 ns |
| Alleppey | 15.71 | (a) | 2.87 ns | —2.95[1] | 5.65[1] | 3.87[3] |
| | | (b) | —7.57[1] | —5.91[2] | —1.72 ns | —5.05[3] |
| Quilon | 15.50 | (a) | 9.95[1] | 5.35[1] | 5.35[1] | 4.11[1] |
| | | (b) | —9.90[2] | —6.61[1] | —3.07 ns | —5.74[2] |
| Trivandrum | 14.10 | (a) | 5.51[1] | 4.23[1] | 1.32 ns | 0.51 ns |
| | | (b) | —2.06 ns | —3.61 ns | 1.53 ns | 2.08 ns |

| | | | | | | |
|---|---|---|---|---|---|---|
| Trichur | 13.98 | (a) | 11.82$^{1}$ | 4.90$^{1}$ | 8.92$^{1}$ | 8.62$^{1}$ |
| | | (b) | —10.56$^{1}$ | —8.49$^{2}$ | —2.69 ns | —4.20 ns |
| Northern districts (includes Palghat, Kozhikode, Malappuram) | 13.56 | (a) | 12.23$^{1}$ | 8.70$^{1}$ | 4.72$^{1}$ | 3.49$^{1}$ |
| | | (b) | —3.23 ns | —3.73 ns | 0.63 ns | —1.41$^{3}$ |
| (i) Palghat only | | (a) | — | — | — | — |
| | | (b) | — | — | — | — |
| (ii) Kozhikode only | | (a) | — | — | — | — |
| | | (b) | — | — | — | — |
| State | 15.42 | (a) | 7.32$^{1}$ | 3.63$^{1}$ | 3.90$^{1}$ | 2.67$^{1}$ |
| | | (b) | —5.85$^{1}$ | —4.83$^{1}$ | —0.90 ns | —2.65$^{3}$ |

TABLE 2-A—(*Contd.*)

| Districts | | Growth Rates of Tapioca @ | | | |
|---|---|---|---|---|---|
| | | In farm price | In farm price relative to farm price of paddy | In retail prices | In wholesale prices |
| Kottayam | (a) | 8.38$^{1}$ | —2.19 ns | 9.09$^{1}$ | 9.96$^{1}$ |
| | (b) | 6.71 ns | 5.28$^{2}$ | 7.63$^{2}$ | 5.27 ns |
| Cannanore | (a) | 11.59$^{1}$ | 4.29$^{3}$ | 6.53$^{1}$ | 10.47$^{2}$ |
| | (b) | 3.84 ns | 4.11 ns | 6.06$^{1}$ | 12.38$^{1}$ |
| Errakulam | (a) | 8.56$^{1}$ | 0.84 ns | 10.72$^{1}$ | 8.12$^{1}$ |
| | (b) | 3.84 ns | 3.31 ns | 6.87$^{1}$ | 8.08$^{2}$ |
| Alleppey | (a) | 10.27$^{1}$ | 3.58$^{3}$ | 10.35$^{1}$ | 9.17$^{1}$ |
| | (b) | 3.07 ns | 1.82 ns | 6.26$^{1}$ | 5.49$^{3}$ |
| Quilon | (a) | 7.74$^{1}$ | —1.69 ns | 10.72$^{1}$ | 9.71$^{1}$ |
| | (b) | 3.28 ns | 3.32 ns | 6.56$^{3}$ | 5.59$^{2}$ |
| Trivandrum | (a) | 8.84$^{1}$ | —0.92 ns | 7.70$^{1}$ | 8.83$^{1}$ |
| | (b) | 2.64 ns | 3.10 ns | 2.43 ns | 2.53 ns |
| Trichur | (a) | 10.51$^{1}$ | 0.39 ns | 12.00$^{1}$ | 9.66$^{1}$ |
| | (b) | 4.36 ns | 3.93 ns | 6.23$^{2}$ | 8.24$^{2}$ |

| | | | | | |
|---|---|---|---|---|---|
| Northern districts | (a) | — | — | — | — |
| | (b) | — | — | — | — |
| (i) Palghat only | (a) | 12.32$^{1}$ | 2.56 ns | 7.70$^{2}$ | — |
| | (b) | 1.73 ns | 0.14 ns | 9.35$^{2}$ | — |
| (ii) Kozhikode only | (a) | 4.71$^{3}$ | —6.97$^{1}$ | 10.35$^{1}$ | 7.05$^{3}$ |
| | (b) | 6.90$^{2}$ | 6.28$^{2}$ | 9.64$^{1}$ | 14.63$^{1}$ |
| **State** | (a) | 8.48$^{1}$ | —1.48 ns | 8.01$^{1}$ | 9.22$^{1}$ |
| | (b) | 4.79 ns | 3.73 ns | 4.78$^{2}$ | 4.40 ns |

*Note*: 1. (a) Trends for 1963-64 to 1974-75.
(b) Trends for 1975-76 to 1981-82.
2. (@) Linear trends with slope expressed as per cent at respective means.
3. (**) Mean yield based on data for 1963-64 to 1981-82.
4. $^{1}$, $^{2}$, $^{3}$=significant at 1 per cent, 5 per cent and 10 per cent level.
ns=not significant.

TABLE 2-B: Growth Performance of Rice in Kerala—1963-64 to 1974-75 and 1975-76 to 1981-82

| Districts | Mean rice yield in kgs per hectare** | | Growth Rates of Rice @ | | | |
|---|---|---|---|---|---|---|
| | | In production | In area | In yield per hectare | In farm price of paddy | In retail prices |
| Palghat | 1841 (a) | 2.40[1] | 1.44[1] | 0.96[2] | 10.92[1] | 11.41[1] |
| | (b) | 1.86ns | 0.46ns | 1.41ns | 1.05ns | 0.82ns |
| Alleppey | 1591 (a) | 3.25[1] | 1.40[1] | 1.87[2] | 8.82[2] | 8.62[1] |
| | (b) | 1.26ns | —1.92ns | 2.93[3] | 0.93ns | 0.81ns |
| Kottayam | 1561 (a) | 5.61[1] | 2.64[1] | 3.10[2] | 10.31[1] | 9.04[1] |
| | (b) | —5.60[1] | —7.98[2] | 2.81ns | 0.82ns | 0.47ns |
| Quilon | 1472 (a) | 1.71[3] | 0.43[1] | 1.29[2] | 9.64[1] | 9.66[1] |
| | (b) | 2.06ns | —0.54ns | 2.63[3] | —0.46ns | 0.24ns |
| Trivandrum | 1443 (a) | 1.02[3] | 0.25[1] | 0.77ns | 10.86[1] | 10.59[1] |
| | (b) | —4.14[2] | —3.44[1] | —0.65ns | —0.98ns | 1.63ns |
| Ernakulam | 1348 (a) | 2.65[1] | 1.42[1] | 1.24[3] | 10.64[1] | 8.80[1] |
| | (b) | 1.21[2] | 0.06ns | 1.16[3] | 0.41ns | 0.49ns |
| Trichur | 1307 (a) | 0.70ns | 0.23ns | 0.42ns | 10.53[1] | 9.04[1] |
| | (b) | —0.26ns | —1.76[3] | 1.49ns | 0.02ns | —0.06ns |

| | | | | | | |
|---|---|---|---|---|---|---|
| Cannanore | 1295 (a) | $1.11^{3}$ | $0.43^{3}$ | 0.68ns | $9.09^{1}$ | $8.94^{1}$ |
| | (b) | $-2.77^{3}$ | $-2.38^{2}$ | $-0.40$ns | $-0.24$ns | $-1.68$ns |
| Kozhikode | 1167 (a) | $2.80^{2}$ | $1.09^{1}$ | $1.73^{3}$ | $10.90^{1}$ | $8.16^{1}$ |
| | (b) | $-0.66$ns | $-3.04^{1}$ | $2.37^{3}$ | $-0.03$ns | $-0.21$ns |
| State | 1483 (a) | $2.30^{1}$ | $1.07^{1}$ | $1.24^{1}$ | $10.19^{1}$ | $9.13^{1}$ |
| | (b) | 0.18ns | $-1.56^{2}$ | $1.72^{2}$ | 0.72ns | $-3.17$ns |

*Note*: (a) Trends 1963-64 to 1974-75;
(b) Trends for 1975-76 to 1981-82.
2. @ Linear trends with slope expressed as per cent at respective means.
3. (**) Mean yield based on data for 1963-64 to 1981-82.
4. $^{1}$, $^{2}$, $^{3}$=significant at 1 per cent, 5 per cent and 10 per cent level.
ns=not significant.

TABLE 2-C: Calorie Yield of Tapioca and Rice in Kerala: Per Hectare Yield and Per Rupee of Expenditure

| Year | Tapioca yield in million calories per hectare | Rice yield in million calories per hectare | Ratio of (2) to (3) | Year | Tapioca calories derived per rupee of expenditure | Rice calories derived per rupee of expenditure | Ratio of (6) to (7) |
|---|---|---|---|---|---|---|---|
| 1 | 2 | 3 | 4 | 5 | 6 | 7 | 8 |
| 1963-64 | 18.87 | 4.85 | 3.89 | 1963 | 11214 | 5164 | 2.17 |
| 1964-65 | 20.72 | 4.85 | 4.26 | 1964 | 9235 | 3802 | 2.43 |
| 1965-66 | 21.16 | 4.30 | 4.92 | 1965 | 5607 | 2582 | 2.17 |
| 1966-67 | 21.18 | 4.69 | 4.67 | 1966 | 6280 | 2149 | 2.92 |
| 1967-68 | 22.14 | 4.80 | 4.61 | 1967 | 5607 | 1663 | 3.37 |
| 1968-69 | 21.60 | 4.95 | 4.36 | 1968 | 4906 | 1860 | 2.64 |
| 1969-70 | 24.78 | 4.85 | 5.11 | 1969 | 5815 | 2084 | 2.79 |
| 1970-71 | 24.69 | 5 13 | 4.81 | 1970 | 5233 | 2232 | 2.34 |
| 1971-72 | 28.11 | 5.35 | 5.25 | 1971 | 5065 | 2276 | 2.23 |
| 1972-73 | 29.32 | 5.45 | 5.38 | 1972 | 4906 | 1966 | 2.50 |
| 1973-74 | 28.99 | 4.97 | 5.83 | 1973 | 3925 | 1442 | 2.72 |
| 1974-75 | 27.78 | 5.23 | 5.31 | 1974 | 3078 | 991 | 3.11 |

| | | | | | | | |
|---|---|---|---|---|---|---|---|
| 1975-76 | 25.89 | 5.26 | 4.92 | 1975 | 2904 | 900 | 2.23 |
| 1976-77 | 24.88 | 5.08 | 4.90 | 1976 | 2857 | 1280 | 2.23 |
| 1977-78 | 22.70 | 5.33 | 4.26 | 1977 | 3140 | 1453 | 2.16 |
| 1978-79 | 23.22 | 5.51 | 4.21 | 1978 | 3203 | 1592 | 2.01 |
| 1979-80 | 26.33 | 5.67 | 4.64 | 1979 | 2653 | 1522 | 1.74 |
| 1980-81 | 23.30 | 5.49 | 4.24 | 1980 | 2386 | 1349 | 1.77 |
| 1981-82 | 23.71 | 5.74 | 4.13 | 1981 | 2041 | 1107 | 1.84 |
| Mean | 24.17 | 5.13 | 4.71 | Mean | 4740 | 1969 | 2.41 |

*Note*: Current retail prices were used for calculating calories derived per rupee of expenditure.
1 kg. of tapioca=1570 calories;
1 kg. of rice =3460 calories.

TABLE 2-D: **Impact of Changes in Rice Prices on Tapioca Prices during 1963-64 to 1981-82**

| District | | Mean tapioca prices (in Rs. per quintal) | Mean Paddy/ rice price (in (Rs. per quintal) | Elasticity | $R^2$ |
|---|---|---|---|---|---|
| Trivandrum | FP | 26.84 | 153.20 | 0.78 | 0.61 |
| | RP | 35.75 | 222.65 | 0.80 | 0.76 |
| Quilon | FP | 25.96 | 142.70 | 0.83 | 0.71 |
| | RP | 37.45 | 218.55 | 0.95 | 0.76 |
| Alleppey | FP@ | 32.37 | 143.37 | 0.92 | 0.65 |
| | RP | 41.65 | 214.00 | 1.00 | 0.70 |
| Kottayam | FP | 29.36 | 130.43 | 0.85 | 0.58 |
| | RP | 45.45 | 218.05 | 1.04 | 0.73 |
| Ernakulam | FP@ | 28.34 | 152.23 | 0.55 | 0.41 |
| | RP | 41.45 | 222.80 | 0.97 | 0.61 |
| Trichur | FP | 29.15 | 126.60 | 0.87 | 0.50 |
| | RP | 35.45 | 218.00 | 0.99 | 0.71 |
| Palghat | FP@ | 26.39 | 129.62 | 0.89 | 0.59 |
| | RP | 37.55 | 198.40 | 0.98 | 0.74 |
| Kozhikode | FP | 28.74 | 128.60 | 0.80 | 0.53 |
| | RP | 42.25 | 223.25 | 0.96 | 0.55 |
| Cannanore | FP@ | 42.22 | 129.20 | 0.87 | 0.41 |
| | RP | 62.75 | 215.70 | 0.82 | 0.60 |

*Note*: 1. (@) Trend based on data for 1966-67 to 1981-82.
2. All retail price equations based on data for 1963 to 1982.
3. All the trends were significant at 1 per cent level.
4. FP Farm Price Equation;
RP=Retail Price Equation.

TABLE 2-E: **Impact of Change in Wholesale Price of Tapioca on Farm and Retail Prices of Tapioca during 1963 to 1982**

| District | | Mean tapioca farm/retail price (Rs. per quintal) | Mean tapioca wholesale price (Rs. per quintal) | Elasticity | $R^2$ |
|---|---|---|---|---|---|
| Trivandrum | FP | 27.24 | 26.71 | 1.01 | 0.97 |
| | RP | 35.75 | 26.71 | 0.95 | 0.94 |
| Quilon | FP | 26.35 | 27.45 | 0.81 | 0.97 |
| | RP | 37.45 | 27.45 | 0.91 | 0.98 |
| Alleppey | FP@ | 32.85 | 35.46 | 0.83 | 0.89 |
| | RP | 41.65 | 32.25 | 1.01 | 0.96 |
| Kottayam | FP | 31.11 | 34.41 | 1.07 | 0.90 |
| | RP | 45.45 | 34.41 | 1.05 | 0.95 |
| Ernakulam | FP@ | 29.23 | 33.83 | 0.74 | 0.91 |
| | RP | 41.45 | 30.99 | 0.99 | 0.96 |
| Trichur | FP | 30.43 | 30.88 | 0.94 | 0.96 |
| | RP | 35.45 | 30.88 | 0.88 | 0.99 |
| Kozhikode | FP@ | 32.28 | 32.64 | 0.98 | 0.90 |
| | RP@ | 46.12 | 32.64 | 0.84 | 0.91 |
| Cannanore | FP@ | 42.95 | 32.99 | 0.62 | 0.70 |
| | RP@ | 68.29 | 32.99 | 0.62 | 0.86 |

*Note*: 1. (@)Trends based on data for 1966 to 1982.

2. All trends are significant at 1 per cent level.

3. FP=Farmprice.

RP=Retail price.

4. Palghat district is not included since wholesale prices of tapioca were quoted only for four years.

## REFERENCES

1. *Poverty, Unemployment and Development Policy—A Study of Some Selected Issues with Reference to Kerala*, Centre for Development Studies, United Nations, 1975 and Orient Longman, 1977, p. 27.
2. Upto 1974-75 the sample size for the Land Utilisation Survey was 0.6 per cent of the revenue villages for each round. Thereafter following introduction of the TRS scheme, the sample size was increased to 10 per cent of the revenue villages in 1975-76; 15 per cent in 1976-77 and 20 per cent in the following years.
3. As per official figures area and production of tapioca in 1962-63 was as follows: A-221 thousand hectares, P-1540 thousand tonnes; in 1963-64 A-210 thousand hectares, P-2524 thousand tonnes.
4. Three more districts, Wynad, Pathanamthitta and Kasargode have been formed recently.
5. The revenue villages lying 76.2 meters above the mean sea level (MSL) and over were treated as highlands, those between 76.2 and 7.62 meters approximately as midlands and the remaining area below 7.62 meters as lowlands (or coastal tracts). In our map in Chapter 3, owing to cartographic limitations we took 0-10 meters, 10-100 meters and above 100 meters to demarcate the lowlands, midlands and highlands.
6. For details, see KNS Nair: *Constraints that are Limiting Agricultural Production and Causing Uneven Distribution of Gains—A Case, Palghat district*, Kerala State, Div. of Agricultural Economics, IARI, New Delhi, 1972 (Unpublished Ph D thesis) and also *The Report of the Committee on Agro-Climatic Zones and Cropping Pattern*, Government of Kerala, Trivandrum, April 1974.
7. *Package of Practices for Tapioca* (Pamphlet), CTCRI, Trivandrum.
8. Consequent on the formation of Malappuram district in 1969 by combining parts of Palghat and Kozhikode, the data on tapioca from 1970-71 for Palghat and Kozhikode, was greatly distorted. Since talukwise figures on tapioca for the period involved were not available, the three districts were combined to overcome this problem, and facilitate trend analysis. The data on tapioca for, 1973-74 and 1974-75 for Kottayam and Ernakulam was slightly distorted owing to the formation of Idukki district in 1972. However, the area under tapioca lost to Idukki was negligible. We have, therefore, ignored this and fitted separate regressions for Kottayam and Ernakulam. As a check, however, we fitted a regression combining Kottayam, Erankulam and Idukki. The results revealed a declining trend in area under tapioca. Our trend analysis separately for Kottayam and Ernakulam too revealed similar results, i.e., a declining trend in tapioca area. In the case of paddy talukwise figures were available and hence we rsconstructed the data for the years affected by reorganisation of districts.

9. See, *Package of Practices for Tapioca* (Pamphlet), op. cit., p. 3.
10. See, NSS 26th round, July 1971-September 1972, No. 265/4, *Fertiliser Use in Agricultural Holdings*, South Zone Rural Sector, Government of India, March 1976.
11. *Extent of Adoption of Improved Agricultural Practices: An Evaluation Study*, Kerala State Planning Board (vide), 'The Third Decennial World Census of Agriculture' 1970-71, Report for Kerala State, Vol. I, General Report, Agricultural Census Division, Bureau of Economics and Statistics, Government of Kerala, Trivandrum, November 1973, p. 88.
12. See also K N Ninan: Agricultural Labourers and Poverty: A Comment, in *Economic and Political Weekly*, September 19, 1981.
13. *Report on the Marketing of Tapioca in India,* Directorate of Marketing and Inspection, Ministry of Food and Agriculture, Government of India, Marketing Series No. 88, October, 1955.
14. *Development of Tapioca-Based Industry in Kerala*, CSIR, Trivandrum 1977.
15. (a) *Poverty, Unemployment and Development Policy* (CDS), op. cit.
    (b) *Food Habits Survey*, conducted in Southern India, Vol. III, Kerala, Tabulation by Operation Research Group, Baroda, Protein Foods Association of India, see also Vol. I, Summary and Deduction.
    (c) Shubh K Kumar, *Impact of Subsidised Rice on Food Consumption and Nutrition in Kerala*, Research Report No. 5, IFPRI, Washington, January 1979.
16. The CDS had also conducted a dietary survey in Trivandrum district.
17. Dietary surveys are usually based on consumption details recorded for a reference day or week or in some cases even more. It is assumed that the consumption pattern for the reference period is representative of the consumption pattern during the whole year. This poses problems particularly when there are seasonal variations in consumption of food items.

# 3

# THE SAMPLE DESIGN, VILLAGES AND FARM HOUSEHOLDS

WE NOW move on to an intensive study of the tapioca economy, based on micro level data. We spell out here the sample design of the study and present a profile of the selected villages and farm households.

## SAMPLE DESIGN

For an intensive study of tapioca cultivators, a multi-stage sampling design was formulated in order to choose the region/sub-region, taluks, villages and the ultimate unit of analysis—the farm household. Earlier we have noted that within Kerala, Trivandrum and Quilon districts accounted for almost 47 per cent of area under tapioca in the state. Crop Location Quotients,[1] calculated to know the concentration of tapioca area across districts (refer Table 3.1) also confirmed the pre-eminent position enjoyed by Trivandrum and Quilon districts in the state's tapioca economy. Both these districts are contiguous and occupy a major portion of the former princely state of Travancore, which traditionally has been the dominant tapioca-growing belt of the state. The two districts are fairly representative of the state. On account of these factors, Trivandrum and Quilon districts put together have been selected as the sample region for our intensive study.

For selecting taluks also Crop Location Quotients were the prime consideration. However, with a view to selecting the sample villages from the three natural zones of the state (viz., Highlands, Midlands and Lowlands), we had also taken into consideration the natural zones into which the taluks fell as also the contiguity of the regions to be selected. On this basis, we selected Quilon, Kottarakara and Pathanapuram taluks in Quilon district, and Nedumangad taluk in Trivandrum district. These taluks have a high concentration of tapioca as evident from the crop location quotients presented in Table 3.1

TABLE 3.1: **Crop Location Quotients Showing Concentration of Tapioca Cultivation in Taluks of Trivandrum the Quilon Districts (based on average for 1971-72 to 1973-74)**

| Taluk | Crop Location Quotient | Taluk | Crop Location Quotient |
|---|---|---|---|
| *Trivandrum district* | 2.91 | *Quilon district* | 2.64 |
| 1. Neyyatinkara | 1.07 | 1. Quilon | 1.40 |
| 2. Trivandrum | 0.64 | 2. Kottarakara | 1.02 |
| 3. Nedumangad | 1.22 | 3. Kunnathur | 0.75 |
| 4. Chirayinkil | 0.83 | 4. Pathanamthitta | 0.47 |
| | | 5. Pathanapuram | 1.68 |
| | | 6. Karunagapally | 0.65 |

*Note*: The crop location quotient for Kottayam district was 1.13; in all the remaining districts it was less than 1.

Coming to selection of villages, we took up those with a good concentration of tapioca cultivation, so that they presented adequate area for an intensive study covering different size groups of farmers. Since village-wise data on area under tapioca cultivation were not available it was not possible to rank villages according to the concentration of the crop. The selection had, therefore, to be made on the basis of discussions with block and

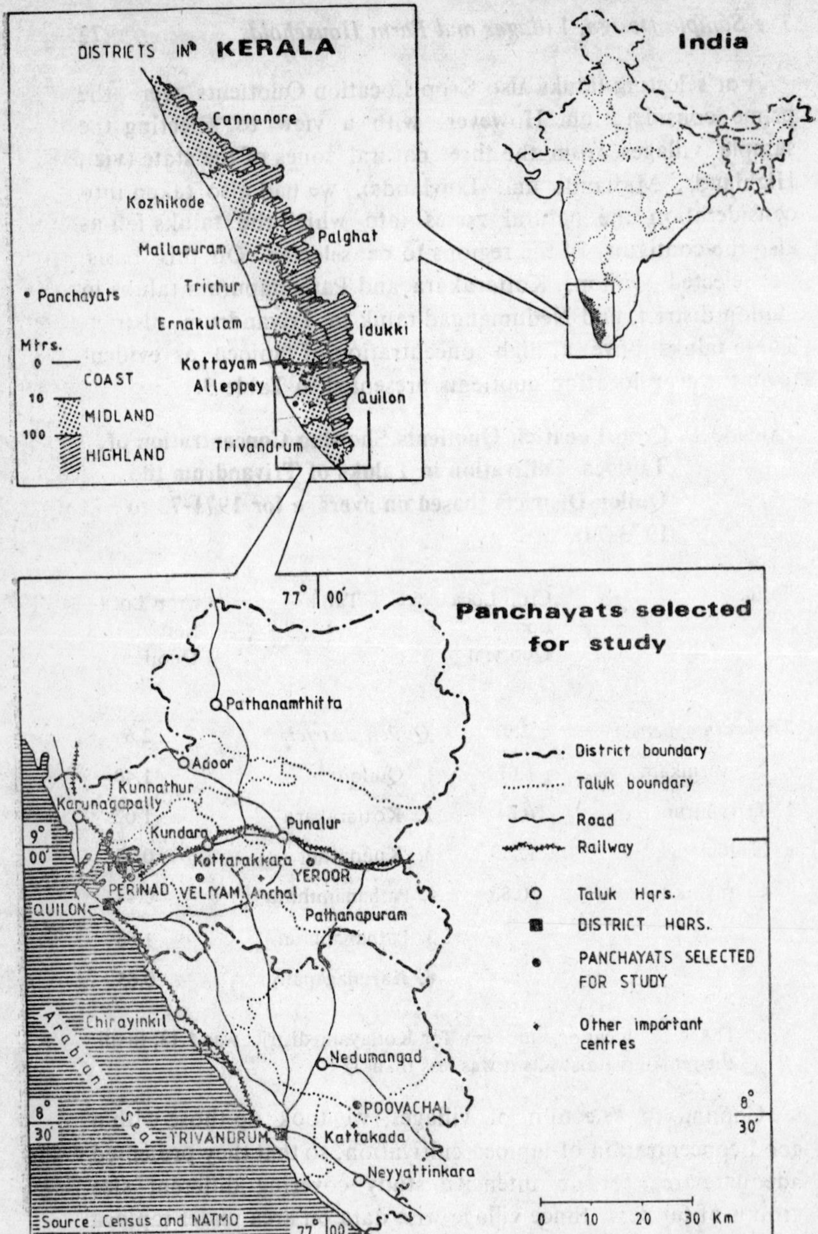


FIG. 1: *Location map of study region*

village level officials, checked through personal visits to prospective villages to be selected. Our choice fell on four villages: Yeroor—a highland village in Pathanapuram taluk (Quilon district), Veliyam and Poovachal—two midland villages in Kottarakara (Quilon district) and Nedumangad (Trivandrum district) taluks respectively, and Perinad—a lowland village in Quilon taluk (Quilon dsitrict).* Since tapioca was predominantly cultivated in the midland belt, we selected two villages from this zone. The villages represent more the natural regions (highland, midland and lowland) rather than their respective districts.

The Village Panchayat area being unwieldly, a suitable hamlet in each village was taken up for intensive study. The hamlets selected were Ayilara (in Yeroor), Muttara (in Veliyam), Cherumood (in Perinad) and Kuzhakad (in Poovachal). To facilitate identification of tapioca cultivators, complete enumeration of farm households was first undertaken in the selected hamlets. Thirty-five farm households were selected from each village on random sample basis from the enumerated list of topioca-growing households with probability proportional to size (PPS) of their operated area, making a total of 140 farm households for the intensive study. Sampling on PPS basis was adopted because otherwise larger holdings which are relatively fewer in number would have less chance of being selected though they actually may be accounting for a greater proportion of output than is signified by their numbers. Secondly, we considered operated area for this purpose rather than area under tapioca for a significant reason. While our purpose is to concentrate on tapioca, it is not at the cost of neglect of the farm economy as a whole. By giving weightage to operated area it was felt that population characteristics would be more truly represented. As such, the role of tapioca in the farm economy of the sample cultivators would be more properly reflected. The required data were collected on the basis of a detailed farm household schedule prepared for this purpose. Thesu rvey was conducted from June 1977 to October 1977. The reference period for the survey was March 1976 to February 1977 which corresponds to

*See Map on page 74

the major sowing and harvesting season of tapioca in Kerala.[2] The reference period, it may be clarified, was agriculturally a normal year for the state.

## THE VILLAGES

The selected villages are representative of their respective regions, as noted earlier. The highland village which has about a third of its geographical area under forests is sparsely populated (438 persons/sq. km. as per 1971 Census). In contrast to this, the two midland villages were more densely populated (average 700 persons/sq. km.) while the lowland village was very densely populated (1500 persons/sq. km.).

Agriculture is the main activity in all four villages. About two-thirds of the workers in the villages were directly engaged in agriculture as cultivators or agricultural labourers except in Perinad, the lowland village, where only a third of the workers were directly engaged in agriculture. This is due to the availability of other avenues of employment in the allied agricultural andnon-agricultural sector in and around the village including amajor tapioca-processing unit. Coir-making and fishing are important subsidiary activities in the lowland village. The plantation sector absorbed a good chunk of the workers in the highland village. Cashew processing was found to be an important source of employment in one of the midland villages (Veliyam), whereas in the other (i.e., Poovachal) services was an important source of employment.

The villages differ from one another in respect of their cropping pattern also. Paddy and Coconut are the dominant crops cultivated in the lowland village, with tapioca being of secondary importance. The midland villages are noteworthy for the diversity of crops cultivated like rice, tapioca, coconut, banana, cashew, pepper, arecanut and vegetables, etc. In the highland village, apart from rice and tapioca, plantation crops like rubber, oil-palm and spices like pepper are the important crops grown here.

Like many other villages in Kerala the sample villages have a good measure of basic amenities. There are markets in all the villages but they aslo have access to neighbouring centres through a network of roads that are served by both public and private transport.

Though the sample villages are typical of Kerala villages it is necessary to note here that Kerala villages in general are atypical of Indian villages in two respects. Firstly, houses here are not built in clusters as one finds in other parts of India but are dispersed. Secondly, unlike most Indian villages Kerala villages are less isolated owing to the well developed infrastructure in terms of road network and transport services; provision of basic rural amenities too are found to be at a much higher level here than in other parts of India.

## PROFILE OF FARM HOUSEHOLDS

The consumption and production activities of agrarian households would be conditioned by demographic, social, economic and cultural forces. The nature and extent of the influence of each of these forces would vary depending on the historical processes distinct to each region. In what follows we have tried to briefly present the socio-economic background of the sample households.

The role of demographic factors like size of family as also its composition has been noted as a determinant of the income earning and saving capacity of households. Table 3.2 shows that inter-size class differences in family size are narrow, being around 6 persons per household. This, of course, is not uncharacteristic of a region said to have witnessed a dramatic demographic transition.[3] While demographic factors like family size as also its composition may shed light on the number of producers and consumers that a household has, its influence in an agrarian economy is primarily felt via its impact in relation to land. Family workers per acre of operated area is inversely related to size of holdings and hence may explain, for instance, as to why small farmers have a general tendency to apply more labour input per acre than large farmers, as observed in several studies. The operated area per capita varies directly with the size of holdings and may explain, for instance, as to why small farmers

TABLE 3.2: **Demographic and Literacy Characteristics of Farm Households**

| Indices | Size classes in acres | | | | | | | |
|---|---|---|---|---|---|---|---|---|
| | 0.0 to 0.5 | 0.51 to 1.0 | 1.01 to 2.5 | 2.51 to 5.0 | 5.01 to 10.0 | 10.01 to 15.0 | Above 15 | All |
| 1. Average family size—No. of persons per household | 5.3 | 6.0 | 6.3 | 7.0 | 6.7 | 6.3 | 4.7 | 6.3 |
| 2. Operated area in acres per capita | 0.06 | 0.12 | 0.26 | 0.51 | 1.05 | 1.94 | 4.94 | 0.52 |
| 3. Family workers per acre of operated area | 5.22 | 1.83 | 0.74 | 0.35 | 0.19 | 0.08 | 0.04 | 0.40 |
| 4. Age structure of household population (% to total population) | | | | | | | | |
| Adults (above 14 years) | 64.2 | 65.6 | 71.8 | 72.1 | 68.1 | 72.0 | 71.4 | 69.2 |
| Children (6-14 years) | 22.6 | 22.3 | 21.0 | 23.4 | 22.7 | 20.0 | 21.4 | 22.2 |
| Children (blow 6 years) | 13.2 | 12.1 | 7.1 | 4.6 | 9.2 | 8.0 | 7.1 | 8.6 |
| 5. Literates to total population excluding children below 6 years (%) | 83.7 | 84.0 | 95.5 | 95.2 | 96.8 | 95.6 | 84.6 | 92.1 |

generally turn to wage income in order to supplement the income they derive from their small holdings. About 70 per cent of the household population consists of adults (i.e., those above 14 years), the rest being children. The number of dependents among households belonging to the lower size groups are generally more than in the case of other size groups.

One of the constraints to higher incomes and productivity in agrarian societies has been, what some call, 'Peasant Conservatism'. It is, therefore, contended that with changing levels of literacy this impediment could be removed. Literacy not only conditions the outlook of the farmer but also influences his responsiveness to economic stimuli. A number of studies suggest a positive association between literacy levels and agricultural productivity.[4] Investment in education in rural areas is, therefore, viewed as a central ingredient in any strategy to increase agricultural productivity.[5] According to Schultz education has a higher pay-off for farmers in a changing modernising environment than in a static, traditional one.[6] As seem from Table 3.2 most of our subjects were literate. The proportion of literates to total population (excluding children below 6 years) was over 92 per cent overall for all households, which is not a typical of a state like Kerala, known for its high levels of literacy. Though we have treated as literate only those who had formal education, it is necessary to clarify that in a region like Kerala where the influence of the media is strong and dissemination of information swift this factor may not be an overriding constraint to higher incomes and productivity. More than literacy and awareness, the reasons for small farmers lagging behind large farmers in adopting new technology, as observed in some studies,[7] may have to be sought elsewhere, particularly in the differential access of the farmers to resources and markets. There are evidences which suggest that when such institutional impediments are removed, small farmers have not faltered in adopting new innovations.[8]

In the pursuit of maximising family income, members of rural households engage in various vocations. These vocations would not only depend upon their skills and aptitudes but also upon the economic base of the regions in which they are cast.

In an agrarian setting such as ours, the occupations of the households would be primarily related to agriculture and its allied sectors, though the degree of its importance will vary across size classes of farmers. Table 3.3 presents the occupational status of the adult population (i.e., those above 14 years) of our households by main activity. It is noted that cultivators (by main activity) accounted for over 15 per cent of the total adult population while agricultural labourers accounted for almost 5 per cent. Proportion of cultivators generally shows an increasing trend with increase in size of holdings (with stray exceptions) upto 10 acres and then again declines. On the other hand agricultural labourers are found only in the three lowest size groups and clearly shows an inverse relationship with farm size. Agricultural labourers, artisans, factory employees, coir workers and those engaged in fishing mostly occur in households among lower size groups while in higher size groups, apart from cultivation, trade, services and household activities account for a sizeable proportion reflecting not only the economic base of the different size groups but also the diversity in economic activities pursued by the households.

While skills and aptitudes possessed by individuals influence the choice of their vocation, they are in no less measure or more influenced by the economic opportunities available in a given region. The proportion of cultivators and agricultural labourers to total adults was relatively the lowest in Cherumood, the lowland village, being 9 per cent and 0.6 per cent respectively. The availability of other avenues of employment in this region like factory employment and allied agricultural activities like fishing, coir making, cashew processing, etc., may partly explain these trends. Thus 29 per cent of the adults in the lowest size group in this village were factory workers; coir workers too accounted for 18 per cent of all adults in this size group; fishing engaged about 3 per cent of the adults in the village as a whole. In Muttara the cashew industry provided gainful employment to over 11 per cent of the adults. Plantation workers like rubber tappers were reported only in Ayilara, the highland village. All this illustrates some of the spatial contrasts in the vocations pursued by our rural folk.

TABLE 3.3: **Occupational Structure of Adult Population (percentage to total adult population)**

| Occupation (by main activity) | Size classes in acres | | | | | | | |
|---|---|---|---|---|---|---|---|---|
| | 0.0 to 0.5 | 0.51 to 1.0 | 1.01 to 2.5 | 2.51 to 5.0 | 5.01 to 10.0 | 10.01 to 15.0 | Above 15 | All |
| Cultivators | 10.3 | 6.8 | 15.2 | 19.0 | 21.7 | 16.7 | 10.0 | 15.1 |
| Agricultural Labourers | 20.6 | 11.7 | 2.3 | — | — | — | — | 4.9 |
| Artisans | 1.5 | 5.8 | — | 0.7 | — | — | — | 1.3 |
| Traders | 2.9 | 3.9 | 7.6 | 2.1 | 4.1 | 5.6 | 30.0 | 4.9 |
| Services | — | 1.0 | 5.3 | 8.5 | 9.3 | 5.6 | — | 5.3 |
| Factory employees | 19.1 | 5.8 | 11.1 | 2.8 | 3.1 | — | — | 7.4 |
| Fishing and Coir workers | 7.4 | 8.7 | 1.8 | — | — | — | — | 2.8 |
| Students | 7.4 | 13.6 | 16.4 | 15.5 | 18.6 | 27.8 | 10.0 | 15.3 |
| Household duties | 22.1 | 32.0 | 27.5 | 32.4 | 28.9 | 22.2 | 40.0 | 29.1 |
| Others | 8.9 | 10.6 | 12.9 | 19.0 | 14.4 | 22.3 | 10.0 | 14.0 |

The production activities of households in an agrarian economy will depend upon the nature and characteristics of the agrarian structure in a given region. A prominent feature of traditional agrarian societies is the highly unequal distribution of productive resources, particularly land. Not only is land a capital asset but also an important input in the production process. Its possession is thus looked upon as a source of social prestige, economic and political power. Many studies on rural poverty point to the close association between rural poverty and the distribution of land holdings.[9] For this reason an analysis of the distribution of land holdings has aroused curiosity among social scientists, particularly economists. We shall, therefore, briefly examine the land characteristics of our sample households.

Table 3.4 which presents particulars about the area owned and operated by our households clearly shows that our study region has some of the attributes characteristic of a traditional agrarian society with a highly skewed pattern of distribution of holdings, both owned and operated. Though the degree of inequality in distribution of land in Kerala may be less than in other regions (under the impact of land reforms) this by far no means disproves the persistence of inequality in land distribution in the region. The two lowest size groups accounting for 32.9 per cent of the sample households owned and operated only less than 6 per cent of the total area owned and operated by all households. On the other hand farmers in the three highest size groups accounting for 20 per cent of total sample households owned and operated as high as 60 per cent of total area owned and operated by all households. The average size of holdings in the smallest and highest size groups ranged from 0.27 acres to 13.85 acres in the case of owned area—and still wider—from 0.30 acres to 23.20 acres in the case of operated area. It is interesting that concentration of land in the hands of the largest size class is greater in respect of operated land rather than owned area. This suggests that leasing-in could be used by large farmers as an instrument to extend their control over land.

TABLE 3.4: **Particulars of Land Owned and Operated by Farm Households**

| Indices | Size classes in acres | | | | | | | |
|---|---|---|---|---|---|---|---|---|
| | 0.0 to 0.5 | 0.51 to 1.0 | 1.01 to 2.5 | 2.51 to 5.0 | 5.01 to 10.0 | 10.01 to 15.0 | Above 15 | All |
| Distribution of sample households—percentage | 14.3 | 18.6 | 27.1 | 20.0 | 15.0 | 2.9 | 2.1 | 100.0 |
| Distribution of owned area—percentage | 1.3 | 4.3 | 14.5 | 22.8 | 35.1 | 11.8 | 10.1 | 100.0 |
| Owned area per household in acres | 0.27 | 0.67 | 1.56 | 3.35 | 6.88 | 12.16 | 13.85 | 2.94 |
| Distribution of operated area—percentage | 1.3 | 4.1 | 13.9 | 22.1 | 32.5 | 10.8 | 15.3 | 100.0 |
| Operated area per household in acres | 0.30 | 0.71 | 1.66 | 3.59 | 7.05 | 12.25 | 23.20 | 3.25 |
| Proportion of owned to operated area | 90.2 | 94.1 | 94.0 | 93.4 | 97.5 | 99.3 | 59.7 | 90.3 |
| Proportion of wet lands to total operated area | — | 0.5 | 8.5 | 8.8 | 19.1 | 30.9 | 17.8 | 15.4 |
| Wet lands operated per household in acres | — | 0.004 | 0.14 | 0.32 | 1.34 | 3.78 | 4.13 | 0.50 |
| Dry lands operated per household in acres | 0.30 | 0.71 | 1.52 | 3.27 | 5.71 | 8.47 | 19.06 | 2.75 |

If we categorise the lands in terms of their qualitative differences—in our case wet lands and dry lands[10]—we note that the unequal pattern of distribution of lands is even more striking in the case of better quality lands. As seen from Table 3.4 the proportion of wet land to total operated area is directly associated with the size of holdings, with the lowest size group not operating any wet lands. Only the large farmers with holdings above 5 acres operated a significant quantity of wet lands. The significance of the possession and cultivation of wet lands or paddy lands has not been adequately realised. These lands lying along the valley or inter-hill basins are generally fertile with the water table being very high since all the rain-water from the hills and slopes is drained into it. They are easily submersible during monsoon months and hence have all the agronomic features conducive to the growth of paddy, the staple food of the people. Wet lands command a high market value and traditionally their possession has been looked upon as a sign of social prestige. The operation of wet lands influences the crop pattern of our farms, as our discussion in the next chapter shows with paddy being conspicuous by its absence from the crop pattern of the lowest size groups. Thus not only is the distribution of land, both owned and operated, highly skewed but also the more prized lands like wet lands are the preserve and privilege of the big farmers.

More than the extent of land operated by a household, the nature and characteristic of the control exercised over the land may influence producer decisions and productivity. It is, however, not clear as to what kind of link exists between tenancy and producer decisions and productivity. The views in this regard vary widely. Some like Marshall look upon certain forms of tenancy like share-cropping as exerting a negative influence on productivity; others like Cheung, however, dispute this. Bardhan—Rudra noted that in Eastern India the institution of share-cropping had adapted itself to a regime of increasing production and profits.[11] According to Hanumantha Rao the scope for decision-making and entrepreneurship under share-cropping is clearly limited unlike in the case of fixed tenancies.[12] In any case if at all tenancy has a negative effect on production and productivity, we have no reason to consider this as an overriding constraint in our study region. Most of the lands operated by our households were owned, accounting for over 90 per cent of total operated area of all households. But the mere fact of a high proportion of owned cultivators does not imply that this will have a positive effect on production and productivity. In fact there are evidences which suggest that not only may tenant cultivators cultivate land more intensively than owner cultivators,[13] but also small owner cultivators may cultivate land more intensively than big owner cultivators.[14]

Though a high proportion of operated area in the highest size group—about 40 per cent—appears to be unowned, this is accounted by lands mostly operated by near relatives and children living elsewhere. Big farmers in order to circumvent land ceiling laws transfer titular ownership to their near and dear ones though effective control of such lands still vests with them. However, in consonance with our operational definition of a household only land owned by the head of the household or other members can be treated as owned holdings. All other lands controlled by the household but legally owned by outsiders would have to be treated as unowned holdings. This above phenomenon represents an illusory type of leasing in of land by households. In the other size groups the leased in area are mostly genuine based on different tenurial terms like wholly cash or kind rent and cash-cum-kind rent.

The portrait of inequality in the distribution of productive resources that we encounter is not confined to land alone. This is even more true in the case of other productive assets too. As evident from Table 3.5 the pattern of investment in farm and non-farm assets (valued at replacement cost)[15] reveals a highly skewed pattern of distribution ranging from Rs. 3468 per household in the lowest size group to as high as Rs. 1.25 lakhs in the highest size group in the case of farm assets and Rs. 15 to Rs. 19,667 similarly in the case of non-farm assets. The disaggregated picture of farm assets which includes agricultural implements, bullock carts, residential buildings[16] including farm structures and livestock reveal a similar trend. Given their relatively better position in respect of land and income, large farmers

**TABLE 3.5 : Particulars of Ownership of Non-land Assets**

| Indices | Size classes in acres | | | | | | | |
|---|---|---|---|---|---|---|---|---|
| | 0.0 to 0.5 | 0.51 to 1.0 | 1.01 to 2.5 | 2.51 to 5.0 | 5.01 to 10.0 | 10.01 to 15.0 | Above 15 | All |
| *Farm Assets (Value in Rs. per household)* | | | | | | | | |
| Agricultural implements | 58 | 117 | 243 | 522 | 1895 | 1536 | 2513 | 582 |
| Bullock Carts | — | — | — | — | 286 | 325 | — | 52 |
| Residential buildings and farm structures | 3265 | 3977 | 12238 | 16426 | 28671 | 41401 | 103333 | 15510 |
| Livestock | 145 | 404 | 557 | 1140 | 1974 | 1739 | 19827 | 1246 |
| All Farm Assets | 3468 | 4498 | 13039 | 18088 | 32826 | 45001 | 125673 | 17390 |
| Non-Farm Assets (i.e., trade implements and Commercial buildings) | 15 | 245 | 679 | 1275 | 2034 | 3000 | 19667 | 1317 |
| *Draught Animals Owned per Household* | | | | | | | | |
| Bullocks | — | — | 0.05 | 0.28 | 0.95 | 1.00 | 0.67 | 0.26 |
| He-buffaloes | — | — | 0.05 | 0.21 | 0.43 | 1.00 | 2.33 | 0.20 |

| | | | | | | | | |
|---|---|---|---|---|---|---|---|---|
| *Farm Assets* (Rs. per acre of operated area)* | | | | | | | | |
| All | 188 | 164 | 160 | 186 | 419 | 237 | 174 | 261 |
| *Farm Assets* (Rs. per family worker)* | | | | | | | | |
| All | 36 | 90 | 216 | 535 | 2216 | 2911 | 4047 | 650 |

*Note*: *Farm Assets here consists of agricultural implements, draught animals and bullock carts only.

prefer to invest on modern agricultural implements, use durable building materials and maintain cross-breed animals all of which are expensive. But small farmers can afford only the traditional agricultural implements and building materials, and local varieties of animals which are relatively much cheaper. On account of these factors the average value of investment per household varies directly with the size of holdings. Interestingly investment in bullock carts is low, confined to only two size groups, perhaps due to the well developed infrastructure in the villages in terms of road network and transport services and hence obviates the need to possess bullock carts.

In many agrarian societies the extent of draught animals possessed by households is often taken as an index of their economic viability. Draught animals are not only a capital good providing capital good but also a capital good providing services.[17] However, our data suggests that possession of draught animals is not favoured by households in this region, particularly the small farmers, for a variety of reasons. The two lowest size groups do not own any draught animals while in holdings 1 to 5 acres too it is negligible. It is only the two highest size groups who own a significant number of draught animals. The indivisibilities associated with maintenance of draught animals, its limited utility in agriculture in Kerala—its use being almost exclusively confined to paddy cultivation—the practice of custom hiring, the scarcity of grazing lands in Kerala—all these factors explain in some way or other as to why possession of draught animals is not favoured by farmers in this region, particularly those belonging to the lower strata.

So far we have focussed attention only on the pattern of distribution of farm assets across size classes of farmers. We may now find out as to how capital is combined with land among different strata of farms. As seen from Table 3.5 average investment per acre of operated area declines and then increases, though this trend is not smooth in the higher size groups. Capital is not perfectly divisible and hence among small farms average investment per acre appears to be high relative to land. On the other hand for reasons stated earlier, big farmers invest on modern high unit value items and average value of investment per acre is high here too but not for the same reason as in the case of small farmers. Another aspect worthy of notice is that capital per family worker varies directly with size of holdings and the differences become very wide in holdings above 5 acres. This suggests that capital is a constraint among small farms but not to the same extent among large farms.

The ranking of the different segments of the peasantry in the agrarian structure determines the terms of their entry to various markets like, for instance, the credit market. Table 3.6 which gives particulars of borrowings by our households shows that the proportion of borrowing households as also amount borrowed per household varies directly with the size of holding though we note fluctuations in the upper brackets. In the lowest size

TABLE 3.6: **Particulars of Loan Borrowings by Farm Households**

| Size classes in acres | Proportion of households borrowing loans | Amount borrowed in Rs. | |
|---|---|---|---|
| | | Per borrowing household | Per sample household |
| 0.00 to 0.5 | 10.0 | 350* | 35 |
| 0.51 to 1.0 | 26.9 | 1050 | 283 |
| 1.01 to 2.5 | 44.7 | 750* | 336 |
| 2.51 to 5.0 | 53.6 | 1228 | 658 |
| 5.01 to 10.0 | 66.7 | 1425 | 950 |
| 10.01 to 15.0 | 25.0 | 2000 | 500 |
| Above 15 | 33.3 | 4000 | 1333 |
| ALL | 40.7 | 1143 | 465 |

*Note*: Out of Rs. 65,170 borrowed by households during the reference year 74.6 per cent were crop loans, 6.9 per cent were for purchase of livestock and equipments, 10.7 per cent for land development measures like digging of wells and 7.8 per cent for consumption and other miscellaneous purposes.

*Crop loans borrowed here were either wholly or partly diverted for consumption purposes.

group only 10 per cent of the households borrowed loans as against 67 per cent in holdings 5 to 10 acres. Since land is often sought as a collateral security for purposes of lending, it is obvious that big farmers enjoy a distinct advantage over marginal and small farmers in credit borrowing.

To sum up: the 140 farm households who constitute the sample for our intensive study come from dissimilar socio-economic backgrounds. This is particularly true with respect to the distribution of productive resources, especially land. The ranking of the different segments of the peasantry in the agrarian structure determines their bargaining strength in the various markets. As such the feasible choices as well as technical options confronting different size groups of farmers differ. It is in this broad perspective that one could gain a proper understanding of the process of decision-making in a peasant economy like what crop or combination of crops they grow, how they allocate resources between alternate uses and what they sell and retain for their consumption, etc.

## REFERENCES

1. i.e., ratio of the proportion of tapioca area to the gross cropped area in the district (or taluk as the case may be) over a similar proportion for the state as a whole. A value of above one would signify a high concentration of the crop in the district relative to the state (or district if in the case of taluks).
2. This does not perfectly correspond with the official agricultural year (July to June). In fact, the convention of observing a single agricultural year for all crops has been questioned on the grounds that the sowing and harvesting seasons of the different crops in Kerala vary. See *Studies on Farm Management in Kerala*, Report for 1962-63, Chapter IV, p. 127.
3. For details see TN Krishnan: Demographic Transition in Kerala: Facts and Factors, *Economic and Political Weekly* (*EPW*), Annual Number, 1976.
4. Cf. Yujiro Hayami: Sources of Agricultural Productivity among Selected Countries, *American Journal of Agricultural Economics*, Vol. 51, 1969, pp. 564-75; Yujiro Hayami and Vernon W Ruttan: Agricultural Productivity Differences Among Countries, *American Economic Review*, Vol. 60, 1970, pp. 895-911; Morlaine E Lockheed, et al.: Farmer Education and Farm Efficiency: A Survey, *Economic*

*Development and Cultural Change*, Vol. 29, No. 1, October 1980, pp. 37-76.

5. John W Mellor: *The New Economics of Growth*, Cornell University Press, Ithaca, N Y, 1976, p. 74 (vide) Morlaine Lockheed, et al., (op. cit).
6. Cited in Morlaine Lockheed, et al., op. cit.
7. V K R V Rao: *Growth with Social Justice in Asian Agriculture*, UNRISD Geneva, 1974, p. 14; Biplab Dasgupta: *Green Revolution*, UNRISD Geneva; B H Farmer (ed): *Green Revolution*? ELBS, Macmillan, 1980, Chapter 8-13; N S Shetty: Agricultural Innovations: Leaders and Laggards, *EPW*, Vol. 3, No. 33, 1968; C Muthaiah: Green Revolution—Participation by Small and Large Farmers, *Indian Journal of Agricultural Economics*, January-March 1971; also see IJAE: Conference Number, October-December 1971, for several studies on the issue; M Schluter and John WMellor: New Seed Varieties and the Small Farmer, *EPW*, March 25, 1972, pp. A. 31-38.
8. Cited in A K Sen: *Employment, Technology and Development*, Oxford University Press, London, 1975, p. 153.
9. *Poverty and Landlessness in Rural Asia*, ILO, 1977, and *Rural Asia: Challange and Opportunity*, Asian Development Bank, 1977.
10. This is only a very broad categorisation. One could further subcategorise dry or wet lands in terms of their qualitative differences.
11. S N S Cheung: Private Property Rights and Share Cropping, *Journal of Political Economy*, 76(6), November-December 1968, pp. 101, 1107-23 (vide) R Albert Berry and William R Cline: *Agrarian Structure and Productivity in Developing Countries*, The John Hopkins University Press, Baltimore and London, 1979, Chapter 2, p. 78; Pranab Bardhan and Ashok Rudra: Interlinkage of Land, Labour and Credit Relations, Analysis of Village Survey Data in East India, *EPW*, Annual No. February, 1978.
12. C H Hanumantha Rao: Uncertainty, Entrepreneurship and Sharecropping in India, *Journal of Political Economy*, Vol. 79, No. 3, May-June 1971.
13. Vyas noted that in Gujarat small tenants cultivatedl and more intensively than small owner-cultivators, see V S Vyas: Tenancy in a Dynamic Setting, *EPW*, June 27, 1970, p. 4-79.
14. C H H Rao, 1971, op. cit., p. 591.
15. Such a valuation would estimate assets at a value higher than in the case of valuation at purchase price. But purchases do not belong to the same time period, and some are farm produced and not purchased.
16. One may object to inclusion of residential buildings as a farm asset. Under Indian conditions there is also a practical difficulty that portions of the residential buildings are used for storing farm produce

or keeping cattle. In Kerala it is common to find traditional houses having specified storage rooms known as Arahs. Cellers and attic of residential houses are also used for storage purposes. Marginal and small farmers often use a portion of their house as cattle shed.

17. K N Raj: *Investment in Livestock in Agrarian Economies*, 1963, Mimeo, 1968 (vide) Bharadwaj, *Production Condition in Indian Agriculture*, Occasional Paper No. 33, Department of Applied Economics, University of Cambridge, Cambridge University Press, 1974. p. 32.

# 4

# LAND UTILISATION

WE DISCUSS here three aspects of the agricultural economy of the sample farm households relating to land use. The first is cropping intensity, about which there has been a lively debate. After briefly reviewing it, we discuss certain limitations of the very concept of cropping intensity as it is measured, particularly in the context of Kerala. This leads us to the discussion of the peculiarities of cropping pattern and cropping systems. It is only the total perspective of land use in all the three aspects together, that gives a proper picture of intensity of land use in Kerala across different size groups of holdings.

## CROPPING INTENSITY

An inverse relationship between cropping intensity and farm size, as observed through farm management data, has attracted explanatory comments from quite a few eminent economists. Since this debate is an offshoot of the debate on productivity in relation to farm size, the explanatory comments in both respects run parallel or almost identical. Though the role of physical factors like irrigation has been acknowledged, the size of holding has been almost tacitly been taken as a determinant (inversely) of cropping intensity, particularly in the context of traditional agriculture as distinguished from modern capitalist agriculture. One version of the argument is that the entrepreneurial factor being limited, as farm size and scale of operation increases the marginal productivity of the co-ordinating, managing and supervising activity of the farmer comes down setting in diminishing returns to scale which in turn limits the intensity of land use. For example, Sampath and Gopinath on the basis of measures of inefficiency adopted in their paper concluded that smaller the size of holdings, less the inefficiency.[1] Almost in the same vein Bhagwati and Chakravarty suggested that larger holdings (which they argued were built up over time through consolidation of small holdings) were characterised by a higher degree of fragmentation of the plots constituting the holdings and this adversely affected efficiency of management particularly on current production operations resulting in poorer productivity of land or less intensive use of land.[2] But as Bharadwaj has pointed out it is not merely the number of fragments that mattered but also size of a fragment and the FMS suggested that average area per fragment increased with size of farms.[3] Moreover by virtue of their control on the supply of land, big farmers are able to control the opportunity of work for local labour thus holding down wages (and under monopsony conditions) resulting in less intensive use of land by big farmers.[4]

The second set of arguments attributed the inverse relationship to qualitative/quantitative differences in factor endowments particularly land and labour. Sen, for instance, attributed this phenomenon to dualism in the labour market.[5] Since use of family labour is not assumed to be wage-determined, its use is extended beyond the point of equality between wage rate and marginal productivity. Labour employed per unit of land would then be higher among the smaller farms compared to larger farms. Apparently such a use of family labour particularly beyond the point of equality with wage, is assumed to have no opportunity cost, the employment opportunities being limited. Hanumantha Rao, in a similar vein opined that small farmers took greater care in performing their tasks and were better managers.[6] The difference in the nature of decision making has been noted as a factor here. The aim of getting subsistence by making the best use of the limited land, involves maximisation of yield per hectare of net sown area. One of the ways of this is through stepping up cropping intensity. The objective of profit maximisation need not involve this. Some suggested that higher cropping intensity among small holdings was due to the fact that smaller holdings constitute better quality of land. In particular, irrigation has been found to be a major determinant.[7] There was some evidence from the FMS to support this. Bharadwaj has, however, stressed the need to make a conceptual distinction between intrinsic differences in soil and man-made differences. If the quality difference is due to past investment, one can overcome the disability through appropriate investment in current inputs. Furthermore, since the economically viable size unit is smaller in the case of better quality land as compared to poorer land it makes possible sub-division. Bhagwati and Chakravarty suggested that when the relatively small operators are forced by circumstances to resort to distress sales to larger holdings, it is the poorer quality land that is transferred, the distressed party preferring to retain the better quality land. There is one more factor. The proportion of leased in land is generally found to be higher among small holdings, and Bharadwaj points out a tenant would prefer to lease in better quality lands since the risk of crop failure for those surviving at the bare subsistence limit could work out much higher for the tenant than the additional cost of tenancy he has to bear.

Prasad observed that lower cropping intensity among big farmers was due to their not making use of irrigation facilities beyond one season.[8] Sau went a step further and argued that big farmers who faced a choice of multiple channels of profit-making would prefer to leave his land idle when he found non-farm activities like money-lending and trading to be more profitable than cultivation.[9]

In any empirical study of cropping intensity, however, one faces a few serious problems of measurement, which the debate reviewed above has side-tracked. Any theoretical explanation of an empirical fact has to be first sure of the nature of empirical fact and the way it is measured. In a State like Kerala, particularly, such empirical problems become conspicuous. Using the index of cropping intensity, traditionally employed, viz., the ratio of gross sown area (net sown area plus double cropped area) expressed as a percentage over net sown area, we get Table 4.1 below for the surveyed villages. The picture here is quite contrary to the one assumed in the debate reviewed above. What in fact we found in these villages is that cropping intensity tends to increase with the size of holding. It is lowest in the smallest two size groups and highest in the last two or three size groups, though between the latter the increase may not be smooth. This is found to be the case in every village and also in all villages taken together. This does not necessarily mean that in Kerala (or villages surveyed at least) the large farmers cultivate land more intensively than the small farmers and that the behaviour/attitudes assumed on the part of large farmers in the debate above do not hold in the case of large farmers of Kerala. This is because we have to take into account the peculiarities of crop pattern and cropping systems in the region, which can introduce complexities in the measurement of cropping intensity. Unless land use in its totality is studied, we cannot derive conclusions about the intensity of land use on the basis of the usual index of cropping intensity alone. Pending the discussion of crop pattern and cropping systems of tapioca in the following sections, we may discuss the limitations of the index of cropping intensity particularly in the context of Kerala and the reasons for the peculiar results in Table 4.1.

The most important determinant of cropping intensity as it is measured is the choice of the crop in the region or size groups of holdings as the case may be. Choice of a seasonal crop like paddy affords a scope for double cropping and this could keep the cropping intensity higher. Cropping intensity is comparable across regions or size groups of holdings only if the scope of such choice is uniform. If, on the other hand, an annual or perennial crop is grown in such regions or size groups of holdings, the cropping intensity as measured could be automatically low even if the land is continuously in use for most parts of the year or throughout the year. This is precisely the case with tapioca cultivation (which is of 8 to 10 months duration) and plantation crops, which dominate in Kerala, resulting in underestimation of land use intensity in Kerala, through cropping intensity index. We have already observed in the last chapter on

TABLE 4.1: **Multiple Cropping Index and Proportion of Wet Land Area to Total Operated Area: by Size Classes of Holdings**

| Villages | Size classes in acres | | | | | | | |
|---|---|---|---|---|---|---|---|---|
| | 0.0 to 0.5 | 0.51 to 1.0 | 1.01 to 2.5 | 2.51 to 5.0 | 5.01 to 10.0 | 10.01 to 15.0 | Above 15 | Total |
| Ayilara | 100 | 100 | 118.26 | 106.25 | 125.89 | 121.81 | – | 117.34 |
| | (—) | (—) | (17.87) | (6.25) | (25.30) | (21.81) | | (17.13) |
| Muttara | 100 | 100 | 106.38 | 108.87 | 118.84 | — | — | 114.21 |
| | (—) | (—) | (5.30) | (8.87) | (18.84) | | | (14.07) |
| Kuzhakad | 100 | 102.56 | 107.27 | 115.38 | 111.21 | 124.49 | 117.81 | 116.75 |
| | (—) | (2.56) | (7.95) | (15.38) | (17.11) | (34.41) | (17.81) | (19.43) |
| Cherumood | 100 | 100 | 100.52 | 100 | 112.05 | — | — | 104.53 |
| | (—) | (—) | (0.52) | (—) | (12.05) | | | (4.53) |
| All Villages | 100 | 100.53 | 108.57 | 108.85 | 119.16 | 123.74 | 117.81 | 114.46 |
| | (—) | (0.53) | (8.52) | (8.84) | (19.06) | (30.87) | (17.81) | (15.41) |

*Note*: Figures in parentheses show proportion of wet land area to total operated area for each size class.

the basis of secondary data that tapioca dominates on the small farms. One can circumvent this difficulty by counting such area twice or thrice depending on the period of crop duration. If, however, the index of cropping intensity is to be used as an indicator of employment absorption in agriculture, such a manipulation would defeat the purpose. This is because the mere fact of the standing crop over the year does not create employment; it may not even indicate production potential where production can be increased by reducing crop duration and increasing the possibilities of double cropping. Both employment and production increase when more than one crop is harvested and area is sown more than once in a year. But this is determined by the availability of irrigation or type of land. Possession of wet lands (or paddy lands) is a privilege which is enjoyed more by larger farmers than the small even in Kerala. It is this fact which is reflected in the lower crop intensity on small farms and higher intensity on larger farms in Table 4.1

Though cultivation of annual/perennial crops does not permit multiple cropping, it helps increase cropping intensity by opening up opportunities for mixed cropping or inter-cropping, a practice quite common in Kerala. The vacant spaces in between rows of annual/perennial crops are made use of by farmers to grow other short duration crops. Thus, for example, cultivation of tapioca opens up prospects for inter-cropping legume crops or groundnut in between rows of tapioca plants. Tapioca can be grown (and is in fact grown) as a subsidiary crop in coconut plantations as also in rubber plantations not more than three years old. This is nothing but one method of intensive use of land. Mixed or inter-cropping helps increase both income and employment and one cannot but treat it also as another method of intensive use of land. Thus there are two problems while considering the question of cropping intensity. One is that cultivation of annual/perennial crop does not permit multiple cropping, and to that extent the cropping intensity index does not show continuous use made of land throughout the year. But on the other hand, cultivation of such crops permits mixed or inter-cropping which is as good as additional cropped area. Both these aspects are, however, not captured by the traditional cropping intensity index. Though we have not coined a new index, our contention is that we cannot jump to conclusions of theoretical or policy significance merely on the basis of the traditional index of cropping intensity. We have to take into account the crop pattern and cropping systems.

## CROPPING PATTERN

The peculiarities of the cropping pattern in Kerala in conjunction with the practice of mixed cropping (as against mono cropping) have raised other problems too. It is thus not uncommon for researchers to find farmers in difficulty when called upon to relate the area occupied by each crop. This problem may not arise in the case of certain seasonal crops like paddy and plantation crops like rubber, tea and coffee which, as a rule, are grown only as a pure crop. In the case of tapioca this problem does not arise only where tapioca is grown as a pure crop. In the case of most other crops, however, one comes across pure plantations only occasionally. Hence, in our survey details were elicited of area occupied by tapioca, paddy and any other crop for which the farmer could indicate the actual or approximate area occupied by the crop. To apportion area under tapioca wherever it was grown as an inter-crop, we took into account the number of stems planted per unit area as well as the spacing pattern. In the case of other crops the residual area (after deductions for tapioca, paddy and other crops for which area occupied was indicated) was apportioned among the remaining crops using the information on number of trees planted and spacing norms. Though the above procedure is not a fool-proof method, it offers a practical solution to a complex problem.

Table 4.2 presents data on the cropping pattern of the sample households. In the context of our earlier discussion it is interesting to note that annual crops like tapioca and bananas, perennial crops like coconut, cashew, arecanut, pepper, rubber, etc., with a production span extending beyond a single season/year dominate the cropping pattern in all size classes, particularly in the lowest size groups. Obviously with such a crop-mix, the

TABLE 4.2: Corpping Pattern: Village-wise and for all Villages (in Per Cent to Total Cropped Area by Size of Holdings)

| Crop | Villages (for all holdings) | | | | All villages Size classes in acres | | | | | | | |
|---|---|---|---|---|---|---|---|---|---|---|---|---|
| | Ayilara | Mutt-ara | Kuzha-kad | Cheru-mood | 0.0 to 0.5 | 0.51 to 1.0 | 1.01 to 2.5 | 2.51 to 5.0 | 5.01 to 10.0 | 10.01 to 15.0 | Above 15 | All |
| Tapioca | 30.0 | 38.3 | 32.5 | 36.2 | 56.1 | 61.8 | 45.8 | 40.1 | 26.9 | 16.0 | 36.0 | 33.9 |
| Paddy | 29.1 | 25.1 | 28.3 | 10.1 | — | 1.1 | 15.8 | 17.2 | 31.1 | 37.2 | 30.2 | 25.3 |
| Coconut | 11.6 | 14.2 | 20.0 | 30.8 | 20.9 | 18.0 | 20.0 | 17.4 | 16.1 | 25.8 | 15.7 | 18.1 |
| Banana | 3.0 | 2.3 | 2.0 | 3.5 | 3.6 | 3.1 | 2.7 | 4.3 | 1.8 | 1.6 | 1.8 | 2.5 |
| Jackfruit and Mango | 2.2 | 2.0 | 1.7 | 1.2 | 3.1 | 2.6 | 2.5 | 2.3 | 1.6 | 1.9 | 0.9 | 1.8 |
| Cashew | 4.4 | 5.7 | 0.5 | 3.4 | 0.8 | 1.2 | 1.6 | 4.8 | 3.6 | 4.0 | 0.7 | 3.1 |
| Arecanut and Pepper | 5.3 | 2.5 | 3.3 | 0.5 | 3.9 | 2.3 | 3.3 | 4.3 | 2.5 | 4.6 | 1.7 | 3.1 |
| Rubber | 9.2 | 3.0 | 6.1 | 11.7* | — | — | 1.1 | 1.6 | 12.3 | 4.9 | 9.8 | 6.7 |
| Other crops | 5.2 | 6.9 | 5.7 | 2.7 | 11.6 | 10.1 | 7.1 | 8.1 | 4.2 | 4.0 | 3.1 | 5.5 |

*Note*: *The area under rubber reported here is actually located in the midland region.

scope for multiple cropping is extremely limited, if not absent, and this factor has to be taken note of in any discussion on the intensity of land use, particularly in a region like Kerala. Leaving aside this aspect it is striking to note the diversity of crops being cultivated by the different size groups of farmers. Crop diversification, it may be noted, is a potent device used by farmers to overcome the perils associated with specialisation in a single crop. Not only food crops but also non-food crops are being cultivated clearly reflecting the diverse requirements of the households for food as well as cash. The immediate implication of crop diversification, however, is that the range of crops the farmer proposes to grow has to compete for the limited resources that he can command. The extent of land that will be devoted to the cultivation of each crop depends on a variety of factors like subsistence requirements, profitability, institutional factors like the nature of access to wet and dry lands, etc.

The cropping pattern does have salient contrasts both with respect to the size groups of holdings and regions/villages. The proportion of cropped area under tapioca cultivation in general (with stray exceptions) shows a declining trend with an increase in the size of holdings upto 15 acres where again it increases. Tapioca occupies a pivotal position in the cropping pattern of holdings upto one acre occupying between 50-60 per cent of total cropped area. From thence its share declines consistently upto holdings above 15 acres where again about 36 per cent of cropped area is put under tapioca cultivation. Thus tapioca is seen to dominate the cropping pattern of the two lowest size groups. In the highest size group too it accounts for a high proportion. The rationale behind allocating a high proportion of a scarce input like land to cultivating a low unit value crop like tapioca may be questioned. An answer to this may call for a look into the motivational forces governing producer decisions which may vary across size groups of holdings and crops. Farmers belonging to the lower size groups may be growing it primarily for subsistence and moreover in the context of their limited resources tapioca may perhaps fit in their limited budget. It is true that they grow cash crops also but this is because of the pressing need to raise cash to meet their current consumption and production needs. An obvious question that one may raise here is as to why they do not concentrate exclusively on cultivation of cash crops and buy their food requirements from the market. But this may make them vulnerable to the vagaries of the market. Since small farmers are risk-averse they may prefer to cultivate a low risk crop like tapioca, which in any case can be raised with a low budget, as noted earlier. Also they mostly grow it as an inter-crop in between rows of coconut trees. These factors may not operate in the case of medium and large farmers who may be growing tapioca mostly as a cash crop with profit maximisation as their aim.

While subsistence or profit consideration may influence the choice of a crop, institutional factors too influence the cropping pattern. This is particularly true in the case of paddy among our sample households. The proportion of cropped area under paddy increases consistently with an increase in the size of holdings upto 15 acres and then declines again, though it still occupies almost a third of the cropped area in holdings above 15 acres. The crop does not figure at all in the cropping pattern of the lowest size group and also in the next size group 0.51-1 acre its share is insignificant.[10] The reasons for the absence of paddy in the cropping pattern of the lowest two size groups have been hinted earlier. Its cultivation is to a large extent determined by the possession (or operation through leasing in) of wet lands. This is the general rule but there are exceptions to this like growing of upland paddy (such a crop may begrown on the lower reaches of hilly tracts) which is a purely rainfed crop. In fact three farmers (in the higher size groups) had reported cultivation of upland paddy. With respect to other crops we do not find any consistent pattern in the proportion of area devoted to their cultivation across size groups of holdings. Though food crops account for a sizeable proportion of cropped area in all size classes, there is no consistent pattern as such.

Incidentally while discussing the role of institutional factors in determining the cropping pattern of the farmers it may be noted that in the case of leased-in dry lands amounting to 8.64

acres, an annual crop like tapioca was preferred. In fact tapioca's share was as high as 80 per cent. In the case of leased-in wet lands only paddy was grown. The disinclination to grow perennial crops in leased-in lands is obvious since such crops involve long-term investment and farmers may not like to risk such investment on lands over which their control is not secure.

Though, as noted earlier, farmers follow a diversified cropping pattern, the options before the farmer on what crop or combination of crops to grow is restricted by the constraint imposed by region. As seen from Table, 4.2 region does have some influence on the cropping pattern. Cultivation of coconut, for instance, is found to be relatively quite high in Cherumood—the coastal village, accounting for as high as 31 per cent of the total cropped area. On the other hand Ayilara the highland village reported the lowest proportion under coconut—over 11 per cent—while the two midland villages feel somewhere in between. Again we note that cultivation of plantation crops like rubber, arecanut and pepper are concentrated in the highlands in Cherumood only a negligible proportion of area is put under arecanut and pepper with rubber not being cultivated at all. Though around a third of total cropped area in each village is devoted to tapioca cultivation this may not fully reflect the regional characteristics (particularly in the case of lowlands) since our sample was only from tapioca cultivators. For the same reason only 10 per cent of cropped area in Cherumood was found to be under paddy cultivation even though the proportion of wet lands to total surface area is higher in the case of the lowlands as compared to other regions.

Other crops like fruit plants and trees, vegetables and miscellaneous crops which includes sweet potato, yam, tamarind, ginger, green gram, etc. are found in all villages.

## CROPPING SYSTEMS IN TAPIOCA CULTIVATION

Another dimension of the intensive use of land is reflected in the cropping systems followed in cultivation. This will be reflected firstly, through higher density of cultivation as in the case of inter-cropping; and secondly, by following a continuous sequence of cultivation. Here, we restrict our attention to tapioca only. Broadly, we can demarcate total area under tapioca into tapioca area grown as pure crop or moro crop and as a mixed crop, i.e., in inter-cropped fields. Where tapioca is grown as a mixed or inter-crop it is often planted as a subsidiary crop in coconut plantations or with rubber plants not more than three years old. Or when tapioca is the main crop, legume crops and groundnut are often grown as inter-crops in between rows of tapioca plants.

Table 4.3 presents the relevant data showing proportion of tapioca area grown as pure crop, the rest of the proportion being mixed crop. For the four villages together, we note that 60 per cent of the total area under tapioca is grown as a pure crop and the rest as mixed crop. Excepting for Cherumood, in all villages a high proportion of tapioca area is grown as a pure crop. This could, quite possibly, indicate that tapioca is being grown as a cash crop in these villages. In Cherumood mixed

TABLE 4.3: **Proportion of Area under Tapioca Grown as Pure Crop*—Percentage to Total in Each Size Class**

| Size classes in acres | Villages | | | | All villages |
|---|---|---|---|---|---|
| | Ayilara | Muttara | Kuzhakad | Cherumood | |
| 0.0 — 0.5 | 31.6 | — | — | — | 8.7 |
| 0.51— 1.0 | 33.3 | 27.0 | 11.9 | 15.1 | 21.6 |
| 1.01— 2.5 | 51.9 | 68.1 | 73.2 | 41.4 | 59.2 |
| 2.51— 5.0 | 75.0 | 42.9 | 27.5 | 33.0 | 44.1 |
| 5.01—10.0 | 48.9 | 73.7 | 76.0 | 57.1 | 67.5 |
| 10.01—15.0 | 3.3 | — | 83.3 | — | 56.7 |
| Above 15 | — | — | 94.9 | — | 94.9 |
| All | 51.3 | 61.4 | 72.8 | 35.7 | 60.0 |

*The percentages presented in the table refer to pure crop only. The remaining part of this in each size-class is as mixed/inter-crop.

cropping is more prevalent accounting for 64.3 per cent of total area under tapioca cultivation in that village. From this it would seem tapioca's importance in this coastal village is mostly as a secondary crop, grown largely in coconut groves, which abound in the coastal belt. Thus overall we note that the midland villages reported the highest proportion of tapioca area grown as pure crop followed by the highland village; while in the case of the lowland village tapioca is mostly important as a mixed crop.

More than inter-village differences, inter-size class differences are interesting. As size of holding increases the proportion of tapioca area grown as pure crop increases though not quite smoothly, perhaps suggesting that tapioca is grown more as a commercial proposition on bigger farms. Taking the figures for the four villages together we note that in the lowest size group only 8.7 per cent of tapioca area is grown as a pure crop while in the highest size group this proportion is as high as 95 per cent. The data for the individual villages also reveal a similar trend though we do come across stray fluctuations. Excepting for Ayilara where 31.6 per cent of tapioca area in the lowest size group is grown as pure crop, in all villages in this size group tapioca is grown only as a mixed crop. On the one hand this suggests that scarcity of land is a constraint in influencing cropping systems, on the other it shows how farmers faced with such a constraint resort to intensive cropping by practising intercropping making the maximum use of their limited land resources. This involves dense cultivation and a very intensive use of land—a phenomenon not captured by the usual cropping intensity index (which we may recall showed lowest values for small holdings).

The fact that tapioca is grown mostly as a mixed crop in the two lowest size groups does not in anyway underrate the importance of the crop in their economy. As noted earlier, tapioca occupies a pivotal position in the cropping pattern of farmers in the two lowest size groups, accounting for a high proportion of total cropped area.

Another dimension of the intensive use of land is reflected in an uninterrupted sequence of cultivation with little time lag between the harvesting of one crop and sowing of the next.

Though this may have a depressing effect on the yield of the subsequent crop, by following suitable crop rotation, and using adequate quantities of plant nutrients, the farmer can overcome this and yet use his land intensively. The data on area under tapioca grown as pure crop was disaggregated into: (1) area under tapioca grown annually as pure crop without any crop rotation, and (2) with crop rotation.

Table 4.4 presents the results of our exercise. Overall for the four villages it was noted that as high as 84.7 per cent of tapioca area grown as pure crop was sown annually without any crop rotation while in the remaining 15.3 per cent tapioca was rotated with other crops. The data for the individual villages, by and large, reveal a similar pattern. Taking the data overall for the four villages, we note that in the two lowest size groups as well as in the highest size group all area under tapioca grown as pure crop is grown annually without following any crop rotation. It is only the mid-size groups with more than 1 acre upto 10 acres who seem to practice some form of crop rotation. In Kuzhakad all size groups who grew tapioca as a pure crop cultivated it without following any crop rotation. In the other three villages it is only holdings between 1 to 10 acres who practise crop rotation. Wherever crop rotation is practised tapioca is rotated with paddy or other crops like banana, tuber crops like yam, sweets potato etc.

To sum up: Land is an important input in the production process and for this reason the pattern and intensity of its use has evinced keen interest among economists. The traditional method to gauge the intensity of land use is to take the ratio of the gross cropped area to net area sown, frequently referred to as cropping intensity index. Using such a procedure we found that large farmers reported higher values as compared to small farmers suggesting that large farmers cultivate land more intensively than small farmers. However, in a region like Kerala where annual and perennial crops dominate the cropping pattern coupled with the practice of inter-cropping involving dense cultivation, the traditional cropping intensity index fails to capture fully the intensity of land use in this region. It is only in the broader light of the crop pattern of the region and cropping

TABLE 4.4: **Distribution of Area under Tapioca Grown as Pure Crop with and without Crop Rotation—(in Per Cent to Total Pure Crop Area in Each Size Class)**

| Villages | | Size classes in acres | | | | | | | |
|---|---|---|---|---|---|---|---|---|---|
| | | 0.0 to 0.5 | 0.51 to 1.0 | 1.01 to 2.5 | 2.51 to 5.0 | 5.01 to 10.0 | 10.01 to 15.0 | Above 15 | All |
| Ayilara: | (a) | 100.0 | 100.0 | 77.1 | 40.0 | 93.0 | 100.0 | — | 67.0 |
| | (b) | — | — | 22.9 | 60.0 | 7.0 | — | — | 33.0 |
| Muttara: | (a) | — | 100.0 | 85.3 | 91.7 | 63.8 | — | — | 73.4 |
| | (b) | — | — | 14.7 | 8.3 | 36.2 | — | — | 26.6 |
| Kuzhakad: | (a) | — | 100.0 | 100.0 | 100.0 | 100.0 | 100.0 | 100.0 | 100.0 |
| | (b) | — | — | — | — | — | — | — | — |
| Cherumood: | (a) | — | 100.0 | 100.0 | 100.0 | 33.3 | — | — | 77.4 |
| | (b) | — | — | — | — | 66.7 | — | — | 22.6 |
| All Villages: | (a) | 100.0 | 100.0 | 90.6 | 74.2 | 70.3 | 100.0 | 100.0 | 84.7 |
| | (b) | — | — | 9.4 | 25.8 | 29.7 | — | — | 15.3 |

*Note*: (a) Area under Tapioca grown annually as pure crop without any crop rotation.
(b) Area under Tapioca grown annually as pure crop with crop rotation.

systems followed that one can gain an adequate perspective of the intensity of land use in Kerala. On the basis of our data, there were sufficient grounds for us to infer that small farmers cultivated land more intensively than large farmers as reflected intheir resort to dense cultivation through inter-cropping as well as following continuous sequence of cultivating crops. Whether this results in higher yields and profits among small farmers has to be examined, which we attempt in our subsequent discussions.

With respect to the cropping pattern of the different strata of farms there are a number of interesting points to note. First, crop diversification is a prominent feature of the cropping pattern of all size groups of farmers suggesting perhaps that it is an adjustment mechanism resorted to by farmers to ward off risks associated with specialisation in a single crop. Second, not only food but also non-food crops are cultivated by the farmers reflecting the diverse requirements of the farm households for food as well as cash. Third, while food crops obviously dominate the cropping pattern in all size groups of farms, an important difference is that among small farms with less than one acre a low value crop like tapioca accounts for the dominant share; among the upper strata of farms a high value crop like paddy figures prominently. Fourth, institutional factors like the nature of access to different types of lands as also the ownership status over lands influences crop choice. Paddy was not cultivated by small farmers owing to lack of access to wet lands. With respect to leased-in lands annual crops like tapioca (in the case of dry lands) and paddy (for wet lands) was preferred; perennial crops were not favoured since they involved long term investment and the risk of being uprooted from their leased-in land acted as a disincentive to cultivating perennial crops in such lands. Thus several factors combine to determine the cropping pattern.

## REFERENCES

1. RK Sampath and C Gopinath: Land Distribution in India—Its Nature and Economic Implications, *Margin*, Vol. II, No. 3, April 1979, NCAER, New Delhi, pp. 43-70.
2. J Bhagwati and S Chakravarty: Contributions to Indian Economic

Analysis: A Survey; *The American Economic Review*, September, 1969.

3. K Bharadwaj: *Production Conditions in Indian Agriculture—A Study Based on Farm Management Surveys*, Occasional paper 33, Department of Applied Economics, University of Cambridge, Cambridge University Press, 1974, p. 16.
4. Sampath and Gopinath, op. cit.
5. A K Sen: Peasants and Dualism with or without Labour, *Journal of Political Economy*, October 1966.
6. C H Hanumantha Rao: Alternative Explanations of the Inverse Relationship between Farm Size and Output Per Acre in India. *The Indian Economic Review*, October 1966 (new series).
7. G Parthasarthy: Size of Land Holding, Intensity and H igh Value Cropping in West Godavari and Mahabubnagar District of Andhra Pradesh, *Agricultural Situation in India*, XXXIII 3 June 1971, pp. 157-166.
8. P H Prasad: *Limits of Investment Planning*, in Ashok Mitra (ed), Economic Theory and Planning, Oxford University Press, 1975.
9. Ranjit Sau: Land Utilisation: A Note, *Economic and Political Weekly*, Vol. XI, No. 36, September 4, 1976, pp. 1473-76.
10. Only one household in this size group reported a negligible area under paddy. Hence, paddy is virtually absent from the cropping pattern of holdings upto one acre.

# 5

# PRODUCTIVITY DIFFERENTIALS AND EXPLANATORY FACTORS

AN IMPORTANT factor influencing the farmer in his area allocation decisions is the productivity of the crops he intends to grow. A knowledge of the yield per unit area would be of immense help to the farmer in evaluating how far remunerative or economical it is to produce a crop; at the same time it provides a convenient measure to identify regions or groups of farmers enjoying a yield advantage with respect to a particular crop or group of crops. There has, in fact, been considerable interest in India and elsewhere on the relationship between size of holdings and productivity. Despite the tremendous research input that has gone into analysing the size-productivity relationship, the debate has remained inconclusive. The broad findings of the various studies in India[1] may be summarised as follows: Firstly, it was observed that the inverse relationship between size of holdings and productivity appeared to hold in the case of FMS data of the fifties and early sixties; but after the advent of the Green Revolution the relationship had got weakened and in some cases reversed. Secondly, the inverse relationship was found to hold true in most regions when value of all crops was aggregated but no systematic, significant or uniform relationship was noticed across individual crops. Our prime concern here is to know as to how yield of tapioca varies across different strata of farms and regions and to identify the factors behind the same. To gain an overall perspective of the behaviour of different groups of farmers we have compared the yield variation of tapioca with paddy and total crops.

## ESTIMATION OF TAPIOCA YIELD

The estimation of tapioca yield has presented problems to researchers in farm surveys particularly on account of the practice of piece-meal harvesting of the crop produce. One of the devices used to arrive at the total output is to estimate the average yield per plant and multiply it with the number of plants cultivated (using some standard norm to arrive at the plant population density per unit area) to arrive at the total yield. However, our field experience revealed that on account of the undulating terrain as also the fact that farmers do not necessarily adhere to any uniform spacing pattern, the plant population density may vary from the standard laboratory ones. To take care of this problem, in addition to the above mentioned procedure to arrive at the tapioca output, we also elicited prior information about the disposal particulars of the farm-produced tapioca. This methodology involves a double check and seems to provide a more reliable estimate of the realised tapioca output.

## YIELD VARIATIONS OVER REGIONS AND FARMS

To start with, we may examine and see whether there are spatial and holding-wise contrasts in the production performance of the farmers with respect to tapioca. For this purpose we may categorise the farm households adopting a two-way classification. On one axis we give class intervals with yield rates as the relevant variable. On the other we give a region-wise and then a holding-wise picture. As seen from Table 5.1 about 60 per cent of the households report tapioca yields ranging from 2 to 5 tonnes per acre. About 23 per cent of the households have yield rates less than 2 tonnes/acre while at the other extreme about 17 per cent households have yield rates ranging from 5 to 10 tonnes/acre and even more. The production performance of the farmers does appear to have certain salient regional contrasts. As obvious from Table 5.1 almost 43 per cent of the farmers in the lowlands fall in class intervals with yield rates upto 2 tonnes/acre. On the other hand, only 11 per cent of the farmers in the midlands report yield rates upto 2 tonnes per acre with a majority of them reporting yield rates ranging from 2 to over 10 tonnes/acre. The highlands fall somewhere inbetween with about 26 per cent of the farmers reporting yields not exceeding 2 tonnes/acre; the rest have yields ranging from 2 to 10 tonnes/acre. If the above analysis is true it seems to suggest that from the viewpoint of productivity tapioca is most suitable to grow in the midlands and relatively the least in the lowlands with the highlands falling somewhere in between the other two regions.

TABLE 5.1: **Classification of Farm Households according to Production Performance of Tapioca—by Regions**

| Tapioca Yield rate classes (kgs/acre) | Highlands % | Midlands % | Lowlands % | Total % |
|---|---|---|---|---|
| 0– 1000 | 5.7 | — | 8.6 | 3.6 |
| 1001— 2000 | 20.0 | 11.4 | 34.3 | 19.3 |
| 2001— 3000 | 20.0 | 22.9 | 20.0 | 21.4 |
| 3001— 4000 | 22.9 | 22.9 | 17.1 | 21.4 |
| 4001— 5000 | 17.1 | 20.0 | 11.4 | 17.1 |
| 5001— 10000 | 14.3 | 20.0 | — | 15.7 |
| Above 10000 | — | 2.9 | — | 1.4 |
| Total | 100.0 | 100.0 | 100.0 | 100.0 |

Table 5.2 presents a similar distribution table with respect to size of holdings. There does seem to be some pattern between yield attainments and size of holdings. A substantial proportion of the households with holdings upto one acre are seen to cluster around size classes with low yield rates. As we move on to higher size classes of holdings the proportion of households with low tapioca yield rates declines perceptibly with most of them

TABLE 5.2: Classification of Farm Households according to Production Performance of Tapioca: By Farm Size Groups

| Tapioca yield rate classes kgs/acre | Size of holdings in acres | | | | | | |
|---|---|---|---|---|---|---|---|
| | 0.0 to 0.5 | 0.51 to 1.0 | 1.01 to 2.5 | 2.51 to 5.0 | 5.01 to 10.0 | 10.01 to 15.0 | Above 15 |
| | *(in percentages)* | | | | | | |
| 0—1000 | 5.0 | 11.5 | — | — | 4.8 | — | — |
| 1001—2000 | 45.0 | 30.8 | 21.1 | 3.6 | 4.8 | — | — |
| 2001—3000 | 15.0 | 11.5 | 29.0 | 28.6 | 19.1 | 25.0 | — |
| 3001—4000 | 25.0 | 15.4 | 21.1 | 32.1 | 14.3 | 25.0 | — |
| 4001—5000 | 5.0 | 11.5 | 21.1 | 25.0 | 23.8 | — | — |
| 5001—10000 | 5.0 | 19.2 | 7.9 | 10.7 | 33.3 | 50.0 | 33.3 |
| Above 10000 | — | — | — | — | — | — | 66.7 |
| Total | 100.0 | 100.0 | 100.0 | 100.0 | 100.0 | 100.0 | 100.0 |

figuring in high yield rate size classes. Thus our results do seem to suggest a clear pattern between tapioca productivity and size of holdings. But the fact that we do find a handful of households in the lower size classes with high tapioca yield rates and conversely some households with large holdings reporting low yield rates may be taken as an indication that size of holdings may not necessarily be the overriding constraint on productivity.

In the context of the size-productivity debate it will be interesting to find out how per acre yield of tapioca varies in relation to size of holding. Table 5.3 presents the productivity of tapioca across size classes of farms for the villages separately and all four villages as a whole. The need to present separate village-wise figures arises in the context of the references to area aggregation bias giving rise to the inverse relation or in other cases nullifying it when present.[2] Overall we note that per acre tapioca productivity increases with an increase in the size of holdings, ranging from 2.6 tonnes per acre in the lowest size class to over 10 tonnes per acre in holdings above 15 acres. When we turn to the village-wise data we do come across fluctuations in this consistent pattern, but in general, high yields are noticed among farmers in the higher size groups. Both midland villages report higher average yields as compared to the highland and lowland villages. Average tapioca yields are relatively the lowest in Cherumood, the lowland village. This seems to lend credence to our argument that tapioca is most productive in the midlands, followed by the highlands and lowlands. The observed variations in tapioca productivity across size classes of farms and regions may be due to factors systematic or random in nature.

To test whether the observed variations in tapioca productivity between regions and farm size groups are significant or not, we conducted a one-way analysis of variance (ANOVA for short) taking into account all 140 sample observations. The computed F value for the Between Regions Yield Variations was 4.73 which was statistically significant at 5 per cent level. The computed F value for the Between Farm Size Group Variations was 5.51 which was statistically significant at 1 per cent level. As an extension of the F test in the ANOVA we used Scheffe test

TABLE 5.3: **Average Productivity of Tapioca (kgs. per acre)**

| Size classes in acres | Villages | | | | All villages |
|---|---|---|---|---|---|
| | Ayilara | Muttara | Kuzhakad | Cherumood | |
| 0.0— 0.5 | 3011 | 3278 | 2069 | 1958 | 2603 |
| 0.51— 1.0 | 3053 | 3514 | 4148 | 3169 | 3369 |
| 1.01— 2.5 | 3722 | 3506 | 3209 | 2403 | 3229 |
| 2.51— 5.0 | 3670 | 3710 | 3569 | 3577 | 3638 |
| 5.01— 10.0 | 3966 | 4918 | 4259 | 3287 | 4469 |
| 10.01— 15.0 | 6167 | — | 5331 | — | 5589 |
| Above 15 | — | — | 10984 | — | 10984 |
| All | 3901 | 4288 | 7089 | 3020 | 5086 |

measures to identify the regions/farm size groups which were contributing to these significant differences. Our choice of the Scheffe test measures stems from the fact that it is considered as a rigorous test and also easy to compute.[3] The test involves testing the means of all possible combinations of regions/farm size groups with thc help of F ratio. The results presented in Table 5.4 indicate that the differences in tapioca productivity between the midlands and lowlands are statistically significant at 5 per cent level, but not so in the case of other combinations. In the case of farm size groups the test indicated that among all possible combinations, differences in tapioca productivity were significant between the three lowest size classes (i.e., holdings 2.5 acres and below) on the one hand and the highest size-class (i.e., holdings above 5 acres) on the other.

Though region effect and farm-size effect on yields are significant as per our above analysis, a limitation of a one-way ANOVA is that it takes note of the effect of only one variable on yields, at a time. One may be interested in knowing whether, given farm size effect, region effect on yield is significant or not. Similarly, given region effect, is farm size effect on tapioca yields significant or not. To find this out we conducted a two-way ANOVA taking region as the block effect and farm size as the treatment effect and alternatively farm size as block effect and region as treatment effect. The model adopted for the analysis is as follows:[4]

$$Y_{ijk}=u+T_i+B_j+e_{ijk}$$

$$k = 0, 1, 2, \ldots\ldots n_{ij}$$

$$j = 1, 2. \ldots\ldots\ldots b$$

$$i = 1, 2, \ldots\ldots\ldots t$$

*where* : $u$ : General mean common to all observations

$T_i$ : Effect of the i-th class treatment

$B_j$ : Effect of the j-th class block

$e_{ijk}$ : random error associated with $Y_{ijk}$ with the conventional distribution properties.

TABLE 5.4 : **Results of Scheffe Test Measures**

*Between Regions:*

| | Mean Yields | | |
|---|---|---|---|
| Highlands | Midlands | | Lowlands |
| (1) | (2) | | (3) |
| 3698.57 | 4194.06 | | 2881.03 |
| 2 Versus 1 | | F Value: | 1.3456$^{ns}$ |
| 3 Versus 1 | | F Value: | 2.7474$^{ns}$ |
| 3 Versus 2 | | F Value: | 9.4491** |

*Between Farm Size Groups:*

| | | Mean Yields | | |
|---|---|---|---|---|
| 0—0.5 acres | 0.51—1 | 1.01—2.5 | 2.51—5 | Above 5 acres |
| (1) | (2) | (3) | (4) | (5) |
| 2833.93 | 3202.71 | 3437.83 | 3843.86 | 5201.98 |
| 2 Versus 1 | | | F Value: | 0.3872$^{ns}$ |
| 3 Versus 1 | | | F Value: | 1.2036$^{ns}$ |
| 3 Versus 2 | | | F Value: | 0.2149$^{ns}$ |
| 4 Versus 1 | | | F Value: | 2.9970$^{ns}$ |
| 4 Versus 2 | | | F Value: | 1.3958$^{ns}$ |
| 4 Versus 3 | | | F Value: | 0.6694$^{ns}$ |
| 5 Versus 1 | | | F Value: | 16.4773* |
| 5 Versus 2 | | | F Value: | 13.5719** |
| 5 Versus 3 | | | F Value: | 12.6365** |
| 5 Versus 4 | | | F Value: | 6.5037$^{ns}$ |

*Note*: *, **=Significant at 1 per cent and 5 per cent level respectively.
ns=not significant

The model assumes no interaction effect. Since there are unequal observations in the cells we have to follow a different procedure from the general two-way ANOVA. The use of the OLS procedure to derive estimates calls for a constant variance if the estimates are to be efficient. On account of unequal observations in cells the constancy of the variance is affected and, though the estimates using OLS may be unbiased they may not be efficient. Moreover, with unequal observations in cells the normal equations are not easily solvable. The above model specifies a procedure to overcome this problem. It consists in inverting the matrix and deriving a set of reduced normal equations which is solvable. It may suffice to mention here that the treatment sum of squares obtained here is adjusted for block effect, i.e., it eliminates block effect by giving the variation solely due to treatment effect. In our case the sum of squares on account of farm size effect is adjusted for region effect. Also the F-ratio computed here pertains to the treatment sum of squares only. It is quite clear that farm-size effect on tapioca yield is significant even when we eliminate region effect (See Table 5.5). This seems to suggest that there are systematic factors that explain the variations in tapioca productivity between farm-size groups.

**TABLE 5.5: ANOVA: Farm Size Effect (adjusted) on Tapioca Yield**

| Source of variation | Sum of squares | Degrees of freedom | Mean sum of squares | F-value |
|---|---|---|---|---|
| Between regions i.e., B (un-adjusted) | 40315141.15 | 2 | 20157570.58 | |
| Due to farm size, i.e., T (adjusted) | 65791720.68 | 4 | 16447930.17 | 4.23* |
| Error | 517452939.14 | 133 | 3890623.61 | |
| Total | 623559800.97 | 139 | 4486041.74 | |

*Note*: *Significant at 1 per cent level.

The above ANOVA model is repeated by interchanging our variables this time treating farm-size as the block effect and region as the treatment variable. This will enable us to know whether region effect on yield adjusting for farm-size effect turns out to be significant or not. Table 5.6 presents the results of our exercise. The treatment sum of squares eliminating block effect is not significant. In other words, region effect on yield, eliminating farm-size effect, does not turn out to be statistically significant. This would suggest that regional variations in tapioca productivity actually reflect variations on account of the structure of holdings in a given region more than variations on account of region effects *per se*. It follows that if, as in our case, high yields (either with respect to individual crops or total crops) are an attribute of large farms, regions where large farms dominate would show up as high productivity regions (with respect to individual crops or total crops as the case may be) as compared to other regions; the same logic would hold ture in the case of small farm dominant regions if high yields are an attribute of small farms. In fact as our Scheffe test measures in Table 5.4 indicated the difference in average yield of tapioca was significant only between midlands and lowlands. This can partly be attributed to the fact that we find more large-sized holdings in the midland villages (ranging from 5 to 30 acres) than in the lowland village.

TABLE 5.6: **ANOVA: Region Effect (adjusted) on Tapioca Yield**

| Source of variation | Sum of squares | Degrees of freedom | Mean sum of squares | F-value |
|---|---|---|---|---|
| Betwen farm size groups, i.e., B (unadjusted) | 87543475.56 | 4 | 21885868.89 | |
| Due to regions, i.e., T (adjusted) | 18561969.38 | 2 | 9280984.69 | 2.39$^{ns}$ |
| Error | 517454356.03 | 133 | 3890634.26 | |
| Total | 623559800.97 | 139 | 4486041.74 | |

*Note*: ns=not significant.

Incidentally while trying to attribute tapioca yield differentials to factors related to size of holdings one may have to distinguish between two kinds of scale effects—one related to the economy of the entire holding, its resources and hence the size of holding; the other to the actual area under the crop. The area under a particular crop does not always vary positively with the size of holdings. To see whether this was true with respect to tapioca we examined the correlation between area under tapioca and size of holdings in our sample taking into account all 140 observations. The correlation was found to be 0.85 and was statistically significant at 1 per cent level. Our results with respect to size of holdings could thus be generally held to be true with respect to size of cropped area under tapioca as well. In fact a regression exercise by us, regressing per acre yield of tapioca on size of holdings and then on size of cropped area under tapioca yielded the following results:

(1) $Y = 2954.97^* + 241.88^* X_1 \quad R^2 = 0.23 \quad N = 140$

(2) $Y = 2970.19^* + 612.60^* X_2 \quad R^2 = 0.23 \quad N = 140$

Where $Y$ = Yield of tapioca in kgs. per acre.

$X_1$ = Operated area in acres.

$X_2$ = Area under tapioca in acres.

*Significant at 1 per cent level.

In both cases we find a positive association between the two variables. The scale effect due to size of holdings may, however, be more important since it determines one's access to resources and markets. Scale effect due to size of area under a particular crop may be important in the case of plantation crops, especially if the heavy dose of overheads required for cultivating such crops cannot be spread over the holding as a whole.

## FACTORS INFLUENCING YIELD VARIATIONS

Quite a number of explanations could be put forward to explain the observed differences in tapioca productivity between different size-classes of farmers. Fristly, it may be attributed to the differences in levels of inputs used in tapioca cultivation. Secondly, it could arise due to qualitative differences in the input-mix as reflected through increasing use of non-traditional inputs like new seeds, chemical fertilisers, etc. Thirdly, interlinked to both the above factors due to differences in the techniques and production practices. Table 5.7 presents the relevant data with regard to the non-land inputs used in tapioca cultivation. It is obvious that both quantitative and qualitative differences in inputs used in tapioca cultivation explain why large farmers generally report higher tapioca yields as compared to those belonging to the lower size classes. The quantum of manure and chemical fertilisers applied per acre show a clear upward trend as we move towards the higher size classes, particularly in holdings above 5 acres, though in the case of manures it initially declines with increasing farm size upto 2.5 acres. The quantum of manure and fertiliser applied per acre are relatively the highest in holdings above 15 acres. Results of regressions presented in Table 5.7 show that per acre input of manure and fertilisers varies positively and significantly with holding size. These differences may arise from the fact that access to resources and markets are non-neutral to scale and hence influences the range and intensity with which inputs are applied. Economic constraints that inhabit small farmers from diversifying and pursuing activities complementary to crop farming like animal husbandry on the one hand and the fact that they have limited access to markets and services on the other have resulted in their applying lower doses of manure and fertilisers. A major chunk of the manure used by them consists of ash, tree refuse and limited quantities of dung. This is not the case with large farmers who are better placed in respect of resource endowments and access to markets enabling them to apply relatively higher doses of manure and fertilisers. Labour input per acre appears to remain constant—around 40 mandays per acre—irrespective of changes in the size of holdings with the exception of holdings above 15 acres, where it shows a steep rise. This phenomenon of labour input per acre remaining constant over certain size ranges is, however, not new and has been observed in the FMS data of certain states for some particular years.[5] Regressing labour input per acre on size of holdings we note that even though the coefficient is positive and significant, the explanatory power of the equation is very small.

**TABLE 5.7: Particulars of Inputs Used in Tapioca Cultivation**

| Size classes in acres | Labour mandays per acre | Manure | | Fertiliser | | Proportion of tapioca area under | |
|---|---|---|---|---|---|---|---|
| | | Per cent of households applying | Quantity applied—kgs per acre | Per cent of households applying | Quantity applied—kgs per acre | Improved varieties | HYV |
| 0.0 — 0.5 | 43 | 100 | 1589 | 10 | 12 | 16 | — |
| 0.51 — 1.0 | 42 | 92 | 1441 | 12 | 19 | 21 | — |
| 1.01 — 2.5 | 39 | 97 | 1369 | 32 | 25 | 15 | 0.03 |
| 2.51 — 5.0 | 43 | 96 | 1649 | 54 | 47 | 21 | — |
| 5.01 — 10.0 | 41 | 95 | 1971 | 86 | 103 | 24 | — |
| 10.01 — 15.0 | 48 | 100 | 2639 | 75 | 86 | 32 | — |
| Above 15 | 72 | 100 | 11058 | 100 | 221 | 41 | 12 |
| All | 47 | 96 | 3301 | 40 | 87 | 25 | 2 |

Regression Results: (1) $Y_1 = 42.3986^* + 0.0060^{**} X$ $R^2 = 0.034$ $N = 140$
(2) $Y_2 = 1213.2936^* + 2.1925^* X$ $R^2 = 0.19$ $N = 140$
(3) $Y_3 = 14.7300^* + 0.0889^* X$ $R^2 = 0.31$ $N = 140$

Where: $Y_1$ = Labour input in mandays/acre; $Y_2$ = Manure in kgs/acre;
$Y_3$ = Fertiliser in kgs/acre; X = Size of holding in cents (1 acre = 100 cents).
*, = **Significant at 1 per cent and 5 per cent level respectively.

The table also throws light on the role played by non-traditional inputs like chemical fertilisers and new seeds. As already stated fertilisers applied per acre increase with an increase in the size of holdings ranging from 12 kgs per acre in holdings below 0.5 acres to 221 kgs per acre in holdings above 15 acres. The most commonly applied fertiliser are tapioca mixtures and bone meal with limited quantities of potash. Not only the quantity but also the proportion of households applying fertilisers is very low among farmers belonging to the lower size groups. Only a tenth of the households with holdings upto one acre apply fertilisers. As against this it is observed that most of the households with holdings above 5 acres apply fertilisers. This clearly suggests that fertilisers have made an important contribution to large farmers in realising higher tapioca yields. In fact as seen from our regressions the explanatory power of the fertiliser equation is relatively higher than the manure and labour equations. The use of improved/HYVs of tapioca may also have contributed to higher tapioca yields among large farmers. Only 2 per cent of area under tapioca was under HYVs of tapioca and this too was accounted by the highest size-class. Lack of consumer acceptability of new varieties,[6] non-availability of HYV stems, as also low priority to popularise them may explain why HYV of tapioca have not made much headway as noticed in other crops, notably paddy. However, improved varieties of tapioca are being grown in significant proportion. On an average not less than 25 per cent of area under tapioca is cultivated with improved varieties particularly M-4 and H-105. The proportion of area under improved varieties of tapioca are found to be relatively higher in holdings above 5 acres. All this goes to suggest that quantitative as well as qualitative differences in inputs applied in tapioca cultivation explain the observed direct relationship between size of holdings and tapioca productivity.

A word about the role of weather may not be out of place since it is weather which sets the pace of agricultural operations. The entire tapioca crop in our sample, with stray exceptions, was grown as a rainfed crop. Though weather variables like quantum of rainfall may indicate at an aggregate level the influence of weather on yield, it cannot shed any light on its influence across holdings. More than the quantum of rainfall either over the year or at critical points in the growth span of a crop, a knowledge about the moisture regimes that exist at different points of the surface (varying according to gradient of slope/surface, porosity and type of soil, etc.) will be useful in understanding weather effect across holdings. It is necessary to state that weather effect on holdings may be due to systematic and not necessarily random factors as is often believed.[7] We, however, donot have such detailed particulars pertaining to individual holdings. But it was apparent to us from our field observations that better endowed lands (like paddy fields and lands adjoining paddy fields with better moisture holding capacity) was effectively under the control of the upper strata. Thus here too big farmers enjoyed an advantage over the small farmers.

With land turning out to be the overriding constraint in agriculture, interest may be centred on how production could be increased through increases in productivity. We have, therefore, fitted some per acre tapioca production functions. Though land is excluded as an explicit variable in this kind of a production function, it implicitly assumes land to be a fixed input while others are variable. Our choice of per acre production functions was prompted by the fact that an earlier exercise by us to fit Cobb-Douglas and linear production functions brought to fore the serious problem of multi-collinearity. When collinearity between explanatory variables is near perfect, it could affect the efficiency of the estimates. However, if non-land inputs are applied in a constant proportion of land, the problem of multi-collinearity may still be serious in the per acre functions. Though one can conceive of such a situation, in practice we encountered no such problem. In fact in our per acre production functions collinearity between independent variables was low (Table 5.10). The results should, however, be read with caution on account of the severe limitations of production function analysis.[8]

Two functional forms—one linear the other log-linear—using the OLS method were fitted. They are as follows:

**(1) Linear Function**

$$\frac{Y}{X_1}=C+b_1\frac{X_2}{X_1}+b_2\frac{X_3}{X_1}+b_3\frac{X_4}{X_1}+e$$

**(2) Log-linear Function**

$$Log\left(\frac{Y}{X_1}\right)=log\ C+b_1\ log\left(\frac{X_2}{X_1}\right)+b_2\ log\left(\frac{X_3}{X_1}\right)+ b_3\ log\left(\frac{X_4}{X_1}\right)+e$$

where: $Y$ =Tapioca output in kgs.

$X_1$ =Cropped area under tapioca in cents (100 cents=1 acre)

$X_2$ =Labour in mandays

$X_3$ =Manure in kgs.

$X_4$ =Fertilisers in kgs.

$C$ =Constant

$e$ =random error term.

Since the feasible choices and technical options open to different size groups of farmers differ it obviously means that each size group of farmers face a unique production function. We have, therefore, fitted separate production functions to each size class. In the case of the two lowest size classes (i.e., 0-0.5 and 0.51-1 acre) fertiliser was not included as a variable in both functional forms due to lack of adequate number of observations. Further, in the case of the three highest size classes where fertiliser was included as a variable, wherever zero observations were encountered, a nominal value was substituted in the case of the log-linear function since log of zero is undefined. Furthermore, we have not included new seeds as a variable since this data is not as dependable as that on other variables. The regression coefficients in the log-linear function directly gives the elasticities of yield with respect to inputs. The results are presented in Tables 5.8 and 5.9 respectively.

There are a number of interesting features to note. Firstly, it is noted that the labour coefficient turns out to be non-significant in all size classes in the case of both linear and log-linear functions (except in the case of pooled log-linear equation for above 1 acre). This seems to suggest that labour may not be expected to make a significant contribution to tapioca productivity even though the coefficients are positive in most cases. This is certainly not to deny the role of labour in the production process in its totality. What is meant is that labour is already employed so much per acre that a further addition to this input is not likely to make a significant addition to yields per acre. In other words, marginal productivity of labour is low, if not zero, especially among small and medium farms. Its impact was seen to be positive and significant only when all farms above one acre were pooled in the log-linear equations. Secondly, the manure coefficient turns out to be positive and significant in all cases with the exception of the highest size class in the log-linear function. Thus additional units of manure may help in making a significant contribution to increasing tapioca productivity. Thirdly, the fertiliser coefficient turns out to be positive and significant in the case of holdings between 1 to 2.5 acres in the linear function and holdings above 5 acres in the case of the log-linear function. But in other size groups it is not significant. This may be because of non-adherence to recommended practices in the use of fertilisers as also the fact that not all households are using it. However, when all holdings above one acre were pooled the fertiliser coefficient was positive and significant in both linear and log-linear equations. Fertilisers, as stated earlier, seems to be emerging as a significant contributor to enhancing tapioca productivity. The correlation coefficients between our explanatory variables as mentioned earlier, suggests that collinearity between variables is low in the per acre production function (see Table 5.10).[9] The Chow's test was conducted to see whether there was statistical support for our reason in fitting separate production functions to each size-class. The test, however, revealed that the difference between the sum of error sum of squares of the separate regressions and pooled regression was not

TABLE 5.8: **Results of Per Acre Linear Tapioca Production Functions**

| Size classes in acres | N | Constant | Regression Coefficients | | | $R^2$ |
|---|---|---|---|---|---|---|
| | | | Labour | Manure | Fertiliser | |
| 0.0 —0.5 | 20 | 1496.02ns | —6.2727ns | 0.9212** | — | 0.19 |
| 0.51—1.0 | 26 | 1159.80ns | 17.9754ns | 0.8639* | — | 0.23 |
| 1.01—2.5 | 38 | 1749.75** | —7.7278ns | 1.1599* | 9.5859** | 0.52 |
| 2.51—5.0 | 28 | 2883.08* | 1.8573ns | 0.4804* | —1.5163ns | 0.58 |
| Above 5 | 28 | 1500.40ns | 28.8391ns | 0.4560* | 8.8811ns | 0.59 |
| *Pooled Regressions*: | | | | | | |
| Below 1 acre | 46 | 1465.69*** | 5.9741ns | 0.8216* | — | 0.24 |
| Above 1 acre | 94 | 2330.44* | 2.8721ns | 0.5681* | 7.3543* | 0.59 |

*Note*: *, **, ***=Significant at 1 per cent, 5 per cent and 10 per cent level respectively.
ns=not significant.

TABLE 5.9: **Results of Per Acre Log-Linear Tapioca Production Functions**

| Size Classes in acres | N | Constant | Regression Coefficients | | | $R^2$ |
|---|---|---|---|---|---|---|
| | | | Labour | Manure | Fertiliser | |
| 0.0 —0.5 | 20 | 4.7940* | —0.3622ns | 0.6048* | — | 0.42 |
| 0.51—1.0 | 26 | 6.0719* | 0.2145ns | 0.1548* | — | 0.18 |
| 1.01—2.5 | 38 | 6.0042* | 0.2756ns | 0.1419* | 0.0283ns | 0.14 |
| 2.51—5.0 | 28 | 6.2839* | 0.3439ns | 0.0880*** | —0.0035ns | 0.09 |
| Above 5 | 28 | 5.4327* | 0.4900ns | 0.0708ns | 0.1506* | 0.43 |
| *Pooled Regressions*: | | | | | | |
| Below 1 acre | 46 | 5.9648* | 0.1899ns | 0.1692* | — | 0.18 |
| Above 1 acre | 94 | 5.9646* | 0.3687** | 0.0999* | 0.0601* | 0.29 |

*Note*: *, **, ***=Significant at 1 per cent, 5 per cent and 10 per cent level respectively.
ns=not significant.

statistically significant at 1 per cent or 5 per cent level of significance in both linear and log-linear equations. Though the Chow's test here does not support us, there is a strong theoretical justification for fitting separate production functions to each size class.

TABLE 5.10: **Correlation between Independent Variables in Per Acre Production Functions (Original Observations)**

| Size classes in acres | Labour and manure | Labour and fertiliser | Manure and fertiliser | Multiple R |
|---|---|---|---|---|
| 0.0 —0.5 | 0.5460* | — | — | 0.56 |
| 0.51–1.0 | 0.0128ns | — | — | 0.57 |
| 1.01—2.5 | —0.1453ns | 0.2173ns | 0.1321ns | 0.76 |
| 2.51—5.0 | 0.2765ns | 0.1694ns | 0.3452*** | 0.80 |
| Above 5 | 0.4484** | 0.3452*** | 0.1360ns | 0.81 |
| *Pooled Regression*: | | | | |
| Below 1 acre | 0.2800*** | — | — | 0.53 |
| Above 1 acre | 0.4730* | 0.3936* | 0.4286* | 0.78 |

*Note*: *, **, ***=significant at 1 per cent, 5 per cent and 10 per cent level respectively.
ns=not significant.

Our discussion so far has only taken note of the influence of varying input levels and input-mix on the yield rates of tapioca across different strata of farms. There are, however, other factors too that influence yield rates like the crop production practices. We may deal with this issue presently.

The first issue worth looking into is as to how the different cropping systems in tapioca cultivation affect tapioca yields. We have already noted that tapioca was being grown annually with or without crop rotation or as a mixed crop with perennial and/or seasonal and annual crops. The popular notion is that frequent cultivation of a soil with a crop observing no crop rotation is unscientific as it depletes the soil of specific nutrients and hence depresses subsequent yields. A substantial proportion of area under tapioca, as noted earlier, is cultivated annually without any crop rotation; the remaining area is grown mostly as a mixed crop and some as pure crop with crop rotation. Table 5.11 indicates the average productivity of tapioca with respect to the three cropping systems cited above. It is interesting to observe that tapioca yields per acre are positively associated with increasing farm size with respect to tapioca area grown as pure crop without observing crop rotation. This suggests that though this method of cultivation is supposed to be exhaustive large farmers on account of their better access to resources and markets are able to replenish the nutrients lost from the soil by applying high doses of manure and fertilisers—a point which has been noted earlier. As regards tapioca area grown as pure crop with crop rotation, it is interesting to observe that average tapioca yields here are relatively higher than yields under the other two cropping systems in the mid-size groups. An obvious question that could be raised here is as to why farmers don't secure higher yields by following crop rotation. Here, however, one has to take note of the small size of holdings and also the rigidities inherent in the cropping pattern of Kerala, dominated as it is by perennial crops, which limits the scope for adjustments in the cropping pattern—at least in the short run.

Though inter-cropping may help increase income and employment it is not clear as to how it affects tapioca yields. Experimental trials in India[10] and Thailand[11] suggest that yields of tapioca when grown as an inter-crop may be less than when it is raised as a pure crop, though total returns from all crops per acre may be more in inter-cropped lands. A look at Table 5.11 reveals no consistent pattern. Though, in general, average tapioca yields are lower than that noted under the other two cropping systems, we do come across a few cases where average tapioca yields are relatively higher. Possibly here one has to take note of the inter-crops too. Cultivation of tapioca in coconut groves—popular in Kerala—may depress tapioca yields on account of the fact that inadequacy of sunlight for proper photosynthesis in tapioca plants (when grown under coconut tress) hinders proper tuber growth resulting in lower yields.[12] The fact that among small farms and in the coastal region, tapioca is mostly grown as an inter-crop with coconut trees may possibly account for the relatively low tapioca yields among these farms and this region in particular.

**TABLE 5.11: Average Tapioca Productivity under Different Cropping Systems**

(*Kgs. per acre*)

| Size classes in acres | Tapioca area grown as pure crop: Without crop rotation | Tapioca area grown as pure crop: With crop rotation | Mixed crop |
|---|---|---|---|
| 0.0— 0.5 | 1500 | — | 2748 |
| 0.51— 1.0 | 3260 | — | 3476 |
| 1.01— 2.5 | 3528 | 3613 | 2682 |
| 2.51— 5.0 | 3752 | 4121 | 3533 |
| 5.01—10.0 | 4296 | 6106 | 3482 |
| 10.01–15.0 | 5331 | — | 6167 |
| Above 15 | 10984 | — | – |
| All | 6025 | 5196 | 3475 |

*Note*: For calculating productivity of tapioca in inter-cropped lands we have taken into account net area sown under tapioca, which was arrived at by taking into account the stems planted per unit area. To ward off possible bias in yield estimates here, the yield of some randomly selected plant on such farms was verified.

The decisions of the farmer as to when and how to sow the crop, the care he bestows on the crop by observing some of the minimum agronomic practices like weeding and interculture, the timing and the mode of harvest of the produce, etc., are other factors which many influence yields and hence merits some attention. It is not clear to us as to how season influences yield.

A substantial number of farmers plant the major crop in the months of Khumbam/Meenam, i.e., February to April. In the lowland and highland villages only the Khumbam/Meenam crop is raised. This is not the case in the midland villages, where in addition to the Khumbam/Meenam crop, quite a number of farmer plant tapioca in the other two seasons as well. But their inability to relate separate yield figures for each season inhibits us from telling much about this. It may, however, be stated that about 5 per cent of the sample households do not observe any seasonal pattern, including the two very large farmers who were able to secure very high yields suggesting that season may not be an overriding constraint on yields. However, given other factors, the tapioca planted in Khumbam/Meenam season may give high yields as it can take advantage of both monsoons. The other popular seasons to grow tapioca are Kanni/Thulam, i.e., September to November, and Karkatam, i.e., July to August.

Tapioca stem-cuttings can be planted in a vertical, slanting or horizontal position. An advantage of planting it vertically is that the tubers may grow in all four directions. Though in the slanting method, tubers may not grow in all directions, they may be relatively longer than in the case of other methods. Most of our farmers planted tapioca stem cuttings vertically perhaps due to the advantage of having tubers grow in all four directions. Proper tillage and sufficiently well formed mounds help in proper tuber formation. Though a majority of our farmers planted tapioca stems on mounds, our observations suggest that the large farmers take care in planting stems on big mounds which is not the case with other farmers. With respect to application of nutrients, experimental trials by CTCRI, Trivandrum suggest that combination of farm yard manure and fertilisers gives higher yields. Among our farmers we noted that the proportion of households applying both FYM and NPK varied positively with the size of holdings ranging from 10 per cent in the lowest size class to 100 per cent in holdings above 15 acres. This is understandable in view of the better resource endowments of the upper strata of farmers.

The timing of harvest of tapioca also influences its yield. Undue delay in harvesting a crop which is fully mature may reduce yields. But our study reveals no instance—at least in our reference year—where harvesting was delayed beyond full maturity. One factor which may have contributed to low tapioca yields among small farmers was the fact that they started piece-meal harvesting of the crop before it was fully mature. An unique advantage of tapioca is that it becomes edible from the sixth month after planting, even though it attains full maturity after 7-8 months only. About 45 per cent of households in the lowest size class, 42 per cent in the size class 0.51 to 1 acre and 18 per cent in the size class above 1 to 2.5 acres commence piece-meal harvesting of tapioca from the sixth month onwards owing to the pressing need for subsistence. This may again explain why small farmers are eager to cultivate tapioca. Obviously no crop other than tapioca becomes edible (and hence gets harvested early) even before reaching full maturity. The preoccupation of the small farmers in meeting their subsistence requirements in the context of their low consumption levels and high marginal propensity to consume may have prompted them to commence early harvesting of tapioca. This factor may have inhibited the small farmers from realising the full potential yield of their tapioca crop. To test whether this factor was significant or not, a difference of means test was conducted to the mean tapioca yields of the two groups of farmers—those harvesting tapioca before it attained full maturity and those harvesting after full maturity only—taking into account all observations with holdings upto one acre only. The test revealed no significant difference in the mean tapioca yields of the two groups of farmers (the t statistic being—0.4617) suggesting, in other words, that low tapioca yields among small farmers are primarily due to other reasons, mentioned earlier.

## YIELD VARIATIONS : INTER-CROP COMPARISONS

Though, as noted earlier, yield of tapioca varies positively with farm size, this does not mean that the relationship will hold true in the case of other crops as well. This is evident from Table 5.12 which presents the average productivity of tapioca, paddy and all crops as a whole expressed in value terms for all size groups. Table 5.12 shows that unlike in the case of tapioca where there was a positive association between tapioca yields per acre and increasing farm size, no consistent pattern is observed in the case of paddy, irrespective of whether it is expressed in terms of per net or gross sown area. Here, perhaps, one has to take note of the fact that the scope for further increases in paddy yields seem very limited, with the result that big farmers in spite of their better resource endowments find technology to be a barrier to securing higher paddy yields. In the case of total crops too, there is no consistent pattern. However, small farmers with holdings less than 0.5 acre were able to realise quite high gross returns per acre, though not the highest. The cultivation of high value crops like coconut and more important the higher density of cultivation through inter-cropping partly explain these trends. Moreover, small farmers may be growing tapioca for subsistence and hence perfer to devote greater attention to the cash crops cultivated by them. Tapioca yields could, therefore, be lower among small farms. Though a high proportion of land among small farms is under tapioca, it may be noted that they do not allocate any exclusive zone for its cultivation; rather, as seen earlier, it is cultivated as an inter-crop with coconut trees reflecting the intensity with which land is utilised among small farms. On account of all these factors small farmers are able to bridge the yield gap to some extent, when value of all crops is aggregated.

To sum up: The much talked of inverse relationship between size of holdings and output per acre does not seem to be a universal phenomenon. Our data suggests that whereas in the case of tapioca yield per acre varied positively with farm size no similar or consistent relationship between yield per acre and farm size was observed in the case of paddy and total crops. Small farmers, however, did report quite high yields (though not the highest) when value of output of all crops was aggregated. The unequal access to resources and markets of the different groups of the peasantry which characterises many agrarian societies is an important factor which influences the range and intensity of input use on farms. However, if this were the only factor one is at a loss to explain as to why small farmers are able to bridge, to some extent, the yield gap observed for tapioca (between small and big farmers) when value of output of

TABLE 5.12: **Value of Crop Output of Tapioca, Paddy and All Crops—By Farm Size Groups**

*(Rs. per acre of cropped area)*

| Size classes in acres | Tapioca | Paddy Per GSA | Paddy Per NSA | All Crops Per GSA | All Crops Per NSA |
|---|---|---|---|---|---|
| 0.0— 0.5 | 691 | — | — | 1735 | 1735 |
| 0.51— 1.0 | 918 | 1795* | 3590* | 1344 | 1351 |
| 1.01— 2.5 | 879 | 1235 | 2448 | 1443 | 1568 |
| 2.51— 5.0 | 994 | 1393 | 2646 | 1303 | 1418 |
| 5.01—10.0 | 1188 | 1405 | 2811 | 1564 | 1853 |
| 10.01—15.0 | 1601 | 1319 | 2638 | 1156 | 1430 |
| Above 15 | 3295 | 1721 | 3442 | 2099 | 2473 |
| All | 1433 | 1435 | 2846 | 1524 | 1744 |

*Note*: 1. GSA: Gross Sown Area
NSA: Net Sown Area
2. Tapioca is an annual crop. Hence, net and gross sown area are the same.
3. All crops include value of crop output of tapioca, paddy, coconut, cashew, arecanut, pepper, rubber, fruits and vegetables, etc.

*Results should be read with caution as it is based on a single observation.

all crops is aggregated. Here, perhaps one has to take note of the behavioural attitudes of the farmers too. Small farmers, as suggested earlier, grow tapioca for subsistence and hence pay more attention to the cash crops cultivated by them. Moreover, in the context of their pressing need for subsistence they cultivate land intensively through inter-cropping and hence maximisation of gross returns per acre may be more important for them. Big farmers grow tapioca as a cash crop and hence are willing to invest more resources on its cultivation.

## REFERENCES

1. To cite a few of the important studies: A K Sen: An Aspect of Indian Agriculture, *The Economic Weekly*, Annual Number, February 1962 and Size of Holding and Productivity, *The Economic Weekly*, Annual Number, February 1964; A P Rao: Size of Holdings and Productivity, *Economic and Political Weekly* (EPW), November 1967; N Bhattacharya and G R Saini: Farm Size and Productivity: A Fresh Look, *E P W*, June 24, 1972; C H H Rao: Alternate Explanations for Inverse Relation between Farm Size and Output Per Acre, *Indian Economic Review*, October, 1966; Krishna Bharadwaj, *Production Conditions in Indian Agriculture*, Occasional Paper No. 33, Department of Applied Economics, University of Cambridge, Cambridge University Press, 1974, Chapter 2; Prannoy Roy: Transition in Agriculture: Empirical Indicators and Results (Evidence from Punjab), *Journal of Peasant Studies*, Vol. 8, No. 2, January 1981; Manabandu Chattopadhyay and Ashok Rudra: Size Productivity Revisited, *EPW*, September 25, 1976 and March 12, 1977; G K Chadha: Farm Size and Productivity Revisited, *EPW*, September 30, 1976; Ashok Rudra and Amartya Sen: Farm Size and Labour Use, *EPW*, Annual No. 1976; Surjit S Bhalla: *Farm Size, Productivity and Technical Change in Indian Agriculture*, in Berry and Cline, *Agrarian Structure and Productivity in Developing Countries*, John Hopkins University Press, Baltimore and London, 1979.
2. See Bhattacharya and Saini, 1972, op. cit., p. A. 63, 71-72; Chattopadhyay and Rudra, 1976, op. cit., p. A. 110.
3. N M Downie and R W Health: *Basic Statistical Methods*, Harper and Row, 1970 (III Edition), p. 221.
4. For details see Franklin A Graybill: *An Introduction to Linear Statistical Models*, Vol. I, McGraw-Hill Book Company, 1961, Chapter 13.
5. M Chattopadhyay and Ashok Rudra, March 12, 1977, op. cit., p. 481.
6. Based on views expressed by the sample farmers.
7. In an interesting Paper V M Rao argues that weather effect across holdings could follow a systematic pattern rather than random due to undulating terrain and high rainfall resulting in different moisture regimes across holdings. Interestingly the example quoted by V M Rao was from South Kanara, a region with a terrain almost comparable to that of Kerala and these results seemed to support his hypothesis that weather effect could vary systematically across holdings. See V M Rao: Farm Production Function Studies—Treatment of Weather and Selection of Functional Form, *EPW*, April 11, 1970.
8. *Cf*: Krishna Bharadwaj: op. cit., and also her *Technical Relations in Agriculture* in C H Shah (ed), *Agricultural Development of India—*

*Policies and Problems*, Orient Longman, Bombay, 1979; Ranjit K Sau: Agricultural Revolution by Production Function, *EPW*, June 26, 1971; Ashok Kumar Hati and Ashok Rudra: Calculations of Efficiency Indices of Farmers, *EPW*, March 3, 1973; Jack R Anderson and N S Jodha: On Cobb-Douglas and Related Myths, *EPW*, June 30, 1973; Ashok Rudra: Hypothesis Testing in Relation to Cobb-Douglas Myths, *EPW*, March 30, 1974; Ashok Rudra: *Indian Agricultural Economics—Myths and Realities*, Chapter 12, Production Function, Allied Publishers, New Delhi, 1982, pp. 254-272; N Krishnaji: Cobb-Douglas Production Function: A Sceptical Note, *EPW*, Vol. XVI, October 17-24, 1981.

9. One of the procedures suggested by Lawrence Klein to see whether collinearity is low or high is to measure it in relation to the multiple R. We have followed this norm. Cited in A. Koutsoyiannis: *Theory of Econometrics*, Macmillan, 1977 (second edition), p. 237.
10. See *Studies on Inter-cropping*, CTCRI Annual Report, 1974, p. 23.
11. T J Goering, *Tropical Root Crops and Rural Development*, World Bank Staff Working Paper No. 324, April 1979, pp. 74-75.
12. See *Breeding for Shade Tolerance in Cassava*, CTCRI Annual Report, 1974, p. 13.

# 6

# COST STRUCTURE AND INCOME

EXPENDITURE on and returns from producing a crop will provide a synoptic view of its economy. We shall, therefore, analyse here the cost structure and income from tapioca cultivation in comparison to paddy and crop farming in general. The contribution of tapioca to the household income as also the source-wise distribution of household income are the other issues dealt with here. Before analysing our data we may clarify the cost and income concepts as well as mode of valuation of output adopted for our analysis.

## COST AND INCOME CONCEPTS

Some issues of theoretical importance and relevant to framing our cost and income concepts may be posed first. In discussions relating to resource use and allocation in agriculture diverse opinions have been expressed on two major questions. Firstly, are the problems of the peasant akin to that of the entrepreneur of the firm or are they different? In particular is profit maximisation the sole motivating force behind producer decisions on the farm (as in the firm) or are there other behavioural maxims like maximisation of gross output or surplus over paid out costs, etc., which guide the decision of the peasant? Secondly, is the use of owned inputs on farms determined by market prices or are there other factors which govern its use?

The absence of any unanimity in answering these questions has been one of the prime reasons behind the controversy about the cost and income concepts adopted by the Farm Management Studies (FMS) in india. In particular Cost C concept adopted by the FMS, consisting of value of purchased inputs plus imputed value of owned inputs like family labour and owned land was singled out for harsh criticism. When profits were calculated with reference to Cost C, much of Indian farming was found to be unremunerative. The validity and relevance of this cost concept in understanding decision making in peasant economies like that of India, with a significant non-monetised sector is therefore questioned.[1]

Controversies have raged as to whether it is the imputation of market wage rate to family labour or rental value to owned land which is responsible for losses reported by farms in the FMS.[2] A basic premise underlying the imputation of value to owned inputs like family labour is the opportunity cost to the farmer for using his labour on his farm instead of hiring it out. The market wage rate was, therefore, assumed to reflect the opportunity cost for use of family labour. Apart from such problems in finding the appropriate rates at which to impute value to these owned inputs, one has to answer the larger question of whether there really do exist opportunity costs. In the conditions obtaining in India, with a vast reservoir of rural unemployed, it may be contended that opportunity cost for family labour will tend to zero, if not zero. In which case imputing wage rate to family labour could be questioned. Similar reservations could be made about imputing rental value to owned land and national interest on owned capital too. As far as farm-produced inputs like seeds and manure are concerned, farmers perceive them to be real costs, since they are actually incurred material costs with a real opportunity cost. One may, therefore, justify its inclusion for estimating cultivation costs.

One aspect which has not received due attention in the FMS is regarding the components of household income. Given the limited coverage of the FMS data their focus was confined to aspects covering crop economy and animal husbandry. The importance of information on the other sources of household income in understanding peasant behaviour needs no emphasis. Sau, for instance, suggests that big farmers in India do not cultivate land intensively like small farmers because of the multiple channels of profit making available to them.[3] Majumdar states that the wage incomes received by many households from wage empolyment is crucial for investment decisions on their farms.[4] In the absence of data on the other sources of household income such observations cannot be verified. An analysis of the composition of household income as also an estimate of the household disposable income (a determinant of consumption and savings) is, therefore, essential.

Despite its shortcomings, the FMS concepts provide a suitable framework for analysing the varying composition of inputs across different strata of farms. Moreover, in the presence of diverse elements in the peasant economy like family or hired labour based farms, tenant or owner operated holdings, they facilitate some homogeneity of comparison. Taking all these factors into account the following cost and income concepts are used in the study:

Cost $A_1$ = Actually paid out costs excluding imputed value of family labour, owned animal labour and farm produced inputs, etc. In other words, it includes value of hired human labour (including imputed value of payments in kind and perquisites to hired labour), value of hired bullock labour, value of purchased seeds, manure, fertilisers, insecticides and pesticides plus actual repair and maintenance charges for non-land fixed farm capital (i.e., farm implements and machinery, irrigation installations and farm buildings) plus charges for hired implements plus land revenue and other land taxes and cesses.

Cost $A_2$ = Cost $A_1$ plus actual rent paid for leased in land plus actual interest paid for borrowed loans.

Cost $A_3$ = Cost $A_2$ plus imputed value of farm produced inputs and owned animal labour.

Cost B = Cost $A_3$ plus rental value of owned land (and unowned land not included in Cost $A_2$) plus interest on owned fixed capital.

Cost C = Cost B plus imputed value of family labour.

Though seemingly these cost concepts resemble the FMS concepts, there are some important differences. Cost $A_1$ here includes only actually paid out costs, whereas in the FMS Cost $A_1$ included not only the actually paid out costs but also the imputed value of farm produced inputs, owned animal labour and notional costs like interest on working capital. Depreciation, though seemingly notional, is a real cost incurred over time depending on the life span of capital and hence actual repairs and maintenance charges of non-land fixed farm capital have been included in Cost $A_1$. The interest paid on borrowed loans as also rent for leased in land are included in Cost $A_2$ rather than Cost $A_1$ on the ground that they are paid out from the surplus generated during the process of production.

These cost concepts have their corresponding income concepts. Value of crop output minus the respective costs yield Incomes $A_1$, $A_2$, $A_3$, B and C respectively. Income $A_3$, B and C are Farm Business Income, Farm Family Income and Net Income respectively as in the FMS. The concepts used in the study will help make a clearer distinction between owned and purchased inputs. The significance of the conceptual distinctions adopted here are obvious. For an owner cultivator maximising surplus corresponding to actually paid out costs, Cost $A_1$ will be appropriate while for a tenant operator it is Cost $A_2$. If, however, farm produced inputs are perceived to be real costs, Cost $A_3$ is appropriate for owner and tenant cultivators. If the farmer is like the entrepreneur in the firm he may be concerned about maximising surplus with respect to Cost C. In estimating Farm Household Disposable Income, we have taken into account the income corresponding to Cost $A_2$ plus income from sources other than cultivation netted for all taxes not included earlier in cultivation costs.

In computing the costs incurred in tapioca cultivation we have not included the imputed value of owned seeds. This is because tapioca stems used for propagation have virtually no value in exchange. Markets for tapioca stems, if any, are of a limited nature, confined to a few pockets and to HYV seeds only. Since we have excluded it from cost the imputed value of stems is not included as a source of income either. However, wherever tapioca stems were actually purchased this has been taken note of.

## VALUATION OF OUTPUT

Output is valued in order to arrive at the income of farmers across size-classes. All farmers do not grow the same crops and hence output of different crops expressed in physical quantities cannot be aggregated and compared. To aggregate and make it comparable across size classes, we express it in value terms. This is arrived at by multiplying the given output with the respective prices. The issue is at what price should output be valued. Should it be valued at a uniform price for all farmers or at prices actually received which differ between farmers depending on the time of harvest and sales and other factors like quality of product, etc.

If we were to adopt differential or actually realised prices in valuing output we may encounter some problems. Firstly, there may be farmers who do not market their produce and in such cases prices may not be available. Secondly, even in the case of those farmers who market a portion of their produce, it is questionable whether we should value the produce retained for home consumption (i.e., non-marketed quantity) at the sale price of the marketed quantity. Valuation of output at differential prices may distort the pattern of distribution of produce in real terms across size-classes. This is because the differences in income may be both on account of differences in output and differential price advantages (or disadvantages).

But valuation of output at a uniform price has its own drawbacks, since it cannot indicate the impact of differential prices actually received by farmers when they market their produce. Our sample study showed that quite a few farmers sold their produce at prices which were different (higher or lower) from the prices which they reported to be prevailing at the time of harvest of their crops. These differences in prices received by farmers for the sale of their produce may be on account of relative market advantages (or disadvantages).

In our analysis we wish to examine all those elements which account for income differences. Hence taking all the above factors into consideration we shall value output at a uniform price; but we also take into account the change in income as a result of a farmer selling his produce at differential prices, i.e., the difference between the uniform price adopted for valuation of output and the sale price or actually realised price per individual farmer multiplied by the quantity of sale constitutes the extra income on account of relative market advantages (or disadvantages).

The uniform price is derived by taking the mean of the prices prevailing in the village at the time of harvest as reported by farmers. For calculating the uniform price the farm harvest prices were preferred because farmers who did not sell their produce obviously could not report sale prices; but even such farmers were able to report the farm harvest prices prevailing at the time of harvest of their crops. Furthermore, the prices prevailing at the time of harvest are generally lower than during other periods and generally bulk of sales by farmers take place in this season. These prices can, therefore, be looked upon as a sort of normal price. It is obvious that if sales are effected immediately after harvest both farm harvest price and sale price may coincide, though this may again depend upon the market channel through which the farmer sells his produce. The uniform prices pertain to each individual village separately, since between villages significant differences in prices may exist.

The advantage of our methodology is that by valuing output at two sets of prices, one at uniform price and the other at actual sale price (only marketed quantity), we can separately study the differences in income that occur due to output variations on the one hand and market advantages (or disadvantages) on the other. With these remarks about our concepts and norms we may pass on to the analysis of our data.

## COST OF CULTIVATION

We may now examine the cost structure of tapioca in comparison to paddy and total crops, using the different cost concepts mentioned earlier. For our analysis cost is expressed in per unit of area and per unit of output so as to reflect two dimensions of the cost structure. Cost per unit area can indicate the intensity with which inputs are applied to land and also the working capital-can-credit requirements of different size groups of farmers. On the other hand, cost per unit of output may be useful in making judgements about production efficiency and as a guide in product price fixation. Moreover, it can also enable us to observe if there are any economies of scale in production.

TABLE 6.1: **Cost of Tapioca Cultivation Using Different Cost Concepts—All Villages**

(*Rs. per acre*)

| Size classes in acres | Cost $A_1$ | Cost $A_2$ | Cost $A_3$ | Cost B | Cost C |
|---|---|---|---|---|---|
| 0.0—0.5 | 131<br>(15.2) | 203<br>(23.6) | 345<br>(40.2) | 607<br>(70.6) | 860<br>(100.0) |
| 0.51—1.0 | 198<br>(24.7) | 219<br>(27.3) | 350<br>(43.7) | 628<br>(78.3) | 802<br>(100.0) |
| 1.01—2.5 | 221<br>(30.5) | 238<br>(32.9) | 353<br>(48.7) | 610<br>(84.1) | 725<br>(100.0) |
| 2.51—5.0 | 367<br>(46.7) | 392<br>(49.9) | 500<br>(63.6) | 750<br>(95.4) | 786<br>(100.0) |
| 5.01—10.0 | 450<br>(53.6) | 456<br>(54.2) | 577<br>(68.7) | 834<br>(99.3) | 840<br>(100.0) |
| 10.01—15.0 | 513<br>(61.6) | 514<br>(61.7) | 582<br>(69.9) | 833<br>(100.0) | 833<br>(100.0) |
| Above 15 | 930<br>(52.0) | 934<br>(52.3) | 1547<br>(86.6) | 1786<br>(100.0) | 1786<br>(100.0) |
| All | 450<br>(46.7) | 464<br>(48.1) | 661<br>(68.7) | 915<br>(95.1) | 963<br>(100.0) |

*Note*: Figures in parentheses give percentages to Cost C.

The question which we may discuss first is about the quantitative variations in per acre cost for tapioca cultivation over land holding groups. For this purpose we may look at Table 6.1 which presents the size class-wise distribution of cost of tapioca cultivation in rupees per acre using the different cost concepts for all four villages as a whole. The per acre costs of tapioca cultivation increases consistently with an increase in the size of holdings upto Cost B but thereafter in Cost C, which includes the imputed value of family labour, distortions creep in affecting this consistent tendency. Cost $A_3$ which includes all paid out costs plus the imputed value of farm produced inputs indicates that farmers with holdings not exceeding 2.5 acres incur only about a half of the per acre costs incurred by those with holdings above 2.5 acres upto 15 acres. The per acre costs rise steeply in holdings exceeding 15 acres being almost five times more than the costs incurred by the lowest three size classes of farmers. The range of difference in per acre costs between the lowest and the highest size groups, however, reduces when costs are computed in terms of Cost B and Cost C.

These trends, by and large, suggest that the resource endowments of the farmers play an important role in their investment decisions. Since, as noted earlier, small farmers have limited access to resources and markets (including credit institutions) they are unable to invest more inputs on tapioca. Moreover, as suggested earlier, tapioca is a subsistence crop for them and hence they may prefer to give more attention to cash crops like coconut. Big farmers are, however, more favourably placed with respect to resource endowments and hence are willing to invest more inputs on tapioca, especially if it is a cash crop for them. In deciding how to allocate the given resources between different crops, farmers have to assess the input requirements of the crop vis-a-vis the demand of other competing crops, the rank to be assigned to the crop in their scale of preferences, the prices of inputs vis-a-vis their expected rate of return, etc. A notable feature of tapioca is that it can even be grown with a small amount of resources. This is a factor of special significance to poorly endowed farmers. It is, therefore, not surprising that small farmers, as noted earlier, allocated a high proportion of their land to tapioca cultivation since it could be easily tailored to suit their limited budget.

Another important dimension of cost is the composition of inputs across different strata of farms, particularly the extent of monetisation of inputs as reflected in the ratio of purchased to owned inputs. Monetisation of inputs, it may be noted, signifies dependence on the market for supply of inputs. Moreover, if it involves use of more hired labour and factory-produced inputs like fertilisers it helps foster intra-rural and inter-rural-urban links. Table 6.1 presents the costs corresponding to each concept expressed as per cent of Cost C. The proportion of purchased inputs to total inputs (see under Cost $A_2$) varies from 24 per cent in the lowest size class to between 52 to 62 per cent in holdings over 5 acres. Cost $A_3$ as a proportion of Cost C is about 70 per cent overall for all farmers implying that inclusion of imputed value of owned inputs other than farm-produced material inputs by themselves account for about 30 per cent of Cost C. For the size classes it ranges from 40 per cent in the two lowest size classes to between 60 to 87 per cent among the upper strata of farms. The prominence of owned inputs in the input structure of small holdings as compared to purchased inputs among bigger holdings suggests that imputation of value to owned inputs for deriving costs and profits and thereafter for making inferences about the production efficiency of the different strata of farms has a built-in bias to present a distorted view of the small farmers' economy particularly if the farmers don't perceive such inputs to be real costs. The importance of the conceptual framework adopted for analysing peasant behaviour in these circumstances, therefore, needs to be emphasised.

The above analysis gives only a broad categorisation of inputs in terms of owned and purchased and does not shed light on the relative importance of different factors in the input structure of different farms. A further break-up of the cost components in tapioca cultivation in relation to Cost C for the different land holding groups is presented in Table 6.2. Taking all farmers together we see that labour, capital in the form of seeds, manure and fertilisers, etc., and land (in that order)

TABLE 6.2: **Cost Components in Tapioca Cultivation: All Villages (as per cent to Cost C)**

| Cost components | | Size classes in acres | | | | | | | |
|---|---|---|---|---|---|---|---|---|---|
| | | 0.0 to 0.5 | 0.51 to 1.0 | 1.01 to 2.5 | 2.51 to 5.0 | 5.01 to 10.0 | 10.01 to 15.0 | Above 15 | All |
| *Land*: | Rented | 8.1 | 1.9 | 1.7 | 2.4 | 0.4 | — | — | 1.0 |
| | Owned | 29.9 | 33.0 | 34.1 | 30.5 | 29.2 | 29.8 | 12.6 | 25.2 |
| *Labour*: | Hired | 9.7 | 18.7 | 24.8 | 37.4 | 36.7 | 43.0 | 28.9 | 31.7 |
| | Family | 29.4 | 21.7 | 15.9 | 4.6 | 0.7 | — | — | 4.9 |
| *Material Inputs*— (i.e., seeds, manure, fertilisers, etc. | Purchased | 4.8 | 4.1 | 4.9 | 8.6 | 16.6 | 18.4 | 23.0 | 14.6 |
| | Owned | 16.6 | 16.4 | 15.8 | 13.8 | 14.5 | 8.2 | 34.4 | 20.5 |
| *Interests, Depreciation, etc.* | Actually paid | 1.0 | 2.4 | 1.5 | 1.4 | 0.4 | 0.2 | 0.3 | 0.7 |
| | Imputed | 0.5 | 1.7 | 1.3 | 1.2 | 1.4 | 0.3 | 0.8 | 1.2 |
| *Land Revenue, Taxes, etc.* | | 0.04 | 0.1 | 0.1 | 0.1 | 0.1 | 0.2 | 0.1 | 0.1 |
| Total Purchased Inputs | | 23.6 | 27.3 | 32.9 | 49.9 | 54.2 | 61.7 | 52.3 | 48.1 |
| Total Owned Inputs | | 76.4 | 72.7 | 67.1 | 50.1 | 45.8 | 38.3 | 47.7 | 51.8 |
| Total | | 100.0 | 100.0 | 100.0 | 100.0 | 100.0 | 100.0 | 100.0 | 100.0 |

account for a lion's share of the costs incurred in tapioca cultivation. Wages paid to hired labour by itself accounts for about 31 per cent of total cost. The rental value of owned land as also imputed value of farm produced material inputs come next in importance accounting for over 25 per cent and 20 per cent of Cost C. Capital costs like interest, depreciation and also land revenue and taxes account for only 2 per cent of Cost C.

Labour is, without doubt, an important item of expenditure in all strata of farms. But a striking difference is that among the three lowest size groups this is mostly accounted for by the imputed value of family labour. In holdings of 0.5 acres or less the imputed value of family labour alone accounts for as high as 29 per cent of Cost C. As against this, we find that among big holdings with more than 5 acres very little or no family labour is employed. Labour required for cultivating tapioca among big farms is, therefore, mostly hired and hence wages paid to hired labour represent a significant expenditure among big farms.

Capital inputs like manure and fertilisers are the next significant component of costs in tapioca cultivation. But what is striking is that the share of capital inputs to total costs is relatively higher among the bigger holdings, at times exceeding or equalising labour costs. Particularly in holdings of over 15 acres its share in total costs goes up to the extent of 57 per cent. This, of course, is not a strange phenomenon. Big farmers are known to use not only more of capital inputs but often also substitute capital for labour; among small farms labour is the major input in tapioca cultivation.

Rental value of owned lands accounts for a sizeable component of total costs—about 30 per cent—in all size classes except in the highest size class. Rent paid for leased-in lands is relatively high in the lowest size class. Other expenditures like depreciation, interest, taxes and cesses, etc., as noted earlier, form a minor component of cost in all size classes.

An interesting issue that needs to be discussed in the context of a crop's economy is whether there are any economies of scale which favour any particular group of farmers in the production of tapioca. Cost per unit of output rather than cost per unit area may be more appropriate in answering the question since any expenditure can be justified only in terms of the output or returns. Here again comparisons are made in terms of Cost $A_3$ and Cost C. As seen from Table 6.3, Cost C per unit of tapioca output more or less shows an inverse relationship with size of holdings, ranging from Rs. 0.33 per Kg. of tapioca in the lowest size class to Rs. 0.16 in the highest size class. Does this imply that economies of scale favour large farms in production of tapioca? In the conditions in which tapioca is grown in Kerala there are sufficient grounds for us to infer that tapioca may not be vulnerable to such scale effects at least to the extent one may observe in plantation and seasonal crops.

TABLE 6.3: **Cost of Production of Tapioca in Rupees per Kg. of Output—All Villages**

| Cost | Size Classes in Acres | | | | | | | |
|---|---|---|---|---|---|---|---|---|
| | 0.0 to 0.5 | 0.51 to 1.0 | 1.01 to 2.5 | 2.51 to 5.0 | 5.01 to 10.0 | 10.01 to 15.0 | Above 15 | All |
| Cost $A_3$ | 0.13 | 0.10 | 0.11 | 0.14 | 0.13 | 0.10 | 0.14 | 0.13 |
| Cost C | 0.33 | 0.23 | 0.22 | 0.22 | 0.19 | 0.15 | 0.16 | 0.19 |

Diseconomies among small farms could arise if there is capital intensification involving use of machinery for some operations like land preparation and harvesting. This is because such capital is not perfectly divisible resulting in high overhead costs among small farms. But our study revealed absence of any form of mechanisation in tapioca cultivation among all strata of farms and the only implements used in tapioca cultivation were those of common usage like hoes and spades. Furthermore, the only capital inputs used in tapioca cultivation were divisible inputs like fertilisers. If economies of scale favour large farms in production of tapioca one is at a loss to explain as to why small farmers, as noted earlier, devoted a high proportion of their operated area to cultivating tapioca. Thus, whatever differential advantage large farms enjoy over small farms in producing tapioca implied by Cost C disappear when costs are reckoned in terms of Cost $A_3$. Thus, even small holdings here report as low per unit costs of production as some of the large farms.

Further to the above discussion one may enquire whether economies of scale may favour small farms in producing tapioca. For instance, if scale has a telling effect upon the entrepreneurial factor it could result in diseconomies among large farms. But as far as tapioca is concerned there is great flexibility in the time of its sowing and harvesting which may not tax the farmers to the extent as in other crops. In fact in the highest size class two farmers who had put 12 acres each under tapioca cultivation tried to cope with this scale of operation by spreading over the whole year the sowing and harvesting of tapioca, taking one acre at a time in each month for sowing as well as harvesting. Thus, taking into account all the above factors, we have reason to believe that economies of scale may not favour any particular group of farms in production of tapioca in Kerala, or at least among our sample farms. This is perhaps one more reason why all strata of farms are inclined to cultivate a low value crop like tapioca. In making the above observations we are, no doubt, aware that in some of the tapioca-growing countries like Thailand and Colombia, tapioca is being cultivated on a plantation scale and also with the help of mechanisation. In such cases economies of scale may be operative. Our observations should, therefore, be read in the limited context of our study region.

Across villages it was observed that the per unit costs of production were relatively high in Cherumood—the lowland village—in terms of both cost concepts perhaps suggesting that efficiency of tapioca production is lower here as compared to other villages.

Let us now focus attention on paddy and find out in what respects its cost structure differs from that of tapioca. Table 6.4 presents the data on the cost of paddy cultivation using the various cost concepts for the aggregate villages. There are two striking features which differentiate paddy from tapioca. Firstly, unlike in the case of tapioca we do not find any strong and clear trend between per acre costs and size of holdings for paddy. Among large as well as small farms per acre costs are quite high. Moreoer, in most cases the per acre costs for paddy cultivation are much higher than observed earlier for tapioca. Paddy requires more resources as compared to tapioca and very often indivisible inputs from part of the input mix. Per acre costs could, therefore, be high for paddy among the relatively small farms too due to high overheads required for undertaking paddy cultivation.

TABLE 6.4: **Cost of Paddy Cultivation Using Different Cost Concepts—All Villages**

(*Rs. per acre*)

| Size classes in acres | Cost $A_1$ | Cost $A_2$ | Cost $A_3$ | Cost B | Cost C |
|---|---|---|---|---|---|
| 0.0 —0.5 | — | — | — | — | — |
| 0.51—1.0 | 1213 | 1213 | 1663 | 2114 | 2114 |
| | (57.4) | (57.4) | (78.7) | (100.0) | (100.0) |
| 1.01—2.5 | 735 | 750 | 870 | 1419 | 1567 |
| | (46.9) | (47.9) | (55.5) | (90.5) | (100.0) |
| 2.51—5.0 | 737 | 776 | 1085 | 1514 | 1551 |
| | (47.5) | (50.0) | (70.0) | (97.6) | (100.0) |
| 5.01—10.0 | 695 | 718 | 1026 | 1576 | 1603 |
| | (43.4) | (44.8) | (64.0) | (98.3) | (100.0) |
| 10.01—15.0 | 1064 | 1086 | 1337 | 1809 | 1809 |
| | (58.8) | (60.0) | (73.9) | (100.0) | (100.0) |
| Above 15 | 943 | 943 | 1315 | 1771 | 1771 |
| | (53.2) | (53.3) | (74.3) | (100.0) | (100.0) |
| All | 816 | 836 | 1131 | 1632 | 1660 |
| | (49.1) | (50.4) | (68.1) | (98.3) | (100.0) |

*Note*: Figures in parentheses give percentages to Cost C.

TABLE 6.5: **Cost Components in Paddy Cultivation: All Villages (as per cent to Cost C)**

| Cost components | | Size classes in acres | | | | | | | |
|---|---|---|---|---|---|---|---|---|---|
| | | 0.0 to 0.5 | 0.51 to 1.0 | 1.01 to 2.5 | 2.51 to 5.0 | 5.01 to 10.0 | 10.01 to 15.0 | Above 15 | All |
| *Land* | Rented | — | — | 0.8 | 2.3 | 1.2 | 1.1 | — | 1.1 |
| | Owned | — | 21.3 | 34.7 | 27.3 | 33.3 | 25.9 | 25.4 | 29.6 |
| *Bullock Labour* | Hired | — | 3.3 | 7.1 | 1.1 | 0.5 | — | — | 0.9 |
| | Owned | — | — | 1.3 | 7.1 | 7.3 | 7.4 | 7.6 | 6.9 |
| *Human Labour* | Hired | — | 49.1 | 27.2 | 29.1 | 25.9 | 28.8 | 37.0 | 29.2 |
| | Family | — | — | 9.5 | 2.4 | 1.7 | — | — | 1.7 |
| *Tractor Hire Charges:* | | — | — | — | – | 0.2 | — | — | 0.1 |
| *Material Inputs* (i.e., seeds, manure, | Purchased | — | 5.0 | 12.3 | 16.9 | 16.5 | 29.8 | 16.1 | 18.6 |
| fertilisers, pesticides etc.) | Owned | — | 21.3 | 6.4 | 12.8 | 11.9 | 6.4 | 13.3 | 10.9 |
| *Interest, Depreciation,* | Actually paid | — | 0.03 | 0.6 | 0.5 | 0.5 | 0.2 | 0.3 | 0.5 |
| *etc.* | Imputed | — | 0.02 | 0.3 | 0.4 | 1.0 | 0.3 | 0.3 | 0.5 |
| *Land Revenue, Taxes, etc.* | | — | 0.001 | 0.02 | 0.04 | 0.1 | 0.1 | 0.04 | 0.1 |

| | | | | | | | | |
|---|---|---|---|---|---|---|---|---|
| Total Purchased Inputs | — | 57.4 | 47.9 | 50.0 | 44.8 | 60.0 | 53.3 | 50.4 |
| Total Owned Inputs | — | 42.6 | 52.1 | 50.0 | 55.2 | 40.0 | 46.7 | 49.6 |
| Total | — | 100.0 | 100.0 | 100.0 | 100.0 | 100.0 | 100.0 | 100.0 |

Secondly, the degree of monetisation of inputs in paddy cultivation (see Table 6.4 below Cost $A_2$ and Table 6.5) is relatively higher than observed for tapioca in all size classes. Cost $A_2$ which includes the value of all purchased inputs accounts for between 44 to 60 per cent of total inputs used in paddy cultivation in all size classes. This, of course, is not unexpected. Paddy cultivation, as is well known, witnessed a major transformation in the mid-sixties and seventies under the impact of new technology. As a result it led to a growth in demand for hired labour and factory-produced inputs like fertilisers and pesticides. Tapioca, on the other hand, did not witness any change on a similar scale. Though fertilisers were used in tapioca cultivation, the quantity used in paddy was higher, partly due to additional demand for the second crop.[5] Furthermore, in tapioca use of pesticides was not reported by any farm. Another reason is that owing to the absence of any critical period for sowing and harvesting tapioca, there is scope to cut down on use of hired labour. Such a situation may not exist for paddy. In these circumstances, there could be a higher degree of monetisation of inputs in paddy as compared to tapioca. It may, however, be noted that among large farms, there is a sizeable proportion of monetised inputs both for tapioca and paddy.

Land, labour and capital account for a major proportion of the total expenditure incurred for paddy cultivation (see Table 6.5). Bullock labour is an important input used in paddy cultivation but not for tapioca. Being an indivisible input small holdings have to bear high overheads on this account. The lower strata of farms (i.e., below 2.5 acres) cannot afford to maintain draught animals, as indicated earlier, and hence mostly hire bullock labour (even though hire charges are high) for ploughing operations in paddy. On the other hand holdings above 2.5 acres rely on owned bullock labour.

It is interesting to note that the imputed value of family lobour does not figure as an item of cost as much as it does in tepioca cultivation, even in farms belonging to the lower size classes. Since the reasons for relatively lower use of family labour in paddy cultivation as against tapioca is discussed in the next chapter, we shall not raise it here. It may suffice to mention here that in view of this factor wages for hired labour is a significant item of expenditure in paddy cultivation among all strata of farms. Material inputs in the form of seeds, manure, fertilisers and pesticides are also a significant cost component in paddy cultivation. Tractor use in paddy is negligible and, therefore, turns out to be a minor cost. So also the interest, depreciation and taxes.

With respect to per unit cost of production we find from Table 6.6 that, just as in the case of tapioca in paddy too, Cost C per unit of paddy output varies inversely with size of holdings though the trend is not smooth. Here, however, one could easily argue that economies of scale may favour large farms in production of paddy as compared to small farms because of the use of indivisible inputs like bullock labour. But Cost $A_3$ per unit of paddy output shows no consistent pattern, with small holdings reporting as high or as low per unit costs as on large holdings. Thus in paddy too, whatever differential advantage large farmers enjoy over small farmers in its production is mainly in terms of Cost C but not Cost $A_3$.

TABLE 6.6: **Cost of Paddy Production in Rupees Per Kg. of Output—All Villages**

| Cost | Size classes in acres | | | | | | | |
|---|---|---|---|---|---|---|---|---|
| | 0.0 to 0.5 | 0.51 to 1.0 | 1.01 to 2.5 | 2.51 to 5.0 | 5.01 to 10.0 | 10.01 to 15.0 | Above 15 | All |
| Cost $A_3$ | — | 1.54 | 1.01 | 1.23 | 1.08 | 1.56 | 1.20 | 1.20 |
| Cost C | — | 1.96 | 1.82 | 1.76 | 1.69 | 2.11 | 1.62 | 1.76 |

We may now take a look at the input structure of the different strata of farms taking all crops as a whole. In computing the cost incurred in cultivation of perennial crops, only maintenance costs (and establishment costs, if any) incurred during the reference year were taken into account. Table 6.7 presents the cost structure of all crops taken as a whole. Per acre costs vary positively with farm size with respect to all cost concepts except in Cost C, signifying how the resources within the reach of farmers influence their investment decisions.

**TABLE 6. 7: Cost of Cultivation for Total Crop Production—All Villages**

*(Rs. per acre)*

| Size classes in acres | Cost $A_1$ | Cost $A_2$ | Cost $A_3$ | Cost B | Cost C |
|---|---|---|---|---|---|
| 0.0 — 0.5 | 170 | 219 | 391 | 679 | 924 |
| | (18.4) | (23.7) | (42.3) | (73.5) | (100.0) |
| 0.51 — 1.0 | 200 | 224 | 397 | 697 | 861 |
| | (23.2) | (26.0) | (46.1) | (81.0) | (100.0) |
| 1.01 — 2.5 | 283 | 312 | 423 | 762 | 900 |
| | (31.4) | (34.7) | (47.0) | (84.6) | (100.0) |
| 2.51 — 5.0 | 406 | 439 | 571 | 881 | 910 |
| | (44.6) | (48.3) | (62.8) | (96.8) | (100.0) |
| 5.01 — 10.0 | 470 | 487 | 635 | 1035 | 1045 |
| | (45.0) | (46.7) | (60.7) | (99.0) | (100.0) |
| 10.01 — 15.0 | 529 | 540 | 667 | 1007 | 1008 |
| | (52.5) | (53.6) | (66.2) | (99.8) | (100.0) |
| Above 15 | 765 | 773 | 1250 | 1568 | 1568 |
| | (48.8) | (49.3) | (79.8) | (100.0) | (100.0) |
| All | 473 | 494 | 684 | 1032 | 1069 |
| | (44.3) | (46.2) | (64.0) | (96.6) | (100.0) |

*Note*: Figures in parentheses are percentages to Cost C.

Secondly, the proportion of owned inputs, as noted earlier, decreases with an increase in farm size; among bigger holdings there is more of monetised inputs. An implication of this, as mentioned already, is that imputation of value to owned inputs is likely to portray the picture of a relatively high cost economy prevailing among small farms. In the case of non-market or owned inputs the level of input use may not be meticulously determined in terms of economic calculus as in the case of purchasedinputs. As such more of them may be used even beyond the point of an economic level. As such their inclusion is likely toinflate costs among small farms. The existence of a significant non-monetised sector in peasant economies like in India, is the prime reason for reservations being expressed about applying the accounting techniques of commercialised farms for analysing the problems of peasant farms. Cost $A_3$ rather than Cost C may, therefore, be more relevant in understanding the economics of peasant farming as against large-scale capitalist farming.

One more question which we may discuss here is about the efficiency with which resources are used in total crop production by the different land holding groups. For this purpose we have computed input-output ratios. The results presented in Table 6.8 are quite interesting. The cost per unit value of output indicates that both in terms of Cost $A_3$ and Cost C there is a

TABLE 6.8: **Input-Output Ratios for Total Crop Production—All Villages**

| Size classes in acres | Cost $A_3$ per rupee of output | Cost C per rupee of output | Output/Input Ratio using | |
|---|---|---|---|---|
| | | | Cost $A_3$ | Cost C |
| 0.0 — 0.5 | 0.23 | 0.53 | 4.44 | 1.88 |
| 05.1 — 1.0 | 0.30 | 0.64 | 3.39 | 1.56 |
| 1.01 — 2.5 | 0.29 | 0.62 | 3.41 | 1.60 |
| 2.51 — 5.0 | 0.44 | 0.70 | 2.28 | 1.43 |
| 5.01 — 10.0 | 0.41 | 0.67 | 2.46 | 1.50 |
| 10.01 — 15.0 | 0.58 | 0.87 | 1.73 | 1.15 |
| Above 15 | 0.60 | 0.75 | 1.68 | 1.34 |
| All | 0.45 | 0.75 | 2.23 | 1.43 |

broadly increasing trend in per unit costs as farm size increases. Alternatively the returns per unit value of input more or less varies inversely wsth farm size. Both these results suggest that when it comes to total crop production small farmers are more efficient in the use of their resources as compared to large ones.[6] An explanation in terms of diseconomies of scale enabling small farms to be more efficient than large ones may not go far. The point is that in their quest for survival small farmers exploit their resources intensively in order to extract as much surplus as possible. They could, therefore, be efficient in the use of their resources. However, the fact of thier efficiency in this context does not necessarily imply that they are viable too. In fact as our results presented later indicate most small holdings are not viable units. Efficiency in this case is not synonymous with viability.

## INCOME FROM CROPS

In making a number of observations on the cost structure of our farms we are, no doubt, aware that any expenditure can be rationalised only in terms of the returns secured. We shall, therefore, take a look at the returns from tapioca and paddy cultivation and crop farming as a whole. Gross value of crop output valued at a uniform price per individual village netted of the cultivation costs gives the returns or income. Table 6.9 presents the data on income from tapioca corresponding to the various cost concepts for all four villages as a whole. The data reveals that tapioca is more or less a profitable crop to grow. But the variations in income corresponding to different concepts are quite wide between different size classes of farms. Obviously income, as expected, consistently declines as we traverse from Income $A_1$ to Income C. Net income corresponding to Cost C are less than half of the income corresponding to Cost $A_1$. The size class-wise differences are even more interesting. Holdings not exceeding 0.5 acres show negative income corresponding to Cost C, and even in terms of Cost B income is quite low though positive. There is a sharp decline in income among the lower size classes as we move from Income $A_3$ to Income C, implying that imputation of value to owned land and/or family labour leads to a steep decline in profits or even results in loss in tapioca cultivation among small holdings. By and large profits are seen to vary positively with farm size though the trend is not smooth in the mid-size groups.

TABLE 6.9: **Profit/Loss from Tapioca Cultivation—All Villages**

(*Rs. per acre*)

| Size Classes in acres | Income $A_1$ | Income $A_2$ | Income $A_3$ | Income B | Income C |
|---|---|---|---|---|---|
| 0.0 — 0.5 | 560 | 488 | 346 | 84 | —169 |
| 0.51 — 1.0 | 720 | 699 | 568 | 290 | 116 |
| 1.01 — 2.5 | 658 | 640 | 526 | 269 | 154 |
| 2.51 — 5.0 | 627 | 602 | 494 | 244 | 208 |
| 5.01 — 10.0 | 738 | 733 | 611 | 354 | 348 |
| 10.01 — 15.0 | 1087 | 1086 | 1018 | 768 | 768 |
| Above 15 | 2366 | 2362 | 1748 | 1509 | 1509 |
| All | 984 | 970 | 772 | 518 | 470 |

The profitability of a crop may vary from region to region. The village-wise figures (see Appendix 1) indicates that Cherumood—the lowland village—conspicuously reported a negative income corresponding to Cost B and Cost C in all size classes except one. Incomes in terms of other concepts too are quite low in Cherumood compared to the other three villages. Low tapioca yields in Cherumood, noted earlier, coupled with relatively higher per unit cultivation costs may account for Cherumood's performance. The second striking feature to note is that the negative income (corresponding to Cost C) from tapioca cultivation reported among small farms with holdings not exceeding 0.5 acres appears to hold consistently in all the four villages (in Muttara though positive, it is negligible), once again reminding us that imputing value to owned inputs like family labour tends to paint a gloomy picture of the small farmer's economy.

From the evidences presented here and elsewhere it appears that yield differentials and cost differentials account for a large part of the observed variations in profitability of tapioca over size classes of farms. Yield differentials have obviously played a bigger role as evinced by the relatively very high profits reported by big farmers, especially those with holdings above 10 acres. It is, therefore, not surprising to find big farmers showing keen interest to cultivate a low value crop like tapioca since they are able to earn high profits by raising yield per acre. Small farmers report losses only when value is imputed to owned inputs. If, however, only actually paid costs are reckoned for profit calculations, they too find it profitable to cultivate; in any case it is not a losing proposition for them.

Since output is valued at a uniform price per individual village, price differentials cannot be cited as a factor for profit variations over size classes within a village. Across villages, however, since individual village prices were taken not of price differentials could be looked upon as a factor for inter-village profit variations. Our data, however, suggests that price differentials between villages oscillated within a narrow range—from 26 paise per Kg. to 30 paise—and hence does not warrant being cited as a significant factor in explaining regional variations in profitability. On the whole, our results seem to bear testimony to the fact that tapioca is profitable to grow in the midlands and highlands but not in the lowlands where relatively higher per unit costs of production coupled with low tapioca yields either resulted in low or negative income from tapioca cultivation.

Coming to paddy we may examine Table 6.10 which presents the income derived from paddy cultivation using the various concepts. As seen from the table, income B and Income C (i.e., corresponding to Cost B and C) are conspicuously negative for paddy in all size groups. The magnitude of negative income per acre among the small farms are as high as that among large farms. Thus if profits are reckoned in terms of Costs B and C, we get a gloomy picture of a crop which has traditionally been looked upon as a remunerative crop. A major reason for the negative income is the inclusion of rental value of owned paddy lands which is quite high—a fact that attests to the price of paddy lands in the land market. If the use of owned inputs on farms is determined by prices there may be some justification in looking upon this trend as evidence of paddy cultivation being a losing proposition. But if the farmers are only concerned with maximising surplus with respect to actually paid out costs (i.e., Cost $A_2$ or Cost $A_3$) then there is nothing to stop us from concluding that paddy was profitable to cultivate at least among our sample farms. In fact, as seen from Table 6.10 Income $A_3$ is positive in paddy. Profits from paddy (corresponding to Cost $A_3$) rise upto holdings of 2.5 acres, then remains more or less constant upto holdings of 10 acres, rises again only in holdings exceeding 15 acres. The returns from paddy cultivation are of a lesser magnitude as compared to tapioca. In terms of Cost $A_3$, for instance, income from paddy cultivation are about a half of that observed for tapioca. Large farmers too report relatively low returns from paddy cultivation compared to tapioca. Constraints to augment paddy yields as also in minimising cultivation costs possibly explain why even large farmers are unable to reap as much profits noticed in the case of tapioca. However, a word of caution may be added here. In comparing the two crops on per acre basis one must not forget the possibility of a second crop of paddy, in a given year, as a result of which income from paddy per annum would be higher than implied by the figures in Table 6.10.

In spite of the possibility of double cropping in paddy, it is apparent from Tables 6.9 and 6.10 that income from paddy cultivation is negative corresponding to Costs B and C, while it is positive in the case of tapioca. Such a negative income arises from paddy in the case of all farmers. Then why should they produce this crop at all? An explanation in terms of limited or even absence of alternatives to paddy in paddy lands cannot go far. The point is that the negative income observed here arises mainly because of the inclusion of imputed rentals of owned lands as a part of cost—and rental rates are high for paddy lands. The surplus over paid-out costs, however, is positive and significant per season in the case of paddy which could make it attractive enough. And it is precisely this potential as also that of double cropping which has kept the rents on paddy lands high.

TABLE 6.10: **Profit/Loss from Paddy Cultivation—All Villages**

(*Rs. per acre*)

| Size classes in acres | Ineome $A_1$ | Income $A_2$ | Income $A_3$ | Income B | Income C |
|---|---|---|---|---|---|
| 0.0 — 0.5 | — | — | — | — | — |
| 0.51— 1.0 | 582 | 582 | 132 | —319 | —319 |
| 1.01— 2.5 | 500 | 485 | 365 | —184 | —332 |
| 2.51— 5.0 | 656 | 617 | 308 | —120 | —158 |
| 5.01—10.0 | 710 | 687 | 380 | —170 | —198 |
| 10.01—15.0 | 255 | 233 | —18 | —490 | —490 |
| Above 15 | 778 | 776 | 406 | —50 | —50 |
| All | 619 | 599 | 304 | —196 | —225 |

But rising labour costs are posing a threat to paddy. We have already noted the high proportion of labour costs in paddy cultivation, and even small farms have to hire labour. A trend towards conversion of paddy lands into coconut groves and annual crops like sugarcane and bananas has been noticed recently.

Coming now to total crops we find that crop farming, in general, turns out to be profitable (see Table 6.11). All size classes report a positive income corresponding to all cost concepts. It is also noticed that per acre profits are relatively the highest in the lowest size group as compared to other size groups. One reason why medium and large farmers report lower profits per unit area as compared to small farms may be due to inclusion of area under non-yielding perennial crops in our estimates. Many of these farms reported tree crops of various ages reflecting the desire to assure uninterrupted flow of income from cultivation of perennial crops over time. The age of the tree crops over size classes may bias the size class-wise picture pertaining to total crops and hence our results pertaining to total crops should be read with caution. In the context of the farms reporting profits one may ask as to whether this does not testify to the validity of Cost C in analysing the behaviour of peasant farms. Here, however, apart from the limitations of the estimates cited above, one may note that the weightage of cash crops in the crop pattern of Kerala are relatively high as compared to other regions of India. But cash crops are cultivated side by side with subsistence crops and are not run on the lines of a capitalist farm. One can still, therefore, question the propriety of applying Cost C for computing profits on such farms.

TABLE 6.11: **Profit/Loss from Total Crop Porduction—All Villages**

(*Rs. per acre*)

| Size classes in acres | Income $A_1$ | Income $A_2$ | Income $A_3$ | Income B | Income C |
|---|---|---|---|---|---|
| 0.0 — 0.5 | 1566 | 1516 | 1344 | 1056 | 812 |
| 0.51— 1.0 | 1144 | 1120 | 947 | 646 | 483 |
| 1.01— 2.5 | 1160 | 1131 | 1020 | 681 | 543 |
| 2.51— 5.0 | 897 | 863 | 731 | 422 | 393 |
| 5.01—10.0 | 1094 | 1077 | 930 | 530 | 519 |
| 10.01—15.0 | 627 | 616 | 489 | 149 | 148 |
| Above 15 | 1334 | 1327 | 849 | 532 | 532 |
| All | 1051 | 1030 | 840 | 492 | 455 |

It would be instructive to compare our findings with the Kerala FMS data. The Kerala FMS data revealed that, on an average, for the period 1962-63 to 1964-65, total crop production reported losses upto holdings of 5 acres and profits beyond this size range, when profits were computed in terms of Cost C.

The Kerala results thus seemed to stand in contrast, to some extent, to the general findings of the FMS for other states in India, where losses were reported for a majority of farms with reference to Cost C. Part of the explanation, as observed earlier, is due to the higher weightage of cash crops in Kerala as compared to other regions. This does not necessarily mean that Cost C is relevant for Kerala agriculture. This is because most cash crops in this region, as observed earlier, are not cultivated on a plantation scale.[7] Moreover, as seen from Table 6.11 the difference between Income $A_3$ and Income C on most farms are quite wide. Hence, profit calculations in terms of Cost C tend to grossly underestimate profits and disposable income realised by farms. In retrospect we may state that Cost B and cost C may be relevant to highly commercialised agriculture where produc tion is market-oriented and profit the sole motive for crop production decisions. To understand the economics of peasant farming Cost $A_3$ (or Cost $A_2$ in the FMS, India) may be more relevant.

## IMPACT OF DIFFERENTIAL PRICES ON PPOFIT/LOSS

In arriving at the profits in the above analysis, we had valued output at a uniform price. However, as explained earlier, when farmers sell their produce they may incur a gain or loss in income depending upon the actual prices received. The question of which size classes of holdings have a better advantage in the commodity market as indicated by actual prices received would be taken up in detail in Chapter 8. We shall restrict our attention here to finding out what difference it makes to the profit or loss if marketed quantity is valued at actual sale prices received by individual farmers, as compared to per acre profit/loss from tapioca, paddy and total crops derived from valuation of output at uniform prices. A few points may have to be clarified here. Whereas the uniform price was applied to all output—marketed or not, the realised or differential prices here are applied only to marketed quantities. Secondly, the uniform price which we used above was not weighted for either marketed quantity or output; it is only a simple average. As such, deviations can occur between the two sets of valuation of output or profit/loss derived therefrom both at individual or size class level and also at aggregate level. But our focus is to see which size classes lose, and also to see if the two sets of valuation go together or diverge significantly.

We have compared the profits (Income $A_3$) from tapioca, paddy and total crops using the two valuation procedures. The results are presented in Figure 2. As seen from the figure the scenario observed earlier more or less stands. The variations in profits over size classes in tapioca more or less follows the same pattern except that when marketed output is valued at actual sale price, profits decline in a number of size classes. In paddy there is an upward valuation of profits for big holdings when marketed quantity is valued at actual sale price. But the pattern is again the same. In the case of total crops the mid-size groups from 1 to 10 acres report a gain in income. These differences may be due to market advantages. Thus, on the whole, our results show that the profits from tapioca, paddy and total crops across size classes of farms, more or less, follow a similar pattern irrespective of whether we use a uniform price or actual sale price for valuing output.

## DISTRIBUTION OF VALUE OF CROP OUTPUT

As noted earlier, crop diversification was being practised by all groups of farmers for reasons spelt out in Chapter IV. Not only low value crops like tapioca but also high value crops like cashew, pepper, rubber, etc., figured in the crop pattern of the farms. It, therefore, seems pertinent to assess the contribution of tapioca to household income vis-a-vis other crops.

Table 6.12 presents data showing the share of each crop to the gross value of crop output per household by size classes of farms. It is significant to note that tapioca despite its low unit value, accounts for about a third of the gross value of crop output per household. Even more significant is the fact that in holdings above 15 acres tapicoa's share in the gross value of crop output per household is as high as 57 per cent. This is, no doubt, due to the very high tapioca yields recorded by these holdings. There is no consistent pattern between size classes but

TABLE 6.12: **Cropwise Distribution of Gross Value of Crop Output—All Villages**

*(Rs. per household)*

| Size classes in acres | Tapioca | Paddy | Coconut | Banana | Cashew | Arecanut | Pepper | Rubber | Other miscellaneous crops | All crops |
|---|---|---|---|---|---|---|---|---|---|---|
| 0.0 — 0.5 | 119 | — | 230 | 22 | 31 | 8 | 61 | — | 60 | 531 |
| | (22.4) | | (43.3) | (4.1) | (5.8) | (1.5) | (11.5) | | (11.3) | (100.0) |
| 0.51— 1.0 | 408 | 14 | 339 | 52 | 48 | 12 | 32 | — | 61 | 966 |
| | (42.2) | (1.4) | (35.1) | (5.4) | (5.0) | (1.2) | (3.3) | | (6.4) | (100.0) |
| 1.01— 2.5 | 725 | 352 | 743 | 139 | 130 | 68 | 109 | 189 | 144 | 2599 |
| | (27.9) | (13.5) | (28.6) | (5.3) | (5·0) | (2.6) | (4.2) | (7.3) | (5.6) | (100.0) |
| 2.51— 5.0 | 1558 | 935 | 1056 | 546 | 402 | 160 | 206 | — | 231 | 5094 |
| | (30.6) | (18.4) | (20.7) | (10.7) | (7.9) | (3.1) | (4.0) | | (4.5) | (100.0) |
| 5.01—10.0 | 2653 | 3632 | 2486 | 332 | 700 | 236 | 153 | 2280 | 529 | 13002 |
| | (20.4) | (27.9) | (19.1) | (2.6) | (5.4) | (1.8) | (1.2) | (17.5) | (4.0) | (100.0) |
| 10.01—15.0 | 3889 | 7440 | 2621 | 472 | 305 | 1375 | 174 | 527 | 728 | 17531 |
| | (22.2) | (42,4) | (15.0) | (2.7) | (1.7) | (7.8) | (1.0) | (3.0) | (4.2) | (100.0) |

| | | | | | | | | | | |
|---|---|---|---|---|---|---|---|---|---|---|
| Above 15 | 32448 | 14228 | 6785 | 1459 | 491 | 181 | 73 | 776 | 943 | 57384 |
| | (56.5) | (24.8) | (11.8) | (2.5) | (0.9) | (0.3) | (0.1) | (1.4) | (1.7) | (100.0) |
| All | 1805 | 1347 | 1102 | 254 | 253 | 132 | 115 | 425 | 226 | 5659 |
| | (31.9) | (23.8) | (19.5) | (4.5) | (4.5) | (2.3) | (2.0) | (7.5) | (4.0) | (100.0) |

*Note:* Figures in parentheses give percentages.

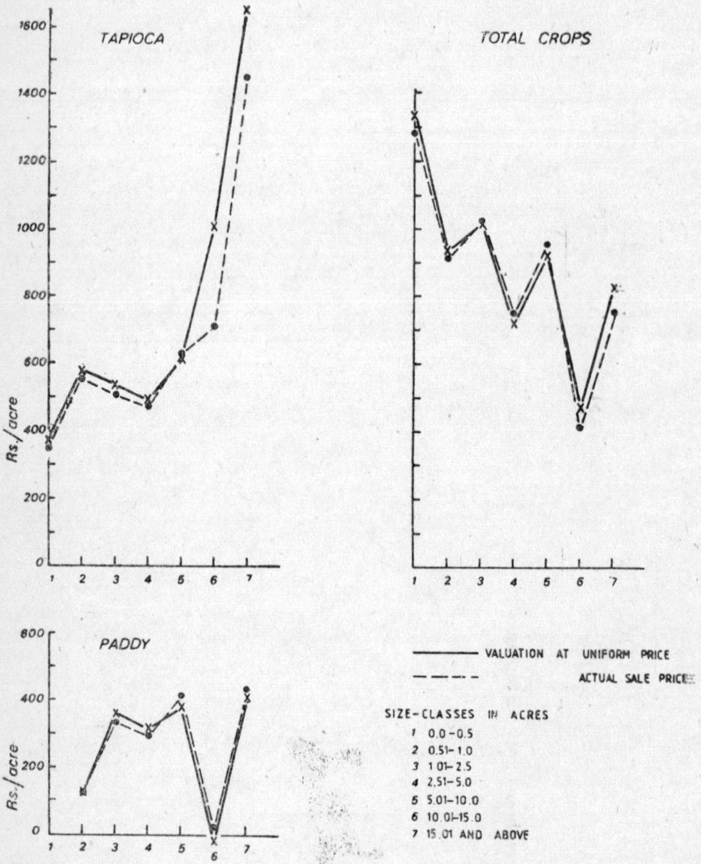


FIG. 2: *Profits (income $A_3$) from crop enterprises*

it is noted that tapioca accounts for not less than a fifth of the gross value of crop output per household in each size class. Apart from tapioca, paddy and coconut also account for a relatively high proportion of the gross value of crop output. What is interesting here is that in the case of coconut, its share in total value of crop output varies inversely with farm size. Coconut is, without doubt, the major cash crop cultivated by small farmers. In view of the relatively higher share of tapioca, paddy and coconut in total value of crop output farmers who grow these crops primarily for sale will be extremely sensitive to any losses incurred in these crops. In the case of tapioca and paddy any sustained losses may motivate the farmer, given other factors, to either stop cultivating or curtail area under that crop. In the case of a perennial crop like coconut, however, decision-making is a more complex phenomenon where in the farmer has to discount the future costs and returns. Hence, a single year's performance may not influence him much in the case of perennial crops.

Since cropping pattern will vary from region to region, it is quite likely that the aggregative picture presented above may conceal regional differences with respect to the contribution of different crops to household income. The village-wise data (not presented here) indicated that in the midland and highland villages tapioca's share ranged from 24 to 43 per cent of the value of all crop output whereas it was relatively lower in the lowland village. Paddy was an important crop in the midland and highland villages but not so in the lowland village where only few farmers cultivated it. Being the dominant crop in the lowlands, the share of coconut in the value of all crop output was relatively higher in this region as compared to other regions. All this illustrates the regional contrasts in the weightage of different crops which determines their relative share in the gross value of crop output.

## HOUSEHOLD INCOME

An examination of the composition of household income assumes significance on a number of grounds. Firstly, it can indicate the economic base of the tapioca-growing households.

Secondly, it can shed light on the nature of diversification of economic activities of the households. To arrive at the income from crop production and animal husbandry we have taken into account the income corresponding to Cost $A_2$. The results of our analysis are presented in Table 6.13.

It is interesting to observe that the percentage share of income from agriculture to total household income increases consistently with an increase in the size of holdings upto 10 acres (the peak being 69 per cent), and thereafter declines though it still continues to make a substantial contribution to household income in absolute terms. Among households with holdings upto one acre, the share of agriculture is lower than 24 per cent. Wage employment is seen to be the major source of income, accounting for almost 36 per cent of household income in holdings upto 0.5 acres. It also figures prominently in holdings between 0.5 to 1 acre. Its contribution is marginal in holdings exceeding 1 to 5 acres and thereafter it does not figure at all. Thus there appears to be a clear cut dichotomy between the small and big holdings with wage employment being a major source of income for small holders, while for big ones agriculture is the mainstay. The dominance of wage income in the lowest size groups may arise from the fact that agriculture by itself, even if profitable, is not able to generate adequate surplus to meet even the basic requirements of these households and hence such land holding groups have to turn to other sources like wage employment for sustenance.

The second point to note is the diverse sources of incomes that households earn by diversifying their economic activities. Though this is true of all land holding groups, it may not be correct to attribute this to the operation of the same phenomenon. This is because among small farmers diversification of economic activities may be undertaken in response to conditions of economic distress. On the other hand, among big holdings it reflects a desire to maximise profits through all possible channels. In fact it is interesting to observe that in holdings above 15 acres, agriculture, animal husbandry and allied activities, trade and business each share around a third of the total household income.

Lastly, as seen from the table, not only does household income vary positively with farm size but also the differences become wider as we move on to bigger holdings, the increase in income being more than proportionate to changes in the farm size in the upper size ranges. In other words, a wide disparity in incomes received is a conspicuous feature of the tapioca-growing households. This is not something unique to tapioca cultivators; on the contrary it reflects more the general malaise of the overall farm economy. What is appalling is that even after diversification of household activities, holdings upto one acre are not able to generate income more than Rs. 3000/-per annum (at 1976-77 prices) which even by official standards is inadequated to meet their basic requirements.[8] It is obvious that for these land holding groups a high proportion of the surplus that they are able to generate will be diverted for consumption purposes. Whether such holdings can become viable in future is, therefore, an intriguing question facing policy makers.

To sum up: The presence of a significant non-monetised sector in peasant economies like that of our study region is the prime reason why reservations have been expressed about the propriety of applying the cost accounting procedures of capitalist farms for analysing the problems of peasant farms. This is because the use of such inputs may not be determined by market prices. As our analysis indicates, owned inputs dominate the input structure of small farms while among big farms there is a preference for purchased inputs. In view of this, comparisons of production efficiency between different groups of farmers has a built-in bias to show small farmers in poor light as compared to big ones. In fact as our analysis revealed, whatever differential advantage large farms enjoyed over small ones in production of tapioca and paddy was only when value was imputed to owned inputs at market prices.

Though, in general, tapioca was profitable to cultivate small farmers with holdings upto 0.5 acre reported losses whenvalue was imputed to family labour at the market wage rate. Profits also varied positively with farm size. Paddy reported losses when value was imputed to owned land and family labour in all strata of farms. Crop farming as a whole was, however,

### TABLE 6.13: Composition of Household Income—All Villages

(*Rs. per household*)

| Size Classes in acres | Agriculture | Animal husbandry & allied agricultural activities | Wage income | Income from trade and business | Remittances | Income from subsidiary occupations/sale of assets/rents, etc. | Total household Income | Total household income (after all taxes) |
|---|---|---|---|---|---|---|---|---|
| 0.0 — 0.5 | 416 | 44 | 957 | 312 | 585 | 336 | 2650 | 2645 |
| | (15.7) | (1.7) | (36.1) | (11.8) | (22.1) | (12.7) | (100.0) | |
| 0.51— 1.0 | 687 | 226 | 469 | 756 | 519 | 224 | 2881 | 2874 |
| | (23.8) | (7.8) | (16.3) | (26.2) | (18.0) | (7.8) | (100.0) | |
| 1.01— 2.5 | 1869 | 285 | 169 | 446 | 1906 | 328 | 5003 | 4969 |
| | (37.4) | (5.7) | (3.7) | (8.9) | (38.1) | (6.6) | (100.0) | |
| 2.51— 5.0 | 2913 | 653 | 11 | 719 | 1805 | 144 | 6245 | 6169 |
| | (46.6) | (10.5) | (0.2) | (11.5) | (28.9) | (2.3) | (100.0) | |
| 5.01—10.0 | 7940 | 251 | — | 848 | 2412 | 80 | 11531 | 11300 |
| | (68.9) | (2.2) | | (7.4) | (20.9) | (0.7) | (100.0) | |

| | | | | | | | | |
|---|---|---|---|---|---|---|---|---|
| 10.01—15.0 | 7764 | 1115 | — | 639 | 2490 | 2250 | 14258 | 13847 |
| | (54.5) | (7.8) | | (4.5) | (17.5) | (15.8) | (100.0) | |
| Above 15 | 23817 | 21925 | — | 27000 | — | 220 | 72962 | 70491 |
| | (32.6) | (30.0) | | (37.0) | | (0.3) | (100.0) | |
| All | 3200 | 795 | 272 | 1174 | 1491 | 288 | 7220 | 7095 |
| | (44.32) | (11.0) | (3.8) | (16.3) | (20.7) | (4.0) | (100.0) | |

*Note*: Income from agriculture is calculated with reference to Cost $A_2$. Income from animal husbandry etc., is netted of actual maintenance costs for livestock upkeep plus owned manure.
Figures in parentheses give percentages.

profitable corresponding to all cost concepts. This is so because losses sustained in one crop are offset by profits in another. These trends, therefore, suggest that a farmer in his quest to maximise surplus or profits from his farming and other economic activities keeps in view an overall perspective and it is this which determines the farmer's behavioural attitudes. This does not seem unrealistic in the Kerala context where mixed cropping and diversification of household activities are widespread, as seen earlier. It may not be out of place to mention here that when profits are reckoned in terms of Cost C they tend to show up losses or if not, underestimate the disposable income available to a household.

An interesting feature of our analysis was the attempt to study the impact of valuation of output at a uniform price as against at actual sale price received (only marketed quantity) on the profits and losses on the farms. When actual sale price was taken note of tapioca still reported profits, though it had declined in a number of size classes. In paddy bigger holdings reported a gain in income while at the level of all crops together the mid-size groups reported a gain.

A highlight of our study was the comparative perspective it provided of the input structure of tapioca and paddy cultivation. A conspicuous feature was the higher degree of monetisation of inputs in paddy as compared to tapioca. This could be explained in terms of the greater impact of new technology on paddy cultivation leading to greater use of market inputs like hired labour, fertilisers, pesticides, etc. Tapioca did not witness a change on a similar scale. Another notable feature of paddy was the use of indivisible inputs like bullock labour which tended to push up per unit costs on small holdings. A common feature of both crops was that among big farms there was a tendency to use more of capital inputs like fertilisers. In otner words, capital intensity was higher among bigger farms; among small farms labour continued to be the major factor of production.

In general, small farmers were found to be efficient in the use of their resources taking into account total crop production. This observation, however, needs to be read within the limited context of our data. Even though crop farming was profitable our results indicate that inspite of diversification of the sources of income the surplus that could be mopped up by holdings below one acre was not adequate enough to assure a reasonable standard of living. This raises doubts about the possibilities of such holdings turning out to be viable.

## REFERENCES

1. Cf: Krishna Bharadwaj, *Production Conditions in Indian Agriculture*, Occasional Paper No. 33, Department of Applied Economics, University of Cambridge, Cambridge University Press, 1974, p. 39, 61; A K Sen: *Employment, Technology and Development*, Oxford University Press, London, 1975, p. 147; N A Majumdar: *Economic Analysis of Farm Management Data*, in *Cost Studies in Agriculture*, Indian Society of Agricultural Economics, Bombay (Seminar Series), May 1961, pp. 163-165.
2. Cf: A K Sen, An Aspect of Indian Agriculture, *The Economic Weekly*, 1962, p. 246 and 1975, op. cit., p. 147; G R Saini: *Farm Size, Resource Use Efficiency and Income Distribution*, Allied Publishers, New Delhi, 1979, pp. 121-123.
3. Ranjit Sau, Land Utilisation: A Note, *EPW*, Vol. XI, No. 36, September 4, 1976, pp. 1473-76.
4. Majumdar, 1961, op. cit., p. 162.
5. For data on fertilisers used in tapioca refer Table 5.7. For paddy theyare as follows:

| Size classes in acres | 0.51 to 1.0 | 1.01 to 2.5 | 2.51 to 5.0 | 5.01 to 10.0 | 10.01 to 15.0 | Above 15 | All |
|---|---|---|---|---|---|---|---|
| Fertilisers Kg. per acre | 60 | 99 | 140 | 179 | 461 | 100 | 213 |

6. These results should, however, be read within the limited context of our data.
7. As per Kerala Agriculture Census 1976-77, 59 per cent of area under coconut, 50 per cent of Pepper, 36 per cent of Cashew, 47 per cent of Arecanut were cultivated in holdings of less than 1 hectare.
8. As per the Sixth Five Year Plan (1978-83) document of the Planning Commission, Government of India, a monthly per capita expenditure

of Rs. 65 (at 1977-78 prices) was accepted as the poverty line to delineate the poor from the rich. Using this norm and assuming an average household of 6 members (as in our case), the minimum annual income for such a household works to Rs. 4680 at 1977-78 prices. It is obvious that our farms with holdings less than one acre fall below this poverty line.

# 7

# LABOUR USE

BEING an important input entering the production process, the pattern and intensity of labour use has generated a lot of interest not only from the veiwpoint of cost minimisation but also from the viewpoint of increasing productivity and employment. It is generally recognised that a rapid generation of employment opportunities holds the key to a viable solution of the poverty problem in many developing countries. The experience of the developed countries suggests that economic growth coincided with a shift of a significant proportion of the labour force from the agriculture to the non-agricultural sector.[1] The sluggish pace of growth of industrial employment coupled with high population growth rates in many LDCs has made it clear that for quite some time agriculture will have to continue to provide employment to many in LDCs. It was in this context that a number of eminent economists put forward the view that the agricultural sector in many LDCs has a latent capacity to absorb more labour.[2] This calls for detailed studies on the pattern and intensity of labour use across crops, regions and farm enterprises to enlighten the policy maker about this latent capacity of agriculture to absorb more labour. Our concern, however, is to know as to what role tapioca can play in generating employment opportunities. This chapter, therefore, seeks to analyse the labour use pattern in tapioca cultivation in relation to other crops.

## LABOUR USE AND YIELD

The findings of a number of studies suggest that there is a positive association between levels of labour use and agricultural productivity. Ishikawa, for instance, found a strong association between intensity of labour use and agricultural productivity in Japan.[3] Vaidyanathan using district level data too found similar results for India.[4] The low level of labour input in Indian agriculture as compared to Japanese agriculture was partly explained by the fact that agricultural productivity in India was quite low when compared to Japan. It was, therefore, contended that increases in productivity would lead to an increase in the intensity of labour use. What we have, therefore, done first is to find out the quantum of employment required for a given increase in yield of tapioca as compared to paddy. In comparing tapioca with paddy we have been prompted by the fact that not only is paddy the most important food crop grown in Kerala but also it has traditionally been looked upon as a labour intensive crop. It can, therefore, serve as a point of reference for tapioca. For our analysis we have fitted linear and log-linear functions to the sample observations. There is no specific reason in the choice of the functional forms. A number of points may, however, have to be noted here. Firstly, in treating labour as a function of yield here, we are no doubt aware that the two variables are inter-dependent in the sense that yield itself depends upon labour in addition to other factors. Our aim here, however, as stated is primarily to see the labour required for a given increase in yield. Secondly, the factors influencing labour use among the different strata of farms may not be the same. If, for instance, small farmers have a general tendency to employ more labour per unit area compared to big farmers, as suggested by some studies,[5] it obviously means that fitting a common function to all observations ignoring such inter size-group differences is not justified. Hence separate regressions have been fitted for each size-group. Thirdly, on account of multiple cropping in paddy, the employment absorption in paddy in a given year is bound to be more. To take note of the impact of cropping intensity on employment our variables are expressed in terms of net area sown. The regression results are presented in Table 7.1.

As obvious there is a positive association between per acre lobour input and tapioca/paddy yields per acre. The coefficients are significant for both crops in all cases except for tapioca in the three lowest size groups. An interesting hint from our results pertaining to paddy is that a given increase in paddy yields leads to a higher volume of labour employment in paddy among the lower strata of farms as compared to the upper strata. This is because output responds less than proportionately to labour input among the lower strata of farms where labour input is already high. Among holdings with size upto 2.5 acres, a one per cent increase in paddy yields leads to a more than proportionate increase in labour employed per acre, the elasticity coefficient being 1.1010. However, a 't' test revealed that the deviation from unity of the elasticity coefficient was not statistically significant, implying that labour increases are proportionate to yield increases. In the next size group (i.e., 2.5 to 5 acres) the elasticity coefficient was 0.93; but the deviation of the coefficient from unity was not statistically significant, in other words an increase in paddy yields will lead to a proportionate increase in labour input per acre. A one per cent increase in paddy yields among big holdings, i.e., above 5 acres, however, leads to a less than proportionate increase in labour input per acre. This may be because big farmers tend to economise on labour use, and instead use more units of capital inputs to increase yield.

The estimates obtained in the tapioca equations suggest that labour absorption in tapioca is not as much as in paddy. Per acre labour input does not seem to be very sensitive to yield increases particularly among holdings upto 2.5 acres. This may be because, as noted earlier, the volume of labour employed in tapioca cultivation is already high and hence a further increase in labour input is not favoured unless yields were to rise significantly as seen among big farms. The explanatory power of the equations is fairly high in the case of paddy but not so for tapioca suggesting that there are other factors which affect labour use in tapioca more. Thus, on the whole, our results indicate

TABLE 7.1: Regression Results Showing Relation between Per Acre Labour Input (Y) and Yield Per Acre (X)

| Size classes in acres | N | Linear | | | Log-linear | | |
|---|---|---|---|---|---|---|---|
| | | Constant | Coefficient | $R^2$ | Constant | Coefficient | $R^2$ |
| *Tapioca* | | | | | | | |
| 0—0.5 | 20 | 43.1043* | 0.0018$^{ns}$ | 0.06 | 2.6343* | 0.1535$^{ns}$ | 0.08 |
| 0.51—1 | 26 | 41.0523* | 0.0012$^{ns}$ | 0.03 | 3.3433* | 0.0529$^{ns}$ | 0.01 |
| 1.01—2.5 | 38 | 37.9946* | 0.0009$^{ns}$ | 0.01 | 2.9144* | 0.0940$^{ns}$ | 0.02 |
| 2.51—5 | 28 | 33.9002* | 0.0028** | 0.16 | 2.1968** | 0.1922*** | 0.10 |
| Above 5 | 28 | 29.6329* | 0.0031*** | 0.37 | 1.4277*** | 0.2789* | 0.27 |
| *Paddy* | | | | | | | |
| Upto 2.5 | 18 | 2.1785$^{ns}$ | 0.1185* | 0.56 | —2.9382* | 1.1010* | 0.62 |
| 2.51—5 | 14 | 36.0007$^{ns}$ | 0.0712* | 0.38 | —1.9476** | 0.9371* | 0.62 |
| Above 5 | 27 | 100.3453* | 0.0257** | 0.16 | 2.6933* | 0.3041** | 0.11 |

*Note*: *, **, ***,=Significant at 1 per cent, 5 per cent and 10 per cent, respectively.
ns=not significant.

that an increase in tapioca and paddy productivity would lead to an increase in labour absorption; but it is not impressive for tapioca. The advantage of multiple cropping in paddy would result in a higher demand for labour in paddy cultivation as compared to tapioca. It may be necessary to clarify that our analysis here is restricted to the production stage only; there is no idea of the employment likely to be generated in the processing stages.

Though our above analysis gives a clue to the likely increase in employment for a given increase in per acre yields of the two crops it does not fully reflect the likely annual employment absorption in tapioca and paddy cultivation. Output can be increased by stepping up yields per acre and/or extending cultivation to more area. With a view to assess the overall annual employment absorption in tapioca and paddy cultivation in response to varying output, we fitted a linear and log-linear function to the sample observations. Here again one may pose a query regarding the need to fit separate functions to each size class. If area expansion is effected within the given holding through cropping pattern adjustments there may be some justification in fitting separate functions. If, however, the area expansion involves an expansion of the holding size itself then the result of the size-class picture may be misleading in view of the changed status of the farmer. It may, therefore, be more prudent to get an overall view of the annual labour absorption. In our functions Y=Total labour input in tapioca/paddy cultivation in mandays; X=Tapioca/paddy output in kgs. The log-linear function, it may be noted, measures the employment elasticity with respect to tapioca and paddy output. The regression results are as follows:

**Tapioca**

$$Y=19.4501^{*}+0.0061^{*}X \qquad \bar{R}^2=0.93;\ N=140$$

$$\log Y=-1.9363^{*}+0.6927^{*}\log X \qquad \bar{R}^2=0.81;\ N=140$$

**Paddy**

$$Y=6.4880^{ns}+0.0823^{*}X \qquad \bar{R}^2=0.90;\ N=59$$

$$\log Y=-1.5796^{*}+0.8823^{*}\log X \qquad \bar{R}^2=0.91;\ N=59$$

*Note*: *Significant at 1 per cent level.
ns=not significant.

The linear functions indicate that every tonne increase in output will require 6 additional mandays of labour for tapioca and 83 mandays for paddy. The employment elasticity with respect to output is 0.69 for tapioca and 0.88 for paddy. In other words, a one per cent rise in tapioca and paddy output would result in 0.69 per cent increase in mandays of labour for tapioca and 0.88 per cent for paddy. The employment elasticity with respect to tapioca and paddy output was not only less than proportionate but also the deviation from unity was statistically significant at one per cent level in both cases.

Thus, by and large, our results seem to suggest that the magnitude of labour absorption in tapioca cultivation is lower than in the case of paddy. An obvious question that could be raised here is as to why farmers don't cultivate a more labour intensive crop like paddy instead of tapioca. This is not a question of relative profitability alone. Here one has to take note of the fact that the two crops are not perfect substitutes in cultivation, and hence any decision to shift a cultivated area from tapioca to paddy or vice-versa has to cope with this constraint. Moreover, as noted earlier, small farmers with holdings less than one acre have no access to paddy lands, the latter being mostly under relatively larger holdings. Secondly, there are other factors which favour tapioca. If the farmer chooses he could rely wholly on family labour to cultivate tapioca. But in paddy on account of peak season constraints as also the need for labour possessing specialised skills, hiring of labour may become necessary. This is another factor why small farmers are keen to cultivate tapioca. The relatively lower labour absorption in tapioca may be an important factor why large farmers show interest in cultivating a low value crop like tapioca since by using more units of capital inputs they can increase per acre yields and profits too. Thirdly, as noted earlier, the prospects for a significant increase in paddy yields taking place in the near future is quite dim. But there is tremendous scope to enhance tapioca productivity by several times and in the process generate more employment opportunities. Thus there are points which can be said in favour of tapioca and against from the employment point of view.

## LABOUR USE AND FARM SIZE

Studies based on farm management data in India have suggested that per acre labour input varies inversely with size of holdings. This trend was sought to be explained in terms of the dualistic nature of the labour market whereby small farmers who were characterised by a surfeit of family labour relative to land tended to use higher doses of labour per unit area.[6] Bharadwaj, however, noted that though the inverse relationship appeared to hold true in the case of total crops, it was not so in the case of individual crops where no systematic or significant relationship was observed.[7] Singh et al., and Gupta using farm level data from Uttar Pradesh noted that per acre labour input increased with an increase in size of holdings upto three hectares and declined again for maize, wheat, paddy and potatoes for some selected years.[8] These results served as an adequate warning that the so-called inverse relationship between per acre labour input and size of holdings could not be generalised. In the following discussion we seek an answer to the following questions: First, how does the pattern and intensity of labour use in crop cultivation vary across different strata of farms and crop operations? Second, what are the qualitative differences in the labour demand schedule of tapioca vis-a-vis other crops as reflected in the demand for different categories of labour?

Table 7.2 presents data pertaining to labour use in crop cultivation among the different strata of farms. Taking into account total labour input we note that as farm size increases the per acre labour input remains more or less constant except in holdings above 15 acres for tapioca and total crops. In the case of paddy, however, per acre total labour input consistently declines upto holdings with 10 acres and then again increases, perhaps reflecting the complementary relationship that exists between levels of labour use and use of modern inputs like fertilisers, which as noted earlier, is in relatively very high doses among the very big holdings. The table further reveals that per

TABLE 7.2: **Particulars of Labour Use in Tapioca, Paddy and Total Crop Production**

*(Mandays per acre of gross cropped area)*

| Size classes in acres | Tapioca | | | Paddy | | | | All crops* | | |
|---|---|---|---|---|---|---|---|---|---|---|
| | Family labour | Hired labour | Total | Family labour | Hired labour | Total | Total per acre of net sown area | Family labour | Hired labour | Total |
| 0—0.5 | 33 | 10 | 43 | — | — | — | — | 32 | 10 | 42 |
| | (76.7) | (23.3) | (100) | | | | | (76.2) | (23.8) | (100) |
| 0.51— 1 | 22 | 20 | 42 | — | 170** | 170** | 340** | 21 | 17 | 38 |
| | (52.4) | (47.6) | (100) | | (100) | (100) | | (55.3) | (44.7) | (100) |
| 1.01— 2.5 | 15 | 24 | 39 | 22 | 74 | 96 | 190 | 18 | 27 | 45 |
| | (38.5) | (61.5) | (100) | (22.9) | (77.1) | (100) | | (40.0) | (60.0) | (100) |
| 2.51— 5 | 5 | 38 | 43 | 5 | 76 | 81 | 154 | 4 | 38 | 42 |
| | (11.6) | (88.4) | (100) | (6.2) | (93.8) | (100) | | (9.5) | (90 5) | (100) |
| 5.01— 10 | 1 | 40 | 41 | 4 | 65 | 69 | 137 | 1 | 44 | 45 |
| | (2.4) | (97.6) | (100) | (5.8) | (94.2) | (100) | | (2.2) | (97.8) | (100) |
| 10.01— 15 | — | 48 | 48 | — | 80 | 80 | 160 | 0.1 | 45 | 45 1 |
| | | (100) | (100) | | (100) | (100) | | (0.2) | (99.8) | (100) |

| | | | | | | | | | | |
|---|---|---|---|---|---|---|---|---|---|---|
| Above 15 | — | 72<br>(100) | 72<br>(100) | — | 100<br>(100) | 100<br>(100) | 199 | — | 72<br>(100) | 72<br>(100) |
| All | 6<br>(12.8) | 41<br>(87.2) | 47<br>(100) | 4<br>( 4.9) | 77<br>(95.1) | 81<br>(100) | 160 | 5<br>(10.2) | 44<br>(89.8) | 49<br>(100) |

*Note*: Figures in parantheses are percentages to respective totals.
*All crops include tapioca, paddy, coconut, bananas, arecanut, cashew, pepper etc.
**Results should be read with caution as it is based on a single observation.

acre family labour input is inversely related to size of holdings for tapioca, paddy and total crops. On the other hand per acre hired labour input is directly associated with size of holdings in the case of tapioca and total crops but not so for paddy where we find no consistent pattern. Family labour accounts for a major share of total labour input among the lower size classes particularly those with holdings upto 2.5 acres. In holdings above 5 acres its share is insignificant or it is not used at all. The supply of family workers varies inversely with size of holdings, as noted earlier, and hence explains why family labour figures more prominently among small farms, while among big farms where labour is a constraint, proportion of hired labour used is more.

On an average tapioca cultivation requires 47 mandays of labour per acre as against 81 mandays for paddy (or 160 mandays if in per net area sown terms). An interesting feature to note is that the share of family labour to total labour input is higher in the case of tapioca as compared to paddy in a given size class of holding. Paddy is a season-bound crop and hence during peak seasons farmers are obliged to hire in labour to supplement their own labour to complete the various operations associated with paddy cultivation in time. This is not the case with tapioca which is a highly adaptable crop. One factor which may explain why tapioca is popular among small farmers is that it is not as demanding in attention and resources as many other crops. As a consequence they are able to make use of their family labour without much need for hired labour and also allocate their labour time to tapioca cultivation possibly during periods when they are free from other pressing work either on or off the farm.

## LABOUR USE AND CROP OPERATIONS

Labour requirements will vary from crop to crop depending on the specific operations that needs to be done. Some crop operations are more labour-intensive than others and hence influences the quantum of labour needed to cultivate various crops. Table 7.3 presents a comparative picture of human labour input in tapioca and paddy cultivation with respect to various crop operations. Land preparation quite understandably absorbs the highest proportion of labour input in both crops—47 per cent of total labour input in the case of tapioca and 35 per cent for paddy. Weeding, interculture and harvesting (in that order) are the other operations which are labour intensive. It is interesting to observe that the labour input per acre in planting and harvesting of paddy (16 and 22 mandays respectively) is quite high when compared to the respective figures for tapioca (4 and 9 mandays respectively). This labour intensity of some operations may partly explain the higher employment absorption in paddy as compared to tapioca. Other operations like replanting, application of pesticides and plant protection measures, etc., are light jobs requiring very little labour.

TABLE 7.3: **Operation-wise Distribution of Human Labour Input in Tapioca and Paddy Cultivation**

(*Mandays/acre*)

| Operation | Total Human Labour Input | |
|---|---|---|
| | Tapioca | Paddy |
| Land preparation | 22 (46.8) | 28* (34.6) |
| Planting | 4 (8.5) | 16 (19.8) |
| Replanting | 0.2 (0.4) | — |
| Weeding, interculture, application of manure and fertilisers | 11 (23.4) | 13 (16.0) |
| Pesticides and plant protection | — | 1 (1.2) |
| Harvesting | 9 (19.2) | 22 (27.2) |
| Transporting to storage place and miscellaneous | 0.8 (1.7) | 1 (1.2) |
| Total | 47 (100) | 81 (100) |

*Note*: Figures in parentheses give percentage to total.
*includes human labour used to operate bullocks.

The second dimension to be noted about crop operation-wise use of labour is the varying composition of labour in response to operation specific requirements. In some operations the share of hired labour may be higher than that of family labour while in others it may be much lower. Table 7.4 presents the crop operation-wise distribution of family and hired labour input for tapioca and paddy across land holding groups. The proportion of hired labour to total labour input is relatively higher for land preparation and harvesting operations as compared to other operations in paddy; in the case of tapioca land preparation accounts for the highest proportion of hired labour. As is well known, land preparation and harvesting are the two operations in the growth span of a crop when demand for labour is at its peak. If family labour is unable to cope with such peak seasonal demands hiring of labour becomes necessary. Interestingly while the hired labour component in total labour input is quite high for land preparation for both tapioca and paddy, a similar trend is not observed for harvesting operations in the case of tapioca. The possibility of time-stretching of harvesting of tapioca obviously enables the farmer to rely more on family labour and hence use less hired labour. Tapioca, it may be recalled, has no critical period for sowing and harvesting, though in Kerala sowing operations are synchronised with particular seasons. Secondly, the proportion of family labour to total labour input in planting, weeding and interculture, and harvesting in paddy is quite low when compared to the respective figures for tapioca. Unlike in tapioca, in paddy transplanting, weeding and harvesting call for specialised skills with which family labour may not be familiar with. As a result they have to hire in labour possessing these skills. Thirdly, an interesting feature to note is that not only big farmers but also small farmers hire in labour for various operations in tapioca and paddy cultivation. This phenomenon of small farmers hiring in labour is, of course, not new. Rudra using FMS data for several states in India noted that even small farmers hired in a significant proportion of labour.[9] Peak season demands for labour witnessed during ploughing and harvesting operations as well as demand for labour possessing specialised skills explain to some extent these trends. It is thus obvious that the supply of family labour in relation to land holdings is not the only factor which influences the pattern of labour use among farms.

The anaylsis presented above suggests that there are dissimilar demands for different categories of labour. Hence any proper assessment of the labour demand schedule for different crops should throw light on this aspect of labour demand. Since labour use is crop and operation-specific the demand schedule confronting different categories of labour also differ. Some operations both on grounds of tradition and some criteria of efficiency are performed by male or female workers. Transplanting, weeding and interculture as also harvesting in paddy cultivation, for instance, have traditionally been a female preserve. Land preparation in paddy cultivation, on the other hand, is a strenuous job involving ploughing of the field, bunding, irrigating the field with required water essential for the paddy plants to sprout or flushing out excess water, basal dressing of the field with required plant nutrients, etc., and hence are usually performed by male workers supplemented with bullock labour. Though land preparation for planting tapioca is not so elaborate an operation as that of paddy, the operations largely consisting of preparatory tillage, formation of mounds on which the stem-cuttings will be put, basal dressing, etc., here too male workers are preferred.

Table 7.5 gives some idea about the demand for different categories of labour and energy in the cultivation of tapioca and paddy. Use of bullock labour is totally absent in tapioca cultivation. But not so in the case of paddy where before sowing, the field is ploughed with the help of bullocks. Tapioca is planted mostly on hill slopes (at least in Kerala) and as an inter-crop with perennial crops and these may have, apart from other factors, resulted in non-use of bullock labour for land preparation in tapioca cultivation. Tractor use is totally absent in tapioca cultivation but makes its presence, though negligible, in paddy cultivation. The social and political milieu in Kerala may not be conducive to mechanisation and also the diseconomies associated with its operation may explain why it does not figure in tapioca and only negligibly in paddy cultivation. Further,

TABLE 7.4: **Percentage Distribution of Family and Hired Labour by Crop Operations**

*Tapioca*

| Crop Operations | | Size classes in acres | | | | | | | |
|---|---|---|---|---|---|---|---|---|---|
| | | 0—0.5 | 0.51—1 | 1.01—2.5 | 2.51—5 | 5.01—10 | 10.01—15 | Above 15 | All |
| Land preparation | FL | 61.7 | 45.4 | 27.1 | 7.2 | — | — | — | 8.5 |
| | HL | 38.3 | 54.6 | 72.9 | 92.8 | 100 | 100 | 100 | 91.5 |
| Planting | FL | 76.2 | 55.3 | 49.0 | 9.1 | 1.5 | — | — | 17.0 |
| | HL | 23.8 | 44.77 | 51.0 | 90.9 | 98.5 | 100 | 100 | 83.0 |
| Replanting | FL | 100 | 100 | 59.4 | 18.2 | 26.1 | — | — | 54.5 |
| | HL | — | — | 40.6 | 81.8 | 73.9 | 100 | — | 45.5 |
| Weeding and | FL | 72.5 | 42.1 | 34.4 | 11.2 | — | — | — | 14.2 |
| interculture | HL | 27.5 | 57.9 | 65.6 | 88.8 | 100 | 100 | 100 | 85.8 |
| Application of | FL | 33.3 | 82.7 | 30.1 | 21.3 | — | — | — | 10.2 |
| manure and fertilisers | HL | 66.7 | 17.3 | 69.9 | 78.7 | 100 | — | 100 | 89.8 |
| Pesticides and | FL | — | — | — | — | — | — | — | — |
| Plant protection | HL | — | — | — | — | — | — | — | — |

| | | | | | | | | | |
|---|---|---|---|---|---|---|---|---|---|
| Harvesting | FL | 100 | 87.3 | 65.5 | 21.6 | 8.5 | — | — | 21.3 |
| | HL | — | 12.7 | 34.5 | 78.4 | 91.5 | 100 | 100 | 78.7 |
| Transporting, etc. | FL | — | — | 100 | 8.8 | 25.7 | — | — | 25.9 |
| | HL | — | — | — | 91.2 | 74.3 | — | — | 74.1 |
| *Paddy* | | | | | | | | | |
| Land preparation | FL | — | — | 35.1 | 1.7 | 1.7 | — | — | 5.1 |
| | HL | — | 100 | 64.9 | 98.3 | 98.3 | 100 | 100 | 94.9 |
| To operate | FL | — | — | 30.1 | 30.2 | 23.0 | — | — | 14.7 |
| bullocks | HL | — | 100 | 69.9 | 69.8 | 77.0 | 100 | 100 | 85.3 |
| Planting | FL | — | — | 14.1 | — | — | — | — | 1.5 |
| | HL | — | 100 | 85.9 | 100 | 100 | 100 | 100 | 98.5 |
| Replanting | FL | — | — | — | — | — | — | — | — |
| | HL | — | — | — | — | — | — | — | — |
| Weeding and | FL | — | — | 20.0 | — | — | — | — | 1.7 |
| interculture | HL | — | 100 | 80.0 | 100 | 100 | 100 | 100 | 98.2 |
| Application of | FL | — | — | 48.1 | 32.9 | 19.7 | — | — | 19.5 |
| manure and fertilisers | HL | — | — | 51.9 | 67.1 | 80.3 | 100 | 100 | 80.5 |

*Note*: FL: Family Labour; HL: Hired Labour.

TABLE 7.4 (*Contd.*)

| Crop Operations | | Size classes in acres | | | | | | | |
|---|---|---|---|---|---|---|---|---|---|
| | | 0—0.5 | 0.51—1 | 1.01—2.5 | 2.51—5 | 5.01—10 | 10.01—15 | Above 15 | All |
| Pesticides and Plant | FL | — | — | 10.8 | 41.4 | 7.4 | — | — | 10.8 |
| protection | HL | — | 100 | 89.2 | 58.6 | 92.6 | 100 | 100 | 89.2 |
| Harvesting | FL | — | — | 14.9 | — | — | — | — | 1.4 |
| | HL | — | 100 | 85.1 | 100 | 100 | 100 | 100 | 98.5 |
| Transporting, etc. | FL | — | — | — | — | — | — | — | — |
| | HL | — | — | — | — | — | 100 | — | 100 |

*Note*: 1. FL: Family Labour; HL: Hired Labour.
2. Wherever labour expended for transport of produce was negligible it has been included with harvesting labour itself.

constraints to the labour supply schedule during peak seasons affect paddy cultivation and may call for limited substitution of tractor power for human or bullock labour in certain operations so as to keep to the production schedule. This factor may not be present in tapioca.

TABLE 7.5: **Labour and Energy Use in Tapioca and Paddy Cultivation: by Categories**

| Item | Tapioca | Padds |
|---|---|---|
| 1. Tractor power (Hours per acre) | — | 0.05 |
| 2. Bullock labour (Bullockdays per acrc) | — | 14.3 |
| 3. Human labour (Mandays per acre) | | |
| — Male | 46.58 | 32·56 |
| — Female | 0.07 | 48.05 |
| — Total | 46.65 | 80.61 |

It is interesting to note that virtually all the operations in tapioca cultivation are done by male workers. Participation of female workers is negligible. This is not the case in paddy cultivation where female labourers outnumber male labourers. This division of labour by sex is rooted in tradition. Generally transplanting, weeding, interculture and harvesting of paddy are performed by female workers. This is not the case in tapioca where the production processes differ from that of paddy. It may be necessary to clarify here that though our data suggests only negligible use of female workers in tapioca cultivation, this does not indicate the potential employment for female workers in the processing stage where generally the cutting of raw tapioca tubers into chips, etc., is done by female workers. On an average, two mandays of labour is required to process 100 Kgs. of raw tapioca tubers into chips. Male labour used in tapioca cultivation in per acre terms is more than in the case of paddy. But on account of double-cropping in paddy cultivation the annual labour absorption for paddy is more than for tapioca. Incidentally, we may mention here that wages paid to female workers are generally lower than those paid to males. This has its consequent impact on the working capital requirements for different crops.

### LABOUR PRODUCTIVITY

We now turn to the question of labour productivity in crop production which is as important as the issue of labour use itself. Increasing labour productivity in agriculture is as much the concern of the policy maker as the question of employment generation. Table 7.6 presents data pertaining to average labour productivity of tapioca, paddy and total crops measured in rupees per manday of labour employed. Average labour productivity of tapioca increases consistently with an increase in size of holdings. In the case of paddy, average labour productivity increases with an increase in farm size upto 10 acres and then declines marginally. The results pertaining to total crops seem a bit curious with average labour productivity being inversely related to size of holdings though the trend is not smooth among the upper strata of farms. Though this is likely to lead us to the conclusion that small farmers have a tendency to maximise gross returns, a word of caution may be added here in interpreting these results. This is because the crops included under total crops consists of several perennial crops of which we have recorded only the labour used during the reference year by way of maintenance cost. It may, therefore, be prudent to confine our remarks to the tapioca and paddy results. Average labour productivity for tapioca is markedly higher than that for paddy in all size classes. It may, however, not be correct to conclude here that labour use efficiency in tapioca is more than that for paddy. This is because the technology for raising paddy is such that it requires a high quantum of labour unlike for tapioca. Both land and labour productivity for tapioca is higher among bigger farms. This, of course, is not strange. When there is increasing use of capital inputs per unit of labour employed, both land and labour productivity could be high among big farms. The correlation coefficient between labour input in mandays per acre and average labour productivity per manday in the case of tapioca was

—0.3 (statistically significant at 1 per cent level) taking into account all 140 observations and—0.6 (statistically significant at 1 per cent level) in the case of paddy for 59 observations. This suggests that average labour productivity of tapioca and paddy increases significantly only when per acre labour input declines. In a way this may be a reflection of the fact that at the present levels of technology, labour is employed in agriculture beyond a point of maximum productivity, and diminishing returns are in operation.

TABLE 7.6: **Average Labour Productivity of Tapioca, Paddy and Total Crops—Value of Output in Rupees Per Manday**

| Size classes in acres | Tapioca | Paddy (including value of by-products) | Total crops |
|---|---|---|---|
| 0.0 — 0.5 | 15.96 | — | 41.22 |
| 0.51— 1.0 | 21.61 | 10.56 | 35.21 |
| 1.01— 2.5 | 22.74 | 12.91 | 31.76 |
| 2.51— 5.0 | 23.15 | 17.16 | 30.86 |
| 5.01—10.0 | 29.14 | 20.47 | 34.19 |
| 10.01—15.0 | 33.39 | 16.52 | 25.64 |
| Above 15 | 46.05 | 17.25 | 29.21 |
| All | 30.72 | 17.80 | 31.31 |

To sum up: Tapioca is not a labour intensive crop like paddy. An acre of land under tapioca requires 47 mandays of labour as against 81 mandays for paddy. If we take into account the additional crops of paddy that can be raised in a given year, paddy will outdistance tapioca further in this respect. The employment elasticity of tapioca and paddy with respect to output was significantly less than unity, being 0.69 and 0.88 respectively.

Since land is limited in Kerala, of more interest would be the increments in labour input arising from increments in per acre yields. Our findings suggest that an increase in per acre yields of the two crops will lead to an increase in per acre labour input but it was not statistically significant for tapioca for holding upto 2.5 acres. An interesting finding was that an increase in paddy yields among farms belonging to the lower strata led to a proportionate increase in labour input while among big holdings with more than 5 acres, it resulted in a less than proportionate increase, perhaps reflecting the tendency among big farmers to substitute capital inputs for labour. For tapioca, per acre labour input rose significantly only in holdings above 2.5 acres. Possibly labour employed in tapioca is already quite high and there is no further scope for further labour absorption.

Despite its less labour intensive nature, tapioca has some points to be said in its favour. Its low requirements of labour may be an important reason why small as well as big farmers find it viable to cultivate the crop. The need to hire in labour with special skills or for meeting peak season constraints characteristic of paddy does not seem to be present—at least to the same extent—in tapioca. Hence, there is more scope for use of family labour in tapioca cultivation. This is a matter of significance to peasant households with meagre resources and where family labour is the main factor of production.

Our analysis also revealed that labour operations in tapioca cultivation are virtually male-dominated; in paddy, planting, weeding, interculture and harvesting are usually tasks assigned to females. Processing of tapioca into chips is, however, usually done by females. Furthermore, unlike in paddy neither bullock labour nor tractor power is used in tapioca cultivation. All this illustrates that the demand for different categories of labour and energy sources will vary across crops.

As regards labour productivity it was observed that average labour productivity of tapioca and paddy increased with an increase in farm size, though this trend was not smooth for paddy among big holdings. Average labour productivity of tapioca was higher than for paddy in all size groups. Our findings suggest that average labour productivity of tapioca and paddy will rise only if labour input were to decline. But this may conflict with the social objective of employment generation.

Increasing employment without, at the same time, producing a decline in labour productivity is, therefore, a tricky question facing policy makers. Possibly efforts should be directed to upgrade technology so as to increase both employment and productivity.

## REFERENCES

1. Colin Clark: *The Conditions of Economic Progress*, Macmillan, London, 1957 (III Edition).
2. Shigeru Ishikawa: *Labour Absorption in Asian Agriculture: An Issues Paper*, ILO Bangkok, 1978; Pranab Bardhan, et al., *Labour Absorption in Indian Agriculture: An Exploratory Exercise*, ILO, Bangkok, 1978; Wilbert Gooneratne (ed): *Labour Absorption in Rice-based Agriculture: Case Studies from SE Asia*, ARTEP, Bangkok, May 1982; Richard T Ward: Absorbing More Labour in LDC Agriculture, *Economic Development and Cultural Change*, (17) January 1969; George Tobias: The Labour Force Explosion Versus The New Technology in Agriculture, *Indian Journal of Industrial Relations*, January 1970; C H Hanumantha Rao: Factor Endowment, Technology and Farm Employment, Comparison of East Uttar Pradesh with West Uttar Pradesh and Punjab, *Economic and Political Weekly*, September 25, 1976; V S Vyas and George Mathai: Farm and Non-Farm Employment in Rural Areas, *EPW*, Annual Number, February 1978, p. 337.
3. Shigeru Ishikawa, *op. cit.*
4. A Vaidyanathan: *Labour Use in Indian Agriculture*, in Bardhan,et al., op. cit.
5. A K Sen, An Aspect of Indian Agriculture, *The Economic Weekly*, Annual Number, February 1962 and Size of Holdings and Productivity, *The Economic Weekly*, Annual Number, February 1964; D Mazumdar: On the Economics of Relative Efficiency of Small Farmers, *Economic Weekly*, Special Number, July 1963.
6. See A K Sen: 1962 and 1964, op. cit., and D Mazumdar, op. cit.
7. Krishna Bharadwaj, *Production Conditions in Indian Agriculture*—Occasional Paper No. 33, Department of Applied Economics, University of Cambridge, Cambridge University Press, 1974.
8. Daulat Singh, et al., Changing Pattern of Labour Absorption on Agricultural Farms in Eastern Uttar Pradesh, *Indian Journal of Agricultural Economics*, October-December 1981, pp. 43-44; BK Gupta: Labour Absorption Under Introduction of the Modern Farm

Technology in District Kanpur (Uttar Pradesh), *Indian Journal of Agricultural Economics*, October-December 1981, p. 55.

9. Ashok Rudra and MM Mukhopadhya: Hiring of Labour by Poor Peasants, *EPW*, January 10, 1976, pp. 33-36.

# 8

# MARKETING, CONSUMPTION AND PROCESSING

HERE we shall take a look at the marketing behaviour of the farmers particularly with respect to marketing of tapioca and paddy in relation to other crops. Our discussion covers questions related to marketed surplus, market dependence, prices received and market channels, processing and consumption.

## MARKETED SURPLUS AND FARM SIZE

To begin with, let us find out as to which group of farmers participate in the tapioca market as sellers and more important what is the relative share of different size-classes of farmers in the sale of tapioca. Table 8.1 which presents the relevant data reveals a number of interesting features. Firstly, the lowest size class do not sell any tapioca obviously because the tapioca they produce on their tiny holdings is not even adequate for their family consumption. The proportion of farm households selling tapioca as also the proportion of tapioca output that is sold varies directly with size of holdings.

It is clear from the table that for holdings above 2.5 acres almost all households ranging from 92 to 100 per cent sell their tapioca produce. Households with holdings between 0.5 to 1 acre sell only 10 per cent of the tapioca output; in the next size class about 29 per cent of tapioca output is sold. The differences become very sharp as we move towards the upper size-ranges.

TABLE 8.1 : **Particulars of Marketing of Tapioca**

| Size classes in acres | Proportion of households who sell Tapioca % | Proportion of tapioca output marketed % | Quantity of tapioca sold per household Kg./HH (Gross marketed quantity) | Value of sales per household Rs./HH | Net marketed quantity of tapioca Kg./HH |
|---|---|---|---|---|---|
| 0—0.5 | Nil | — | — | — | — |
| 0.51—1 | 15.4 | 10.5 | 157.7 | 40 | 130.0 |
| 1.01—2.5 | 57.9 | 29.0 | 772.1 | 199 | 756.8 |
| 2.51—5 | 92.9 | 64.5 | 3678.9 | 878 | 3668.1 |
| 5.01—10 | 95.2 | 71.7 | 7156.9 | 1954 | 7156.9 |
| 10.01—15 | 100.0 | 91.3 | 12393.8 | 3098 | 12381.2 |
| Above 15 | 100.0 | 97.3 | 105240.0 | 28649 | 105240.0 |
| All | 56.4 | 72.7 | 4657.4 | 1244 | 4645.6 |

*Note* : Gross Marketed Quantity is actual quantity marketed.
Net Marketed Quantity is gross net of repurchases and receipts in kind.
HH=Household.

Over 70 per cent of tapioca output in holdings 5-10 acres is sold and thereafter virtually the entire output is sold. Both the quantity as well as value of tapioca sales per household are quite high in holdings above 5 acres. On an average 56.4 per cent of the households sell about 73 per cent of their tapioca output—about 4.6 tonnes per household or in value terms Rs. 1244 per household. The above trends suggest that marginal and small farmers grow tapioca primarily for self-consumption. But medium and large farmers grow tapioca primarily for the market. Obviously for these farmers price and profitability are an important consideration in crop production decisions especially since a predominant portion of their tapioca output is intended for the market. It is paradoxical that even with regard to the marketable surplus of an inferior food crop like tapioca consumed mostly by low income people, big farmers exercise an effective control over its supply. Similar results have been suggested by Nadkarni with reference to millets in Ahmednagar, Maharashtra.[1]

In the context of the high proportion of tapioca sold by the big farmers one may be interested in knowing as to what factor sustains the tapioca market. It is doubtful whether the demand from low income people by itself may sustain the market for tapioca. It, therefore, seems possible that the demand from agro-based industries is another important outlet for the tapioca marketed by big farmers. In fact as our discussion later shows, agents buy a sizeable chunk of the tapioca sold by some of the big farmers. It is quite possible that this is meant for use in agro-based industries.

Though a significant proportion of tapioca output is marketed it is not clear whether the marketed surplus is a commercial surplus or a distress sale. When, owing to pressing need for cash, farmers are compelled to sell their produce and repurchase later for their own requirements it may suggest occurrence of a distress sale.[2] Our data indicates that about 5 per cent of the tapioca-selling households repurchase tapioca in the market. However, the fact that repurchases have taken place need not necessarily reflect occurrence of distress sales. For instance, when fields are located at a distance from residences, farmers may find it more convenient and economical to sell the tapioca produced

TABLE 8.2: **Particulars of Marketing of Paddy**

| Size classes in acres | Proportion of households selling paddy to paddy-growing household % | Proportion of paddy output marketed % | Quantity of paddy sold: Kg./paddy-growing household | Value of paddy sales: Rs./HH | Gross marketed rice Kg./paddy-growing household | Net marketed quantity of rice: Kg./paddy-growing household |
|---|---|---|---|---|---|---|
| 0—0.5 | — | — | — | — | — | — |
| 0.51—1 | Nil | — | — | — | — | — |
| 1.01—2.5 | 17.7 | 6.8 | 37.2 | 52 | 24.8 | 6.2 |
| | (7.9) | | (16.7) | (23) | (11.1) | (2.8) |
| 2.51—5 | 28.6 | 10.4 | 122.8 | 138 | 81.9 | 60.2 |
| | (14.3) | | (61.4) | (69) | (41.0) | (30.1) |
| 5.01—10 | 65.0 | 26.4 | 679.9 | 872 | 453.5 | 453.5 |
| | (61.9) | | (647.5) | (831) | (431.9) | (431.9) |
| 10.01—15 | 100.0 | 48.3 | 2336.3 | 3023 | 1558.3 | 1558.3 |
| | (100) | | (2336.3) | (3023) | (1558.3) | (1558.3) |

| | | | | | | |
|---|---|---|---|---|---|---|
| Above 15 | 100.0 | 39.4 | 3570.0 | 4760 | 2381.2 | 2381.2 |
| | (100) | | (3570) | (4760) | (2381.2) | (2381.2) |
| All | 45.8 | 29.0 | 610.3 | 790 | 407.0 | 396.5 |
| | (19.3) | | (257.2) | (333) | (171.5) | (167.1) |

*Note*: Figures in parentheses give respective figures expressed in terms of total sample households.
HH=Household.

in their far-flung fields and meet their own requirements from nearby markets. In fact there were two such cases among our tapioca-selling households who purchased their requirements from nearby retail shops or markets. Among the households selling tapioca who repurchase the commodity from the market we find that most of them operate holdings below 5 acres. But the net marketed surplus in all size classes are positive. This is confirmed further by examining the individual household data and hence cannot be attributed to any bias in presenting data in the from of group averages. This may suggest that no distress sale has occurred. However, even if net marketed surplus were to be positive it is not a sufficient condition to indicate absence of distress sale, if any. This is because, at times, on account of pressing need for cash, farmers may sell at a lower price, without necessarily repurchasing the commodity.

Coming to paddy, we find from Table 8.2 that, as in the case of tapioca, the proportion of paddy-growing households who sell paddy varies directly with the size of holdings ranging from 17.6 per cent in holdings between 1.0-2.5 acres to 100 per cent in holdings above 10 acres. On an average about 46 per cent of the paddy-growing households, i.e., 19 per cent of the total sample households sell paddy. The proportion of paddy output that is marketed is much lower than in the case of tapioca, especially among large farmers. On an average only 29 per cent of paddy output is sold whereas in the case of tapioca—as noted earlier—it is as high as 73 per cent.

About 18.5 per cent of the paddy-selling households repurchase rice in the market. Again as in the case of tapioca we note that repurchases mostly take place among households with holdings 1 to 5 acres. The net marketed surplus of rice—as in the case of tapioca—is positive in all size-classes. In other words, sales exceed repurchases.

An interesting dimension of the sale of superior cereals like wheat and rice is that farmers may sell them and use the cash derived therefrom to buy inferior foods. Nadkarni, for instance, noted that in Ahmednagar (Maharashtra) small farmers sold a high value and superior cereal like wheat and used the income derived therefrom—either whole or part—to purchase inferior cereals and millets for their family consumption.[3] Here we have a phenomenon of small farmers taking advantage of market opportunities by growing superior cereals for sale and buying inferior cereal from the market for their own use. In our study area, however, most of the paddy sellers are medium and large farmers who did not have to depend on tapioca for subsistence. Out of 27 paddy-selling households, only one household purchased tapioca and that too a big farmer because his tapioca was produced on far-flung fields and hence he preferred to sell this entirely and buy some from a nearby market for his own use.

TABLE 8.3: **Distribution of Value of Crop Sales by Crops**

| Size classes in acres | Value of crop sales to total value of all crop sales | | | Total value of all crop sales |
|---|---|---|---|---|
| | Tapioca % | Paddy % | Other crops % | |
| 0—0.5 | — | — | 100.0 | 100 (125) |
| 0.51—1 | 13.7 | — | 86.3 | 100 (295) |
| 1.01—2.5 | 15.1 | 2.7 | 82.2 | 100 (1322) |
| 2.51—5 | 32.4 | 3.5 | 64.1 | 100 (3019) |
| 5.01—10 | 23.0 | 11.5 | 65.5 | 100 (8508) |
| 10.01—15 | 26.0 | 31.6 | 42.5 | 100 (10756) |
| Above 15 | 70.0 | 12.0 | 18.0 | 100 (40985) |
| All | 35.6 | 10.9 | 53.5 | 100 (3497) |

*Note*: 1. Figures in parentheses give total value of all crop sales in Rs. per household.

2. Value of paddy sales includes value of by-products, i.e., straw.

3. Other crops consist of coconut, cashew, arecanut, fruit crops, pepper, rubber, etc.

In order to find out the importance of tapioca as a cash crop among different strata of farms, we have compared the value of its sales with that of other crops. As seen from Table 8.3 on an average the value of tapioca sales to total crop sales accounts for about 36 per cent; the same in the case of paddy was only 11 per cent; while other crops account for about 53 per cent of the total value of all crop sales. The size-classwise picture reveals notable differences. Value of tapioca sales to total crop sales generally increases with an increase in farm size (with some stray exceptions). It is significant to note that among holdings above 15 acres almost 70 per cent of the value of crop sales is accounted by tapioca, indicating how important a cash crop it is for big farmers. In the case of paddy too we note that generally the value of paddy sales (including by-products increases with an increasein size of holdings upto 15 acres and then declines again. This seems to suggest that big farmers who have a surplus even after setting apart some for their household needs may not like to part with a superior commodity like rice; rather they would prefer to retain the larger portion of their paddy output to meet their current and future consumption needs. It may be noted that rice can be stored for a longer period without any appreciable loss. The same cannot be said about tapioca chips which in spite of its longer storage life when compared to that of raw tapioca tubers does not have a comparable storage life like rice.

Value of other crop sales which largely consists of cash crops varies inversely with size of holdings. This is quite interesting. For farmers belonging to the lower size classes the income from sale of cash crops is an important source of income to them—apart from wage income and other miscellaneous sources. Very rarely do they sell food crops and if at all they sell, it may be on account of distress conditions. They may even sell and yet repurchase in the market or they may sell superior cereals or cash crops and use the proceeds therefrom to buy inferior foods like tapioca. It is thus obvious that for such households cultivation of cash crops assumes the form of a compulsive production decision so as to enable them to raise cash required to meet their current consumption and production needs. Medium and large farmers too grow both food and cash crops. But they grow food crops not only for self-consumption but also for selling. One reason why the large farmers with holdings above 15 acres rely on tapioca as a major source of income may be that despite its low unit value it assures a stable source of income on account of relatively low instability in its prices, as noted earlier. This is not the case with many high value crops like cash crops which are also associated with high instability in prices. It would be interesting to link up our discussion here with some of our earlier findings. Since big farmers grow tapioca as a cash crop, they are willing to invest more resources on its cultivation. Tapioca yields, in that case, can be higher among big farms as compared to small ones. Small farmers, however, look upon tapioca as a subsistence crop and hence may prefer to devote more attention and resources to cash crops like coconut. It is, therefore, not surprising that when value of output of all crops was aggregated small farmers reported quite high returns (though not the highest) but not so in the case of tapioca where yields were low as compared to the yield levels among bigger holdings.

## PRICES RECEIVED AND MARKET CHANNELS

When a farmer markets his farm produce he may earn extra income depending on the price at which he is able to sell his produce. The question is who are the farmers who are able to benefit from market advantages as a result of their involvement in the market as sellers and more important which are the crops which help fetch a better price in the commodity market. A number of studies do indicate that poor peasants are paid less for their produce than is paid to large farmers. Sarkar's study on marketing in West Bengal and Bihar did reveal such price discrimination in the commodity market not only within similar crops but also by similar market channels.[4] Subba Rao's study on marketing of rice in Andhra Pradesh did not suggest any significant difference in prices received by different size groups but spatial differences were found to be significant which could notbe explained by transfer costs alone.[5] Price differentials may reflect qualitative differences, spatial and temporal differences, transfer costs, character of agencies involved in the market, the relative bargaining power of different segments of the peasantry, etc. We may first of all find out how tapioca fares in the market and then compare its performance with other crops sold by the farm households. Table 8.4 indicates the prices received for sale of tapioca by different size groups of farmers for the villages separately and all villages as a whole. Farmers in the lowest size class, as mentioned earlier, do not sell any tapioca since they grow it primarily for self-consumption and hence we find no observation in the lowest size class. Farmers in the other size groups do sell tapioca. When we take the figures for all villages together we note that though the average prices received by small farmers with holdings between 0.5 to 2.5 acres are slightly lower than those received by other farmers, in general the price differentials over size classes are quite small. This suggests that no group of farmers enjoy any distinct market advantage while selling tapioca. However, a word of caution may be added here. In aggregating the data over villages it is quite possible that spatial differences may be camouflaged. Villages may differ from one another in terms of the relative strength of different land holding groups, market access, the relative importance of different crops, extent of commercialisation, etc. It may, therefore, be more meaningful to look at the village-wise figures.

TABLE 8.4: **Average Price Received for Sale of Tapioca**

(*Rs. per tonne*)

| Size classes in acres | Ayilara | Muttara | Kuzhakad | Cherumood | All villages |
|---|---|---|---|---|---|
| 0. 0—0.5 | — | — | — | — | — |
| 0.51— 1.0 | 250 | — | 267 | — | 262 |
| 1.01— 2.5 | 247 | 240 | 287 | 244 | 261 |
| 2.51— 5.0 | 233 | 263 | 306 | 246 | 272 |
| 5.01—10.0 | 235 | 280 | 300 | 217 | 264 |
| 10.01—15.0 | 200 | — | 300 | — | 275 |
| Above 15 | — | — | 267 | — | 267 |
| All | 237 | 268 | 291 | 238 | 266 |

The average price received for sale of tapioca in the midland villages, Muttara and Kuzhakad are higher than in the other two villages. On an average tapioca sellers are able to secure an additional 30 to 50 rupees per tonne in the midland villages as compared to the other villages. These spatial differences in prices received may be on account of qualitative differences in the product or character of agencies involved. Interestingly big farmers in Muttara and Kuzhakad (except those above 15 acres) were able to secure a slightly higher price for tapioca sold. We may recall here that the proportion of big holdings is relatively higher in both midland villages. The scale of their output does seem to have some influence on the prices received by them. But the fact that these prices differentials are narrow suggest that scale has only a weak influence. In contrast to the scenario in the midland villages we find that in Ayilara and Cherumood prices received by big farmers are slightly less than those realised by the relatively smaller ones. This may be explained by the following factors. In the highland village transportation of large quantities of tapioca tubers from hills to village marketing centres presented serious problems. In such a situation agents or traders who came to the farm sites were willing to bear the transport costs by offering a lower price for the commodity. In such instances prices realised by big farmers were lower than that of other farmers. In the lowland village, Cherumood, the only bulk buyer of tapioca was a processing unit located in the village. But the price offered was low. Big farmers who sold their produce to the processing unit thus reported lower prices. Apart from these reasons, there was another factor. In 1977-78 owing to a glut in the market prices fell to as low as Rs. 200 per tonne. Big farmers who had delayed harvesting of tapioca in a number of cases had to sell tapioca at this low price.

From the evidence presented above, it is obvious that it is not possible to make any single generalisation on the question of market advantage favouring any particular group of farmers. As far as tapioca is concerned one may be interested in knowing as to why in spite of the concentration of the marketable surplus of tapioca among big farmers, they are not able to report any distinct market advantage over small farmers as reflected in the prices received by them. Though big farmers can delay harvesting of tapioca in expectation of better prices it may be noted that tapioca cannot be stored in the ground indefinitely as beyond a certain stage the culinary and starch value of tapioca tubers will exhibit a downward trend. This perishable nature of tapioca limits the options of the farmers to secure higher prices. For the same reason retentions of tapioca tubers at any point of time are low. Thus, tapioca growers may often have to play the role of price takers rather than price setters. Moreover, demand for tapioca may be elastic and hence big farmers may not want to use their control over the tapioca market to jack up tapioca prices. However, in spite of these apparent disadvantages in marketing of tapioca, we have noted earlier that big farmers were able to realise high profits from tapioca cultivation.

Table 8.5 presents similar data for other crops. Here again we are aware of the limitations in aggregating data over villages. But our interest is only to see how other important crops as a whole stand in comparison to tapioca. As seen from the table

**TABLE 8.5: Average Price Received for Sale of Other Crops**

| Size classes in acres | Paddy | Coconut | Cashew | Arecanut | Pepper | Rubber |
|---|---|---|---|---|---|---|
| | Rs. per quintal | Rs. per 100 nuts | Rs. per kg. | Rs. per 1000 nuts | Rs. per kg. | Rs. per kg. |
| 0.00— 0.5 | — | 73 | 4.72 | 27.50 | 3.53 | — |
| 0.51— 1.0 | — | 78 | 4.82 | 24.50 | 3.30 | — |
| 1.01— 2.5 | 142 | 78 | 4.54 | 27.50 | 3.71 | 6.00 |
| 2.51— 5.0 | 116 | 74 | 4.71 | 25.87 | 4.03 | — |
| 5.01—10.0 | 131 | 73 | 4.28 | 28.89 | 4.61 | 5.96 |
| 10.01—15.0 | 138 | 73 | 4.08 | 27.50 | 3.33 | 6.00 |
| Above 15 | 131 | 75 | 5.00 | 25.00 | 3.40 | 6.00 |
| All | 131 | 75 | 4.58 | 27.19 | 3.83 | 5.98 |

there is, in general, no marked variation in prices realised by different size-classes of farmers. So far as paddy is concerned the highest price realised is Rs. 142 per quintal in the size class 1.01 to 2.5 acres; while the lowest price of Rs. 116 per quintal is reported in the next size class, i.e., 2.51—5 acres. Whether this is due to market advantages or qualitative differences in product sold is difficult to say owing to the limitation of our data. In most of the other crops like coconut, cashew, arecanut, etc., price differentials are small. Thus, in general, though there are slight variations in prices received for sale of crop produce by different size groups of farmers, they are not conspicuous enough as to warrant the conclusion that scale is an important factor influencing the prices received by farmers.

The price which a farmer receives when selling his crop produce not only hinges upon market accessibility but, more important, upon the market channel to which he chooses to sell his crop produce. For instance in a study on market access in Maharashtra it was noted that farmers who had chosen marketing society as their outlet for cotton sales realised more favourable prices compared to those who disposed of their cotton to itinerant traders at the farm site.[6] Suman Sarkar's study cited earlier noted that in West Bengal and Bihar "not only to different agents within the same market pay different prices, the same agent also offers different prices to different classes of producers at the same time. The conditions of the market are such that monopsonistic or oligopsonistic buying of product by traders from the producer is possible."[7]

Let us now find out whether the prices farmers receive for the sale of their crop produce bears any relation to the choice of market channel. We, however, restrict our analysis to only tapioca and paddy. Table 8.6 indicates the relative importance of different market channels in the sales of tapioca and paddy effected by different size groups of farmers. Firstly, taking tapioca by itself we note that village consumers, village traders and agents are the three market channels who buy tapioca sold by the farmers. But the relative importance of the channels differ across size classes of farmers. In the lower size classes in

TABLE 8.6: Particulars of Tapioca and Paddy Sales by Market Channels

| Size classes in acres | Tapioca: Distribution of Household % | Tapioca: Distribution of Quantity sold % | Tapioca: Average price received Rs./Kg. | Paddy: Distribution of Household % | Paddy: Distribution of Quantity sold % | Paddy: Average price received Rs./Kg. |
|---|---|---|---|---|---|---|
| 0.0 — 0.5 | nil | — | — | nil | — | — |
| 0.51— 1.0 | VC 75.0 | 85.4 | 0.27 | nil | — | — |
| | VT 25.0 | 14.6 | 0.25 | | | |
| | A — | — | — | | | |
| 1.01— 2.5 | VC 59.1 | 52.9 | 0.27 | 66.7 | 40.8 | 1.49 |
| | VT 27.3 | 31.8 | 0.25 | 33.3 | 59.2 | 1.33 |
| | A 13.6 | 15.3 | 0.24 | — | — | — |
| 2.51— 5.0 | VC 26.9 | 27.3 | 0.25 | 75.0 | 47.6 | 1.14 |
| | VT 46.2 | 41.3 | 0.30 | 25.0 | 52.4 | 1.11 |
| | A 26.9 | 31.4 | 0.25 | — | — | — |
| 5.01—10.0 | VC 20.0 | 7.7 | 0.24 | 30.8 | 24.2 | 1.18 |
| | VT 5.0 | 0.7 | 0.25 | 69.2 | 75.8 | 1.40 |
| | A 75.0 | 91.6 | 0.27 | — | — | — |

| | | | | | | | |
|---|---|---|---|---|---|---|---|
| 10.01—15.0 | VC | 25.0 | 5.2 | 0.30 | 100.0* | 92.0 | 1.24 |
| | VT | 50.0 | 60.5 | 0.30 | — | 8.0 | 1.60 |
| | A | 25.0 | 34.3 | 0.20 | — | — | — |
| Above 15 | VC | 66.7 | 55.5 | 0.25 | — | 25.2 | 1.33 |
| | VT | 33.3 | 44.5 | 0.30 | 100.0* | 74.8 | 1.33 |
| | A | — | — | — | — | — | — |
| All | VC | 38.0 | 36.3 | 0.26 | 44.4 | 43.5 | 1.24 |
| | VT | 29.1 | 34.3 | 0.28 | 48.2 | 56.5 | 1.73 |
| | A | 32.9 | 29.4 | 0.26 | 7.4@ | — | — |

*Note*: * includes one house who sell part to village consumers and part to village traders.
@ pertains to the households who sell a portion of paddy to village consumers and another to village traders.
VC: Village Consumers: VT: Village Traders; A: Agents.

general proportion of households selling tapioca as well as proportion of tapioca output sold directly to village consumers at the farm site is distinctly higher than the upper size ranges where the village trader-cum-agent combine enjoy a bigger sway in buying tapioca sold by the farmers. On the other hand in the case of paddy, agents don't figure at all with the entire output being marketed either to village consumers at the farm site or to village traders. But there is no consistent trend with regard to the proportion of households selling paddy and the proportion of paddy output sold across different market channels. Though a higher proportion of households with holdings below 5 acres sell paddy direct to village consumers, the proportion of output marketed is lower as compared to the share of the village trader. When farmers sell their produce direct to village consumers at the farm site, they need not incur any marketing costs. Village traders and agents too come to the farm site to buy farm produce but they often offer a lower price on the grounds that they have to bear the transporting costs. Some of our farmers bemoaned that agents not only offered lower prices but also resorted to cheating by under-weighing as also claiming some extra quantity of tapioca per unit of quantity sold in order to compensate for transportation and marketing losses. But the reason why agents still play a big role in the tapioca market in spite of these complaints may be due to the fact that they are in a position to buy a large quantity of tapioca at a given point of time. Big farmers may prefer to sell to them since they need not then take the trouble of having to sell tapioca in smaller quantities to a larger number of prospective buyers. Though the prices offered by village traders and agents are generally lower than that of village consumers among the small holdings, the average price offered for tapioca by agents or village traders appears to be relatively high among big holdings. This may be because when the volume of sales is high agents or village traders are willing to offer a better price since they can take advantage of the economies of scale of transporting a large output. Further it may reflect on the quality of the tubers sold by these farmers.

## PROCESSING

One point which may be raised in the context of our above discussion is with respect to the form in which tapioca is marketed. If tapioca were processed into dry chips they could be stored to fetch a better price. Tapioca chips unlike raw tapioca tubers have a longer storage life, though not as long as that of other commodities like rice. Hence, the disadvantage associated with selling highly perishable crops like tapioca can be overcome, to some extent, by converting the harvested tubers into sundried or parboiled dry chips. Table 8.7, however, suggests that the major portion of tapioca is sold as tubers rather than dry chips. This may be because farmers find it difficult to cope with the processing of such a large output owing to lack of infrastructure for processing the tapioca. Only 5 per cent of the tapioca produced on the farms was processed into chips. Perhaps it may not be economical to sell processed tapioca. The average price of dry chips in 1976-77 was Rs. 0.8 to 1, as compared to Rs. 0.3 for raw tubers. If we take into account the rate of recovery of processed product from tapioca tubers (which is around 35-40 per cent) and the processing costs, it may not be viable to sell

TABLE 8.7: **Distribution of Tapioca Marketed as Raw Tubers and Dry Chips—Percentage to Total Marketed Quantity**

| Size classes in acres | Raw tubers (%) | Dry Chips (%) | Total |
|---|---|---|---|
| 0.0 — 0.5 | nil | nil | — |
| 0.51— 1.0 | 100.0 | nil | 100.0 |
| 1.01— 2.5 | 92.4 | 7.6 | 100.0 |
| 2.51— 5.0 | 93.0 | 7.0 | 100.0 |
| 5.01—10.0 | 99.0 | 1.0 | 100.0 |
| 10.01—15.0 | 100.0 | nil | 100.0 |
| Above 15 | 100.0 | nil | 100.0 |
| All | 98.3 | 1.7 | 100.0 |

tapioca in the form of dry chips. Moreover, the consumer tastes and preferences—at least in our study region—is to consume tapioca mostly in tuber form rather than as dry chips. Farmers may, therefore, prefer to sell tapioca in the form of tubers.

## MARKET DEPENDENCE

Let us now turn our attention to the question of market dependence and find out as to which group of farm households depend on the market for their requirements of tapioca and rice and what are its policy implications. To answer this question we may examine Table 8.8 which presents data on market dependence for tapioca and rice for different land holding groups.

TABLE 8.8: **Particulars of Market Dependence for Tapioca and Rice**

| Size classes in acres | Proportion of households who purchase tapioca (%) | Quantity of tapioca purchased (Kgs. per household per annum) | Proportion of households who purchase rice (%) | Quantity of rice purchased (Kgs. per household per annum) |
|---|---|---|---|---|
| 0.0 — 0.5 | 95.0 | 618 | 100.0 | 273 |
| 0.51— 1.0 | 61.5 | 357 | 100 0 | 339 |
| 1.01— 2.5 | 15.8 | 48 | 97.4 | 375 |
| 2.51— 5.0 | 3.6 | 11 | 89.3 | 314 |
| 5.01—10.0 | nil | — | 23.8 | 65 |
| 10.01—15.0 | 25.0* | 13* | nil | — |
| Above 15 | nil | — | nil | — |
| All | 30.7 | 170 | 80.7 | 276 |

*Note*: There was only one household here, an exceptional one. Here the farmer sold his entire tapioca output grown in his far-flung fields. For his own use, he bought about 50 Kgs. per annum from nearby markets.

On an average about 31 per cent of the farm households buy tapioca from the market at the rate of about 170 kgs per household per annum. On the contrary the proportion of households depending on the market for their rice requirements is more than 80 per cent indicating not only the relative scarcity of this food compared to tapioca but also possibly the distinct food preference of the people in this region. Proportion of households buying tapioca and rice in the market is inversely related to size of holdings. The same trend holds in the case of quantity of tapioca purchased per household per annum too but not in the case of rice where we note that quantity of rice purchased per household per annum rises upto holdings with 2.5 acres and then declines. Being a high value and superior commodity rice is not easily within the reach of the low income strata. However, with public distribution system having taken strong roots in the state, the ration subsidy is akin to an income effect raising the possibility of substitution of rice for tapioca. Even so the low income strata cannot afford to buy their entire requirements of rice and hence try to compensate this by purchasing a cheap cereal substitute like tapioca which provides more calories per unit of expenditure. Among large farmers particularly those with holdings above 5 acres, very little rice is purchased as they appear to be self-sufficient in their household requirements of rice while in holdings above 10 acres, no rice is purchased. Proportion of households among higher size classes purchasing rice is quite low being 24 per cent. On the contrary all households in the lowest size group buy rice in the market.

In the case of tapioca almost 95 per cent of households with holdings upto 0.5 acre depend on the market to meet the larger part of their tapioca requirements while in the next size class 62 per cent of the houseaolds depend on the market. Thereafter the proportion of households depending on the market for tapioca are not many. The quantity of tapioca purchased per household per annum too is relatively higher in the lower size class—about 618 kgs. per household per annum. Part of the reason, as hinted-earlier, is that tapioca being a low value crop is within the reach of the low income groups. Holdings below 0.5

acre grow tapioca but still meet a larger part of their requirements from the market. On the other hand for their rice requirements they are wholly at the mercy of the market, since they do not have lands suitable to cultivate rice. In holdings above 0.5 acre, a large part of the tapioca requirements of the households is met from their own farm. This is not the case with rice, where households with holdings upto 2.5 acres meet either whole or a large part of their rice requirements from the market. Beyond this size range households are more or less self-sufficient in respect of both commodities.

The above findings suggest that any price support policies will have to take cognisance of the fact that the lowest income groups primarily depend on the market for the supply of their wage goods, in our case tapioca and rice. Any steep rise in the price of tapioca would have its consequent impact on their levels of nutrition and real income. Given the limitations of our data we have not been able to say anything about the demand for tapioca generated by other consumers. But our analysis of the market channels wherein we saw the role of agents in the tapioca trade may be taken as a suggestive clue that part of the tapioca bought by agents is intended for use in agro-based industries.

## ON-FARM UTILISATION OF TAPIOCA

An analysis of the on-farm utilisation of tapioca may throw further insights into the possibilities of diversifying the utilisation of tapioca. Table 8.9 which presents the relevant data indicates that on an average about 70 per cent of the tapioca retained by producers is set apart for self consumption by household members. About 17 per cent is used as livestock feed while 13 per cent is given as perquisites to wage labour and farm servants. The size-class-wise profile reveals that large farmers with holdings exceeding 5 acres utilise a substantial quantity retained for home use as livestock feed and also for giving it as perquisites to labour during cultivation operations. This is quite interesting. Obviously the big farmers are aware of the beneficial effects of giving limited quantities of tapioca as feed to livestock which admittedly has no adverse effect on growth or yield of the animals. Some portion is set apart for being given as perquisites to labourers. Often rice meals given to them are supplemented with tapioca. To the labourer this practice of getting perquisites is advantageous since it serves as a cushion against inflation. For the farmer too, this is advantageous since he need sacrifice less of rice, a superior commodity, for being given as perquisite to labourers and substitute this with a low value and inferior food crop like tapioca. Thus, not only can he conserve a superior commodity like rice for his own use but also find an outlet for his tapioca produce. There are two important implications which stem from the above analysis. Firstly, if the crop is to maintain the growth momentum generated during the sixties and early seventies than the market outlets for the crop and its products should be diversified. Encouraging farmers to divert a portion of their tapioca produce for use as animal feed is one such instance. Secondly, even if a stage is reached when tapioca may become uneconomic to cultivate, big farmers may still continue to grow some tapioca not only to meet their own family consumption requirements (owing to the cultural affinity towards consuming tapioca in Kerala) but also, more important, to meet the needs of wage labour, thus reducing the risk of having to make a larger outlay of rice by way of perquisites to labourers.

## CONSUMPTION

Here we shall examine the role of tapioca and rice in the diet of the people of this region by examining the nutrient intake of the people measured in terms of calories derived. The data on output retained for self consumption plus the quantity purchased during the reference year (i.e., 1976-77), were made use of for this analysis. As an additional check these estimates were compared with additional information of the average daily consumption by household members. In case of wide difference between the two estimates a final figure was arrived at on the basis of clarifications with the respondents. To facilitate comparison between households consisting of people of different age groups the household population has been standardised into nutrition/consumption units using the procedure suggested by the ICMR.[8] We follow the standard practice of calculating a common wastage rate at 10 per cent for both tapioca and rice so as to make an allowance for cooking and plate wastage.

TABLE 8.9 : **Particulars of Tapioca Retained for on-farm Consumption—by Category of Use**

*(Per cent distribution to total)*

| Size classes in acres | For consumption by household members % | For livestock feed % | Perquisites to labourers % | Total |
|---|---|---|---|---|
| 0 — 0.5 | 100.0 | — | — | 100 (448) |
| 0.51— 1 | 82.5 | 17.4 | 0.1 | 100 (1339) |
| 1.01— 2.5 | 89.0 | 8.4 | 2.6 | 100 (1892) |
| 2.51— 5 | 76.7 | 15.1 | 8.2 | 100 (2024) |
| 5.01—10 | 36.2 | 36.6 | 27.2 | 100 (2819) |
| 10.01—15 | 77.4 | 10.5 | 12.1 | 100 (1187) |
| Above 15 | 14.4 | — | 85.6 | 100 (2920) |
| All | 70.0 | 17.4 | 12.6 | 100 (1750) |

*Note*: Figures in parentheses give quantity retained for On-farm consumption in kgs. per household.

TABLE 8.10: **Consumption of Tapioca and Rice (in calories per day per consumption unit)**

| Size classes in acres | Tapioca (after wastage) | Rice |
|---|---|---|
| 0 — 0.5 | 869 | 491 |
| 0.51— 1 | 1042 | 540 |
| 1.01— 2.5 | 1143 | 745 |
| 2.51— 5 | 911 | 780 |
| 5.01—10 | 640 | 1409 |
| 10.01—15 | 611 | 1676 |
| Above 15 | 364 | 2484 |
| All | 932 | 850 |

*Note*: Wastage rate is calculated at the standard rate of 10 per cent of quantity consumed to make allowance for cooking and plate wastage.
1 kg. Rice=3460 calories;
1 kg. Tapioca=1570 calories.

Table 8.10 presents the calorie intake of the farm households derived from consumption of tapioca and rice by size classes of farmers, taking holding size as a proxy for income. The results show that calories derived from tapioca per day per consumption unit increases with an increase in size of holdings upto 2.5 acres and then declines steeply in holdings beyond 5 acres. In the case of rice, however, calorie intake varies positively with farm size. Thus it is the mid-size groups who consume relatively more tapioca than either the lowest or highest size-classes. Lack of adequate purchasing power to buy even a law value food like tapioca may explain why tapioca consumption is lower in the lowest size class compared to the mid-size groups between 1—2.5 acres. The same cannot be said about big farmers who because of their higher position in the income nexus prefer a superior commodity like rice rather than an inferior food like tapioca. It is interesting to note that in holdings upto 5 acres tapioca outstrips rice in terms of its calorie contribution. In the two lowest size groups calories derived from tapioca are almost twice that derived from consumption of rice. Even though the public distribution system has taken strong roots in the state, in the absence of an effective demand for rice owing to low purchasing power, the households in the two lowest size groups are compelled to buy a cheap cereal substitute like tapioca which provides more calories per rupee of expenditure. Households below one acre, it may be recalled, fall below the poverty line adopted by the Planning Commission to delineate the rich from the poor. Despite its inferior status big farmers too consume some tapioca though not to the same extent as in other size groups—because of the cultural affinity attached to consumption of tapioca in Kerala. The consumption figures for both tapioca and rice in holdings above 5 acres appear to be high compared to other estimates. Given the general tendency to overestimate consumption as also the fact that we have not been able to adjust the figures for guests served in the household, the calorie intake among the big farmers would be less than implied by our figures.

Consumption rates of tapioca appear to be influenced by that of rice. As seen from the table as consumption rates of rice increases consumption of tapioca rises initially but then falls and the declines are quite sharp particularly when rice consumption is very high. This would imply that consumption of tapioca is closely related to the consumption of rice. Obviously if rice were available and within the reach of the households they would consume more of rice and reduce their intake of tapioca. But the fact that rice is not that readily available as tapioca coupled with its high unit value have resulted in tapioca figuring prominently in the diet of the lower size groups.

The consumption pattern of a sub-sample of the households consisting of only cultivating agricultural labour households was examined and it revealed the important role of tapioca in the diet of these vulnerable sections. It was noted that these households consumed a high proportion of tapioca deriving 1335 calories per day per consumption unit as against 420 calories in the case of rice. In other words, the share of rice in calorie intake was only a third of that derived from tapioca. Tapioca may continue to play an important role in the diet of these groups but with changing incomes, tastes and preferences this situation may change.

To sum up: While small farmers grow tapioca for subsistence, medium and large farmers grow it primarily for sale. What is noteworthy is that even with regard to the marketable surplus of an inferior food, big farmers exercise a firm control over its supply. The marketed surplus of paddy too was concentrated among big holdings though the proportion of output marketed was less than that of tapioca. Though repurchases take place in the case of both tapioca and paddy, it has not been possible to cite this as clear evidence of a distress sale. For small farmers cash crops like coconut are the main commodity of sale. The participation of small farmers in the commodity market as sellers of cash crops blurs to some extent the differentiation of the commodity market. However, the value of sales per household varies directly with farm size.

As regards market dependence there is no doubt that the bulk of those who depended on the market for their requirements of tapioca and rice belonged to the lowest size groups of farms. Big farmers were more or less self-sufficient in their requirements of both commodities.

An interesting part of our analysis was the attempt to find out which crops and strata of farms were able to benefit from price advantages in the commodity market. As far as tapioca is concerned it was not possible to make any generalisation as to whether price advantage favoured any particular group of farmers. In the midland villages where there were relatively more big holdings, big farmers were able to secure a slightly higher price for tapioca. This is partly due to the fact that agents or village traders who bought a substantial proportion of the tapioca sold by big farmers were willing to offer a better price, since they could take advantage of the economies of scale in transporting tapioca. But price differential over size-classes were small suggesting that scale has only a weak influence. In the lowland and highland villages, owing to transportation problems and lack of bulk buyers, big farmers reported lower prices as compared to other farmers. In the case of most other crops like coconut, cashew, arecanut, rubber, etc., price differentials over size-classes were narrow suggesting that scale has no perceptible influence on the price received by farmers in the commodity market.

Other noteworthy points were that there was a clear preference for marketing tapioca in the form of tubers rather than chips. With respect to no-farm utilisation of tapioca, big farmers used it mostly as animal feed and for being given as perquisites to labour.

Our analysis also gave a comparative perspective of the consumption of an inferior food vis-a-vis a superior food. Consumption of tapioca initially increased with an increase in farm size when purchasing power improved and thereafter declined. In the case of rice it increased continuously. Tapioca was found to be the main source of calories for the lower strata of farmers. Thus income does play an important role in the consumption behaviour of households.

## REFERENCES


1. M V Nadkarni: *Marketable Surplus and Market Dependence in a Millet Region*, Allied Publishers, New Delhi, 1980, p. 148.
2. Such a conceptual distinction between a commercial surplus and distress sale has been suggested by VKRV Rao in his foreword to Dharam Narain's book, *Distribution of Marketed Surplus of Agricultural Produce by Size-level of Holding in India*, 1950-51, Asia, 1961.
3. MV Nadkarni, op. cit., p. 147.
4. Suman Sarkar: Marketing of Foodgrains: An Analysis of Village Survey Data for West Bengal and Bihar, in Review of Agriculture, *Economic and Political Weekly* (*EPW*), Vol. XVI, No. 39, September 26, 1981, pp. A. 103-108.
5. K Subba Rao: *Rice Marketing System and Campulsory Levies in Andhra Pradesh*, Allied Publishers, Delhi, 1978.

6. U Aiyasami and H G Bohle: Market Access as Constraint on Marginal and Small Farmers, Review of Agriculture, *EPW*, Vol. XVI, No. 13, March 28, 1981.
7. Suman Sarkar, Op. cit., pp. A-103-108.
8. See C Gopalan *et al.*, *Nutritive Value of Indian Foods*, National Institute of Nutrition, Indian Council of Medical Research, Hyderabad, India, 1977, pp. 10-11.

# 9

# SUMMARY AND CONCLUSIONS

DESPITE its potential in meeting the food needs of less developed countries (LDCs), particularly in providing a cheap source of calories for the poor, tapioca not only continues to receive a low priority in the development plans of LDCs but it is also not well-researched (particularly in economic aspects), unlike other field crops. Apart from its importance in supplying calories at a very low cost, the crop's economic significance is enhanced by its ability to give high yields per unit of area, as also its suitability to marginal lands and regions with uncertain weather conditions. Whatever be the significance of tapioca as a source of food for the poor, it can be produced in significant quantity only if it is remunerative to produce it. It is for this reason that this study attempted a comprehensive economic analysis of the crop covering its production, consumption and marketing, using both secondary and primary data. It provided further insights by comparing it with the rice economy.

The study has been ideally conducted in Kerala State (India)—a region accounting for 75 per cent of total area under tapioca in the country during 1979-80 to 1981-82. In the state itself, tapioca is the most important food crop after rice, occupying a tenth of the state's total cropped area and also a major supplier of calories at low cost to the poor. During critical phases in the State's agricultural history, when famine-like conditions prevailed or when rice (the most preferred food) was scarce or expensive, it was tapioca which came to the rescue of the poor in Kerala by providing an alternate and cheap source of calories, thereby preventing any alarming decline in their levels of calories intake.

Our study indicated two phases in the growth of tapioca and rice in Kerala. The first phase covering the period 1963-64 to 1974-75 witnessed a significant rise in production of tapioca and rice, the growth rates being higher in the case of tapioca. What was remarkable about the growth in this period was that the increase in tapioca production had not only occured through an increase in tapioca area but also through a significant increase in yields per hectare, a fact of significance to a region like Kerala where the pressure of population on land is acute. It is also noteworthy that yields in Kerala rank among the highest in the world. Secondly, in per capita terms production of tapioca registered a positive and significant growth, while that of rice was stagnant, indicating the important role tapioca has played in augmenting per capita food availability in Kerala. Thirdly, the growth of tapioca was not confined to the traditional tapioca—growing areas of the Travancore belt but extended to newer areas, particularly the northern parts of the state. Lastly, the increase in tapioca area did not occur at the expense of rice area; on the other hand in districts like Alleppey rice may have displaced tapioca in dry-cum-wet (or marginal paddy) lands. Though there was a significant increase in area and yields of rice also, they were not as impressive as that of tapioca owing to scarcity of lands suitable to cultivate rice and limited scope for further increasing yields under present levels of technology. Per hectare yields of tapioca, as stated earlier, increased faster than that of rice; but the rate of growth in tapioca prices was less than that of paddy/rice. In other words, yield advantage rather than price advantage has favoured the growth of tapioca in this period while in the case of rice price advantage has been more important.

The second phase covering the period 1975-76 to 1981-82, witnessed a significant decline in tapioca production owing to a significant reduction in the area under the crop. In spite of an increase in rice yields, production of rice was stagnant owing to a significant decline in rice area. In per capita terms production of both crops registered a significant decline. The factors that have contributed to the reduction in area under the two crops are not the same. As far as tapioca is concerned, the high rate of growth in tapioca production during the preceding period (which was even higher than the growth rate of population) may have led to a glut in the market in the absence of measures to absorb the additional output and hence led to a decline in tapioca area. Here one may also note the class-specific nature of the demand for tapioca, consumed as it is by low income people, which may have inhibited the crop from maintaining its growth momentum observed during the preceding period. All this would suggest that market will act as a constraint on the growth of the crop in the long run, unless the markets for the crop and its by-products are diversified. A decline in yields and an insignificant growth in tapioca prices were among other factors that may have induced farmers to shift to cultivation of more remunerative crops like cocoa, cashew, rubber, etc. Declining paddy prices, increasing costs of cultivation, etc., are some of the factors that have induced rice cultivators to shift to more remunerative crops like coconut, sugarcane, etc.

The second aspect of the growth of tapioca is not only the unevenness of its growth across districts (especially during Period I, i.e., 1963-64 to 1974-75) but also the different factors that have influenced its growth behaviour. Districts where yield rates were high relative to the state average generally reported either a low growth or decline in tapioca area during Period I. The steep rise in yield rates in these districts may have induced the farmers to curtail area under a low value and inferior food crop like tapioca and shift the area so saved to cultivation of more remunerative crops. In the case of yields, however, all districts with the exception of one recorded a positive and significant growth in tapioca yield rates. During Period II (i. e., 1975-76 to 1981-82) all districts reported a decline in tapioca area; in the case of yields five districts reported a decline and the remaining districts reported a positive growth though the trends in both cases were not significant. An interesting feature was that districts which reported high instability in tapioca yields reported a decline in tapioca area (during Period I), suggesting in other words that in the case of low value and inferior food crops like tapioca high instability in yields may act as a disincentive to its production. Another noteworthy feature was that price instability in tapioca was lower than that of paddy and this factor may partly explain the crop's popularity among small farmers who are known for their risk-averse behaviour.

The two most distinguishing features of the tapioca economy are that firstly, its cultivation is mostly concentrated among marginal and small holdings perhaps because it consumes Very little of resources; in the case of rice it is mostly cultivated by medium and large holdings partly due to the fact that access to paddy lands is skewly distributed. Secondly, tapioca is mostly consumed by low income people because it is cheap relative to rice. Per rupee of expenditure tapioca provides more calories than rice. But a disquieting feature is that calories per rupee of expenditure on tapioca has shown a declining trend over the past two decades owing to a rise in retail price of tapioca. However, since rice retail prices also increased fast, tapioca still continues to maintain its edge over rice, though not to the same extent as during the early sixties.

Though all strata of farms grow tapioca small farmers grew it for subsistence while medium and particularly big farmers grew it for the market. Tapioca yields per acre varied positively with farm size and the yield differentials between farm-size groups were found to be statistically significant. The higher intensity of inputs among bigger holdings, particularly of capital inputs like manure and fertilisers as also the use of the modern yield augmenting inputs like fertilisers and improved strains partly explain these yield differentials. It is obvious that the range and intensity with which inputs are applied is determined by the resource endowments of the different segments of the peasantry which is skewly distributed. Moreover, small farmers grow tapioca for subsistence and hence prefer to devote more attention to cash crops like coconut. The limited resources (particularly non-land resources) they have tended to be concentrated in cash crops. Yield of subsistence crops in such case can be lower among small holdings. Big farmers grow tapioca as a cash crop and hence are willing to channel more resources to its cultivation so as to maximise yields and profits.

Since land is an overriding constraints in agriculture (especially in Kerala), increasing interest would be centered on how production could be increased by raising yields per acre. Our evidence suggests that an increase in labour input may not have any significant impact on yields per acre. This is not to deny the role of labour in the production process. All that we mean to say is that it is already employed at high levels (especially among small farms) and there is very limited scope for further increases under present levels of technology. Manure and particularly fertilisers were found to have a positive and significant impact on tapioca yields in most farm size groups. An increase in these two inputs may, therefore, help in increasing tapioca yields.

A look at the input structure in tapioca cultivation showed that among small farms the share of owned inputs was higher as compared to big farms where purchased or market inputs were more important. Furthermore, among big farms the share of capital inputs like manure and fertilisers were relatively high as compared to small farms where labour was more important. A comparison of the input structure of tapioca with that of rice showed that there was a higher degree of monetisation of inputs in rice cultivation among all strata of farms. This can be explained in terms of the greater impact of new technology on rice cultivation leading to more use of purchased inputs like hired labour, new seeds, fertilisers, etc. Tapioca, on the other hand, did not witness a change on a similar scale. Big farms, however, used more of purchased inputs for both tapioca and rice. Another conspicuous feature of rice cultivation was the use of indivisible inputs like bullock labour which tended to push up per unit costs; in tapioca use of bullock labour was not reported.

On the whole tapioca cultivation was found to be profitable. Profits were relatively higher in the midlands and highlands as compared to the lowlands where lower receipts and higher unit cost of production cut down profits or resulted in losses. Per acre profits also varied positively with farm size. Small farmers, with holdings below 0.5 acre, however, reported losses when value was imputed to family labour at the market wage rate. In the case of rice, losses were reported in all size groups when value was imputed to owned land. This procedure of imputing value to owned inputs has been frequently questioned on the ground that in the use of owned inputs market prices do not enter the calculus of the farmer. In other words, it is the paid out costs of out-of-pocket expenses which guides the decision of peasants. Small farmers growing tapioca and paddy growers (all size-classes), as noted earlier, report a surplus when only paid out costs are reckoned. Further whatever differential advantage big farmers seem to enjoy over small farmers in production of tapioca disappear when only paid out costs are taken note of.

Tapioca is not a labour intensive crop like rice. The advantage of multiple cropping in rice cultivation gives a further edge to rice in this respect. An interesting finding was that an increase in rice yields per acre would lead to a proportionate increase in labour input among small and medium holdings whereas among big holdings it was less than proportionate owing to substitution of capital inputs for labour inputs. In the case of tapioca the increase in labour input was not impressive. Unlike in rice, very little female labour was employed in tapioca cultivation; use of bullock labour was not reported. All this shows that the demand generated for different categories of labour and energy sources will vary across crops. Though tapioca is not as labour absorbing as rice it has its apparent advantages. Unlike in rice where peak season constraints and need for labour possessing specialised skills necessitates hiring in of labour, tapioca does not have such requirements of a similar scale and hence can be grown by relying mostly or wholly on family labour. This is a fact of significance to poor peasant households who look upon family labour as their main resource in production.

Looking from the consumer viewpoint there are a number of points.* Firstly, tapioca is considered as a rice substitute in Kerala and hence the consumption rates of tapioca will be influenced by

*See, K N Ninan: Agricultural Labourers and Poverty, *Economic and Political Weekly*, September 19, 1981.

that of rice. Rice is a superior commodity with a positive income elasticity of demand. Tapioca, on the other hand, is regarded as an inferior good with a negative income elasticity of demand. In other words, as incomes rise (or farm size taking it as a proxy for income) consumption of tapioca will decline while that of rice will increase. Secondly, its consumption is localised. Consumption of tapioca will figure more prominently in tapioca-producing regions. If, however, there is a distinct preference for a commodity as in the case of rice, a flow of it will take place from surplus to deficit regions. Markets for tapioca are, however, localised because of its perishability and low unit value. Thirdly, consumption of inferior foods like tapioca will figure more prominently during times of economic distress as borne by the experience of Kerala during the mid-sixties. We also have historical evidence of the role of potatoes during the Irish famines. However, our own evidence and that of others indicate that its consumption is quite high in tapioca-producing regions even during agriculturally normal years. In fact as our study revealed, tapioca provided more calories than rice to households with holdings upto 5 acres; for cultivating agricultural labour households tapioca supplied three times more calories than rice. The data, as we know, pertains to 1976-77, an agriculturally normal year. This being so, the only inference we can draw then is that in brought years or during times of hardship, the poor have to forego what little rice they consume and rely more on tapioca for sustenance.

There is another factor to be taken note of while discussing the diet patterns in Kerala, namely the presence of an effective public distribution system. The ration subsidy here is akin to an income effect with possibility of substitution of rice for tapioca. In spite of this the lower strata of farmers are unable to meet their full requirements of rice owing to limited purchasing power and hence try to compensate this by consuming more tapioca. As noted earlier, tapioca provided more calories than rice for households with holdings upto 5 acres; for cultivating agricultural labour households it was the major source of calories. This shows that even though the establishment of a public distribution system to supply wage goods at fair or subsidised prices to weaker sections may help to lessen the burden of the poor, it should not make policy makers immune to the more important goal which is to raise the effective demand of the poor by increasing their incomes.

The marketable surplus of tapioca, as observed earlier, was concentrated among big farms. This was true of rice as well but the proportion of output marketed was less than that of tapioca. Small farmers do participate in the commodity market as sellers of cash crops like coconut. The bulk of the buyers of tapioca and rice are marginal and small farmers. There is thus no complete identity of interest between small and big farmers.

The problems faced in marketing the crop are many. Its perishability and low unit value as also its bulky nature are factors which have impeded the marketability and large-scale industrial utilisation of the crop. Though the processing of the commodity may help in overcoming these disabilities, very little tapioca was processed on farms. Bulk of sales was in the form of raw tubers. Inadequate infrastructure, uneconomic price as also a preference for tubers may account for the low processing of tapioca on farms. The perishable nature of tapioca also limits the scope of the seller to bargain. Though the data aggregated over villages revealed no perceptible difference in prices received by different size-groups of farmers, the disaggregated picture indicated that in villages with transportation problems or where monopsony elements were present, big farmers with a significant marketable surplus of tapioca accepted lower prices for tapioca. In other cases traders and agents did offer better prices to big farms because of the advantage of economies of scale in transporting bulk quantities. In the case of other crops like coconut, cashew, arecanut etc., is was observed on the basis of data aggregated over villages that scale did not have any perceptible influence on the prices received by different size-groups of farmers.

In reflecting on the future of tapioca in Kerala a number of points may be mentioned. There is no doubt that unless the crop assures a reasonable rate of return compared to other alternatives, farmers particularly those who grow it for the market, will accord it a low priority, and more so because it is a low value crop. By increasing yields and/or lowering unit costs of production it will be possible for tapioca to be competitive. In other words, a low cost high yield technology holds the key to the future of tapioca. Such a technology already, exists. There is tremendous scope to enhance tapioca yields per acre by two to three times as compared to present levels by adopting the new varieties and through use of the package of practices and the complementary inputs that go with it. Accent will have to be paid to stepping up yields per acre, rather than extending cultivation to newer areas, so as to make rational and optimum use of a scarce input like land. This is all the more important in a state like Kerala where not only there is tremendous pressure of population on land but also because tapioca has to vie with other food crops and foreign-exchange earning cash crops for the limited space available. Thus new technology can bring about a rapid transformation of the tapioca production scenario. However, though new technology is supposed to be scale neutral, access to resources is not and hence the gains from new technology are likely to be skewly distributed unless changes are effected in the institutional framework too. If small farmers, who constitute the bulk of tapioca producers are to benefit from new technology in tapioca production, there will have to be direct institutional intervention so as to give them ready and favoured access to new inputs. An increase in tapioca yields per acre among small farms will not only help reduce their dependence on the market for their tapioca requirements but also may enable them to generate a marketable surplus to earn more income.

The thrust to tapioca production brought through adoption of new technology will generate new problems. One such problem is to find a market to absorb the increased production. It is doubtful whether the demand from low income groups and specific regions may sustain the growth of the crop. It is obvious that unless the markets for tapioca and its products are diversified, market will act as a constraint on the growth of the crop in the long run. Technical advances in the knowledge of the various uses of the crop and its by-products have increased so much and indicates immense scope to diversify the market outlets for the crop. While the larger portion of tapioca would, no doubt, be continued to be used for food purposes, efforts should be made not only to encourage its use as an animal feed but also to develop agro-based industries based on the tapioca resources of the state. This will not only help to absorb the additional tapioca output but also act as a catalyst for rural change by increasing income and employment. Furthermore it will help promote a closer integration between Agriculture and Industry.

However, any large-scale industrial utilisation of the crop may push up its price and put it beyond the reach of the poor. In order to prevent such a situation, governments may have to make compulsory levies on big producers and distribute the produce so acquired through fair price shops so as to protect the interests of the consumers, bulk of whom belong to the low income strata. At the same time the interests of the growers, particularly those who have a significant and identifiable marketable surplus of tapioca, will have to be protected by assuring a reasonable margin of profit. This calls for a minimum price support policy to protect the interests of the growers as well. It is thus obvious that the broad contours of a governmental policy will have to consist in harmonising the conflicting interests of the producers and consumers.

The gist of the measures advocated above indicates that there will be increasing commercialisation of the crop not only in terms of monetisation of inputs but also in producing more for the market. An interesting question that could be raised here is as to whether commercialisation will lead to an increase in instability. Since the thrust provided to tapioca production by new technology will essentially involve dependence on factory-produced inputs like chemical fertilisers any bottlenecks in its supply at critical times will, no doubt, introduce some element of instability to its production. Since commercialisation involves more of market-oriented production, any market uncertainty may affect the output of the crop. Diversification could enable farmers to adjust to such risks.

There is no doubt that tapioca has played an important role in the food economy of Kerala not only by increasing per capita food availability but also by putting within the reach of the poor a rather inexpensive source of calories. If developing countries can take a cue from the Kerala experience and reorient their food strategies giving equal emphasis, if not more, on production of cheap food substitutes like coarse cereals and cereal substitutes, it can make all the difference on the nutrition levels and real incomes of the poor.

Since tapioca is not a labour intensive crop like paddy (at least in Kerala), it may not play any significant role in generating rural employment. Our statement in this regard needs to be qualified since we have not examined the employment potential in processing industries. Also we may note that the prospects for increasing rice output either through extending rice area or raising yields is extremely limited in Kerala. But there is immense scope to raise tapioca yields considerably; further the crops' ability to grow in inferior soils or regions with uncertain weather conditions suggest that tapioca can play an important role in absorbing unutilised or underutilised labour. It may also be noted here that research hitherto has been concentrated on evolving high-yielding varieties of tapioca only. It is time to explore the possibilities of evolving short-duration varieties of tapioca so as to facilitate multiple cropping with its consequent impact on incomes and employment. Though tapioca needs less labour per unit area than rice under present levels of technology, peasant households who look upon family labour as their main factor of production are attracted to the crop not only because of its relatively low requirements of hired labour as compared to rice, but also because it helps utilise family labour which may otherwise have remained idle in the absence of other alternatives for employment. However, as stated earlier, they grow it mainly for subsistence. Big farmers too are attracted to the crop because labour costs are relatively low as compared to rice and hence they are able to increase their profits also. Incidentally it may be noted through our evidence that labour productivity of tapioca and paddy will increase significantly only if labour input were to decline. In other words, it indicates that under present levels of technology labour may be used beyond a point of maximum productivity and diminishing returns are operating in agriculture. It is thus obvious that while exploring the possibilities of absorbing more labour in agriculture, policy makers should not lose sight of the more important objective of generating employment in the non-agriculture sector, which holds the key to a solution of the problem of rural unemployment in developing countries.

A word or two about the relative efficiency of small and large farms, the future of the peasantry in Kerala, etc. may not be out of place. In spite of the tremendous research input that has gone into analysing the relationship between size of holdings and productivity, the debate has remained inconclusive. The differing results in various studies hav e provided ammunition to support different schools of thought, the inverse relationship to make a case for small-farm based agriculture, the direct relationship to justify large-scale capitalist or collectivist farming. Our own evidence suggests that though yield of tapioca varied positively with farm size, small farmers were able to bridge, to some extent, the yield gap when value of output of all crops was aggregated, though the advantage was still in favour of bigger holdings. The cultivation of high value crops, the higher intensity of cultivation by intercropping (which of course was not reflected in the traditional cropping intensity index on account of its limitations) are factors which explain why small farmers are able to narrow the yield gap when it comes to total crops. Our evidence suggests that in the case of total crop production small farmers are more efficient in the use of their resources as compared to relatively bigger holdings. This is evinced by the fact that returns per unit value of input varied inversely with farm size. An explanation in terms of diseconomies of scale enabling small farmers to be more efficient than large ones may not go far. The point is that in their quest for survival small farmers use their resources intensively so as to extract as much surplus as possible from their miniscule holdings. This involves an intense cultivation of land and also a diversification of their sources of income. It may be noted here that among small holdings diversification of economic activities is in response to conditions of economic distress whereas among bigger holdings it is undertaken to take advantage of the multiple channels of profit-making. In spite of their efficiency and the diversification of their sources of income small farmers are not able to generate a surplus which can assure them a reasonable standard of living. In other words, efficiency in this context is not synonymous with viability. Whether such holdings can become viable is, therefore, an intriguing question? In this context reference may be made to the Japanese experience where small farms were able to become viable units by diversifying their economic activities. The experience of our farmers suggests that a mere diversification of economic activities is not enough. What is needed is to diversify into high-pay off activities so as to enable small farmersto generate a surplus to meet their current consumption and production requirements as also encourage capital formation.

## *APPENDIX—I*

### Profit/Loss from Tapioca Cultivation: Village-wise by Size-Classes of Holding (Rs. Per Acre)

| Size classes in acres | Income $A_1$ | Income $A_2$ | Income $A_3$ | Income B | Income C |
|---|---|---|---|---|---|
| *Ayilara*: | | | | | |
| 0.0 — 0.5 | 717 | 456 | 420 | 209 | —56 |
| 0.51— 1.0 | 703 | 698 | 584 | 274 | 40 |
| 1.01— 2.5 | 751 | 701 | 614 | 353 | 246 |
| 2.51— 5.0 | 700 | 660 | 613 | 360 | 234 |
| 5.01—10.0 | 705 | 704 | 650 | 342 | 338 |
| 10.01—15.0 | 1293 | 1293 | 1183 | 883 | 883 |
| Above 15 | — | — | — | — | — |
| All | 768 | 738 | 667 | 389 | 296 |
| *Muttara*: | | | | | |
| 0.0 — 0.5 | 808 | 808 | 575 | 345 | 1 |
| 0.51— 1.0 | 857 | 857 | 732 | 495 | 263 |
| 1.01— 2.5 | 770 | 766 | 660 | 431 | 271 |
| 2.51— 5.0 | 631 | 625 | 474 | 234 | 220 |
| 5.01—10.0 | 847 | 844 | 687 | 446 | 437 |
| 10.01—15.0 | — | — | — | — | — |
| Above 15 | — | — | — | — | — |
| All | 776 | 773 | 625 | 385 | 338 |

(APPENDIX-*I*—(*Contd.*)

| Size Classes in acres | Income $A_1$ | Income $A_2$ | Income $A_3$ | Income B | Income C |
|---|---|---|---|---|---|
| *Kuzhakad*: | | | | | |
| 0.0 — 0.5 | 514 | 514 | 370 | 143 | −257 |
| 0.51— 1.0 | 954 | 886 | 793 | 603 | 448 |
| 1.01— 2.5 | 700 | 686 | 584 | 347 | 241 |
| 2.5—1 5.0 | 611 | 574 | 461 | 233 | 233 |
| 5.01—10.0 | 597 | 565 | 538 | 345 | 345 |
| 10.01—15.0 | 995 | 994 | 944 | 716 | 716 |
| Above 15 | 2366 | 2362 | 1748 | 1509 | 1509 |
| All | 1453 | 1437 | 1117 | 888 | 866 |
| *Cherumood*: | | | | | |
| 0.0 — 0.5 | 282 | 279 | 129 | −200 | —347 |
| 0.51— 1.0 | 561 | 543 | 377 | 64 | —48 |
| 1.01— 2.5 | 385 | 380 | 214 | —89 | —172 |
| 2.51— 5.0 | 538 | 524 | 423 | 113 | 113 |
| 5.01—10.0 | 412 | 411 | 246 | —86 | —86 |
| 10.01—15.0 | — | — | — | — | — |
| Above 15 | — | — | — | — | — |
| All | 460 | 451 | 304 | —10 | —61 |

# BIBLIOGRAPHY*

Afran, D K: Cassava and its Economic Importance, *The Ghana Farmer*, Vol. XII, No. 4, 1968.

Agro-Economic Research Centre, University of Madras: *Study of Tapioca Cultivation in Kerala*, Madras, 1976.

Aiyer, A K Yegna-Narayan: *Field Crops of India*, Bangalore Printing and Publishing Company Ltd., 1969.

Andersen, Per-Pinstrup and Diaz, RO: *Present and Potential Labour Use in Cassava Production in Colombia*, Paper presented at III International Symposium on Tropical Root Crops, Ibadan, Nigeria, December 2-9, 1973.

Araulla, E V, Nestel, B and Campbell, M (ed): *Cassava-Processing and Storage*, IDRC—031e, IDRC, Ottawa, Canada, 1974.

Ayres, John: Manioc, *Food Technology*, April 1972.

Bailey, K V: Rural Nutrition Studies in Indonesia, Background to Nutritional Problems in Cassava Areas, *Tropical and Geographical Medicine*, Vol. 13, 1961.

Behrman, J R: *Supply Response in Underdeveloped Agriculture—A Case Study of Four Major Annual Crops in Thailand—1937-1963*, North-Holland Publishing Co., Amsterdam, 1968.

Booth, R H: *Cassava Storage*, CIAT, Cali, Colombia, Series EE-16, September 1975.

Butler, E J, Brown, E E and Davis, L H: *An Economic Analysis*

*Only a select list of literature directly dealing with tapioca (particularly its economic aspects) or which cover the crop in their discussion/analysis are listed here. This also includes a list of official reports and other data sources used in the study.

*of the Production Consumption and Marketing of Cassava (Tapioca)*, Department of Agricultural Economics, University of Georgia, Research Bulletin 97, June 1971.

Catambay, AB: Cost of Harvesting Cassava with a Plow, *Philippine Agriculturist*, Vol. 21, 1932.

—— and Yango, C E: Cost of Harvesting Cassava with Animal-drawn Plough, *Philippine Agriculturist*, Vol. 23, 1935.

Central Tuber Crops Research Institute, Trivandrum: *Proceedings of Short-specialised Training Course on Tapioca Production Technology*, October 14-18, 1974.

——: Annual Reports for the years 1968 to 1974.

Centro International de Agricultura Tropical, Cali, Colombia: *2000 Abstracts on Cassava*, Vol. I, Series H E—26, December 1975.

Chidambaram, M: Marketing of Tapioca and Its Products in Tamil Nadu, *Rural Development Review*, Cards, Coimbatore, January-March 1983.

Council for Scientific and Industrial Research: *Development of Tapioca-based Industry in Kerala*, Trivandrum, 1977.

Coursey, D G: The Status of Root Crops—A Culture-Historical Perspective, *Journal of Root Crops*, Vol. 2, No. 1, 1976, Trivandrum.

—— and Haynes, P H: Root Crops and their Potential as Food in the Tropics, *World Crops*, July/August, 1970.

—— and Booth, R H: *Post-Harvest Losses in Perishable Tropical Produce*, in Proceedings of the VI British Insecticides and Fungicide Conference, London, 1971.

Delcasso, M and Silvestre, P: *Economic Problems Encountered in the Intensive Cultivation of Cassava by IRAT/TOGO*, Paper Presented at Seminar on Roots and Tuber Crops at University of Ibadan, 22-26 February 1971.

Diaz, R O: *World Cassava Production and Yield Trends 1960-68*, Bulletin RB-I, CIAT, Cali, Colombia, October 1972.

—— and Andersen, PP and Estrada, R D: *Cost and Use of Inputs in Cassava Production in Colombia—A Brief Description*, Series EE-5, CIAT, Cali, Colombia, September 1974.

Falcon, Walter P and others: *The Cassava Economy of Java*, Stanford University Press, California, 1984.

Food and Agriculture Organisation, Rome: *The EEC Tapioca Market—Possibilities and Limits*, Rome, 1971.

——: *Processing of Cassava and Cassava Products in Rural Industries*, Agricultural Development Report, No. 54, 1956.

——: *Production Year-book*, Vol. 35, 1981, FAO, Rome, 1982.

George, PS: *Public Distribution of Foodgrains in Kerala—Income Distribution Implications and Effectiveness*, Research Report No. 7, IFPRI, Washington, March 1979.

Goering, T James: Tropical Root Crops and Rural Development, *World Bank Staff Working Paper* No. 324, April 1979.

Gopalan, C and others: *Nutritive Value of Indian Foods*, National Institute of Nutrition, ICMR, Hyderabad, 1977.

Hali, R: *Survey of Important Markets in Kerala*, Agricultural Marketing Section, Department of Agriculture, Kerala, 1967.

Hassain, Z: *The Cultivation and Importance of Cassava in the Tropics*, Institute of Tropical Crop Husbandry, University of Gottingen, Germany, 1967.

Hau Ofa, Epeli: *Corned Beef and Tapioca—A Report on the Food Distribution System in Tonga*, Monograph No. 19, Development Studies Centre, Australian National University, Canberra, 1979.

Hendershott, CH and others: *A Feasibility Study on Manioc Production in North-East Brazil*, AID Contract No. AID/LA-681 (Brazil), University of Georgia, Athens, 1971.

——: *A Literature Review and Research Recommendations on Cassava*, AID Contract CSD/2497, University of Georgia, Athens, 1972.

Holleman, LMJ: *Report to the Government of the Dominican Republic on a Survey on Cassava Production and Processing*, FAO, Rome, 1964.

India, Government of, Directiorate of Marketing and Inspection, Ministry of Food and Agriculture: *Report on the Marketing of Tapioca in India*, Marketing Series No. 88, October 1955.

——: Directorate of Economics and Statistics, Ministry of Food and Agriculture: *Studies in the Economics of Farm Management, Kerala*, Report for 1962-63, 1963-64, 1964-65 and combined report for 1962-63 to 1964-65, 1973.

——: India, Government of, Ministry of Agriculture and Irrigation: *All India Reporton Agriculture Census 1970-71*, New Delhi, 1975; and *Agriculture Census 1976-77*, New Delhi, 1985.

——: Directorate of Economics and Statistics, Ministry of Food and Agriculture: *Area and Production of Principal Crops in India* (Reports for various years).

——: NSS, 17th Round September 1951—July 1962, *Integrated Household Survey*, No. 148, Tables with Notes on Consumer Expenditure, 1974.

——: NSS 26th Round, July 1961—September 1972, No. 265/4, *Fertiliser Use in Agricultural Holdings in South India*, Rural Sector, 1976.

——: NSS 28th Round, October 1973—December 1974, No. 240, *Tables on Consumer Expenditure*, 1977.

Ingram, Jean S and Humphries, J R O: Cassava Storage—A Review, *Tropical Science*, Vol. XIV, No. 2, 1970.

International Development Research Centre, Ottawa, Canada: *Root Crops in Eastern Africa*, IDRC, 177e, 1981.

International Society for Tropical Root Crops: *Proceedings of the I, II, III, and IV International Symposium on Tropical Root Crops*, held at Trinidad (1967), Hawaii (1970), Ibadan (1973) and Colombia (1976) respectively.

Iyer, A Padmanabha: The Cultivation of Tapioca in Travancore, *The Mysore Economic Journal*, October 1916.

Jones, William O: *Manioc in Africa*, Stanford University Press, California, 1959.

——: Manioc: An Example of Innovation in African Economies, *Economic Development and Cultural Change*, Vol. V (2), 1957.

——: *Starchy Root Crops in the Dietaries of Developing Countries*, in Proceedings of the I International Symposium on Tropical Root Crops, Vol. 2, University of West Indies, Trinidad, 1969.

——: *Marketing Staple Food Crops in Tropical Africa*, Cornell University Press, Ithaca and London, 1972.

Kay, DE: *Cassava in TPI Crop and Product Digest*, No. 2, Root Crops, Tropical Products Institute, London, 1973.

Kerala, Government of Trivandrum, TMEB, Board of Revenue, Department of Food: *Report of the Sub-Committee of the Tapioca Market Expansion Board*, 1972.

——: *Report of the Committee on Agro-Climatic Zones and Cropping Pattern*, April 1974.

——: Directorate of Economics and Statistics: *Agricultural Statistics in Kerala*1, 975.

——: *Statistics for Planning*, 1972, 1977, 1980, and 1983.

——: *The Third Decennial World Census of Agriculture 1970-71*, Report for Kerala State, Vol. I and Vol. II, November 1973 and *Agriculture Census 1976-77*, Kerala State, General Report Vol. I, 1982.

——: *Season and Crop Reports*, various issues from 1965-66 to 1975-76.

——: *Report on Crop Estimation Survey*, Various issues from 1965-66 to 1975-76.

——: *Basic Statistics Relating to Kerala Economy*, *1956-57 to 1973-74*, 1975.

Krochmal, Arnold: Labour Input and Mechanisation of Cassava, *World Crops*, September 1966.

Kumar, Shubh K: *Impact of Subsidised Rice on Food Consumption and Nutrition in Kerala*, Research Report No. 8, IFPRI, Washington, January 1979.

Leslie, Kenneth A: *The Significance of Root Crops in the Tropics*, in Proceedings of International Symposium on Tropical Root Crops, University of West Indies, Trinidad, April 2-8, 1967, 1969.

Magoon, ML: *Role of Root and Tuber Crops in Human Nutrition*, in Proceedings of International Symposium on Sub-tropical and Tropical Horticulture, New Delhi, 1967.

——: *Recent Trends in Cassava Breeding in India*, in Proceedings of International Symposium on Tropical Root Crops, Vol. I, 1969.

Mencher, Joan P: Lessons and Non-Lessons of Kerala—Agricultural Labourers and Poverty, *Economic and Political Weekly*, Special Number, October 1980.

Mencher, Joan P. Agricultural Labourers and Poverty, *Economic and Political Weekly*, January 2-9, 1982.

Nair, KNS: *Constraints that are Limiting Agricultural Production and Causing Uneven Distribution of Gains—Palghat District* (*Kerala*), Division of Agricultural Economics, IARI, New Delhi, 1972 (Unpublished PhD thesis).

Nestel, Barry: *Current Trends in Cassava Research*, IDRC-036e, IDRC, Ottawa, Canada, 1974.

—— and Cock, J: *Cassava—The Development of an International Research Network*, IDRC-059e, IDRC, Ottawa, Canada, 1976.

—— and Graham, M (ed): *Cassava—An Animal Feed*, IDRC-095e, IDRC, Ottawa, Canada, 1977.

Ninan, KN: Agricultural Labourers and Poverty—A Comment, *Economic and Political Weekly*, September 19, 1981.

——: Agricultural Labourers and Poverty, *Economic and Political Weekly*, July 10-17, 1982.

——: Labour Use in Agriculture—Case Studies of Tapioca and Paddy, in review of agriculture, *Economic and Political Weekly*, December 22-29, 1984.

Ofori, CS: The Effect of Ploughing and Fertiliser Application on Yield of Cassava, *Ghana Journal of Agricultural Sciences*, Vol. 6, 1973.

Oommen, MA: The Economics of Cropping Pattern—A Case Study of Kerala, *Indian Journal of Agricultural Economics*, Conference Number, January-March 1963.

Panikar, PGK: Economics of Nutrition, *Economic and Political Weekly*, Annual Number, February 1972.

——: Employment, Income and Calorie Intake among Selected Agricultural Labour Households, *Economic and Political Weekly*, Special Number, August 1978.

—— and others: *Population Growth and Agricultural Development—A Case Study of Kerala*, Centre for Development Studies, Trivandrum, FAO, Rome, August 1977.

Phillips, Truman P: *Cassava Utilisation and Potential Markets*, IDRC-020e, IDRC, Ottawa, Canada, 1974.

——: *A Profile of Thai Tapioca Production Practices*, Paper

presented at IV International Symposium on Tropical Root Crops, CIAT, Cali, Colombia, August 1-8, 1976.

Pillai, PR Krishna: *Tapioca in Kerala*, Bureau of Economics and Statistics, Trivandrum, 1972.

Protein Foods Association of India: *Food Habits Survey*, Vol. I and Vol. III, Kerala, ORG, Baroda.

Raj, KN: Poverty, Politics and Development—Western Europe in First Half of 19th Century and South Asia in Second half of the 20th Century, *Economic and Political Weekly*, Annual Number February 1977.

Raj, KN *etal*: *Poverty, Unemployment and Development Policy—A Study of Selected Issues with Reference to Kerala*, Centre for Development Studies, Trivandrum, United Nations, 1975 and Orient Longmans, 1977.

Rao, VKRV: *Food, Nutrition and Poverty in India*, Vikas Publishing House, New Delhi, 1982.

Renvoize, Barbara S: The Area of Origin of Manihot Esculenta as a Crop Plant—A Review of the Evidence, *Economic Botany*, Vol. 26 (4), 1973.

Sawyer, AM: Tapioca Cultivation in Travancore, *Indian Forester*, Vol. XXI, 1895.

Scharenguivel, AG: An Evaluation of the Returns to Investment of Planting 20,000 acres of jungle land with Tapioca, *Review of Agricultural Economics*, Malaysia, Vol. 4 (1), 1970.

Smith, C Earl: The New World Centers of Origin of Cultivated Plants and the Archaelogical Evidence, *Economic Botany*, Vol. 23 (3), 1968.

Terry, ER and others (ed): *Tropical Root Crops—Research Strategies for the 1980* (Symposium Proceedings), IDRC-163e, IDRC, Ottawa, Canada, 1981.

———: *Tropical Root Crops—Production and Uses in Africa* (Symposium Proceedings), IDRC-221e, IDRC, Ottawa, Canada, 1984.

Travancore-Cochin, Government of: *Report of the Tapioca Enquiry Committee*, Trivandrum, 1952.

Venugopalan, S and others: A Study of Marketing of Tapioca in Trivandrum District (Kerala), *The Journal of Scientific Research*, Banaras Hindu University, Vol. XII (2), 1960-61.

Walker, H: *The Market for Cassava*, Report No. G 21, Tropical Products Institute, London, 1966.

Weber, Edward J and others (ed): *Cassava Cultural Practices* (Workshop Proceedings), IDRC-151e, IDRC, Ottawa, Canada, 1980.

# INDEX